REFRAMING
BEAUTY

This is a work of nonfiction. The events and conversations in this book have been set down to the best of the author's ability, although some names and details may have been changed to protect the privacy of individuals. Every effort has been made to trace or contact all copyright holders. The publishers will be pleased to make good any omissions or rectify any mistakes brought to their attention at the earliest opportunity.

Printed in Australia
Cover design by Shawline Publishing Group Pty Ltd
Images in this book are the copyright of Shawline Publishing Group Pty Ltd
Illustrations within this book are the copyright of Shawline Publishing Group Pty Ltd
First Printing: November 2022

Paperback ISBN 978-1-9228-5054-6
eBook ISBN 978-1-9228-5056-0

A catalogue record for this
work is available from the
National Library of Australia

REFRAMING BEAUTY

ANITA SELZER

*For my precious granddaughters who give me joy
and light up my life*

'You're More Than Your Body'
Mel Grieg, radio personality
(Herald Sun, March 7, 2021)

'And More Than Your Face'
Anita Selzer

PROLOGUE

MOTIVATORS

A couple of things prompted me to write this book. Firstly, I am disturbed by how Western culture tends to highly value a woman's external beauty, sending the message that women are prized for their appearance. This message surrounds us and is literally in our faces everywhere, especially on billboards. Despite feminism and the struggle to secure women's rights and the various gains both have made for women, the societal value attributed to external beauty has nevertheless remained intact. And it impacts women and girls negatively as the following findings indicate. This needs to change. We need to dismantle and overthrow this value.

A recent study by Girl Guiding disclosed that 35% of girls aged 7–10 across the UK believe they are valued for their appearance more than their character and achievements. Over half the girls (52%) reported feeling they are not good enough. And 38% of the girls in this study shared they didn't feel pretty enough. Another 23% said they feel the need to be perfect. This cohort of girls said 'the most important thing to improve their lives now would be to stop judging girls and women on the way they look.'

How sad is it that 'the most important thing' these girls would like to change in their lives is the judgment on the way they look. How damaging must this feeling be to their psyche? Their comments almost sound like a cry for help.

Another study of girls, 10–11 years old in four primary schools in South Wales, reported that they use face filters so that they can feel and look prettier. One girl said she wanted her face to look thinner including her nose. Another commented that she wanted to hide any spots on her face. The recommended use of the face filter app is 13 but somehow these younger girls could access it. Beauty filters are executed through an app that adds a filter to photos or videos, placed over the body or face of a person changing their appearance. Faces and bodies can be shrunk, sharpened, enhanced and recoloured through the use of the app.

Do we want augmented reality driving our girls' future as the yardstick of how they see themselves? Fabricated through filters? Is this what we want for our daughters and granddaughters?

An Australian study of 16–18-year-olds revealed many want cosmetic procedures so they can look like their filtered selfies, psychologist Gemma Sharp says. In Western Australia, cosmetic surgeon Dr Vivek Eranki of Cosmetique cosmetic surgery clinic informs that 15-year-olds have approached his clinic wanting botox and fillers. In 2020, he saw a huge demand from young girls wanting these injectables, part of a global trend in his view. He said that celebrity Kylie Jenner had it done when she was 17 – live streaming the experience, removing the stigma and phobia of getting the needles and increasing the demand for them. And, he added, a recent UK study showed that 58% of young girls find getting injectable treatments the same as getting their hair and nails done. It 'shows how normal injectable treatments have become and it's scary.'

Don't these findings tell us that there is something very wrong with societal messages that these girls are internalising about the value of external youthful beauty?

According to a survey of 13–19-year-old girls conducted by a mental health organisation in the UK, 46% reported that they worried about their body image. '54% said the images on social media have caused them to worry' about it. A study found that, globally, 54% of girls 10--17 years old do not have high body esteem according to an international survey. 7 out of 10 of those girls think 'there is too much importance placed on beauty as a source of happiness.' 14 countries were represented in this survey showcasing diverse cultures, beliefs, social pressure and economic development.

The same study disclosed that, globally, 55% of girls will not spend time with family and friends, nor participate in activities outside the home, if they don't feel happy about the way they look. 80% of these girls have low body esteem.

How troubling are all these findings that stretch across the globe! What must that kind of thinking do to the mental health of these young girls? Not much good, according to Dr Daron Gersch who informs that the mythical perfect body doesn't exist and chasing it leads to poor self-esteem, impacting on other aspects of life. He says eating disorders like anorexia, bulimia and binge eating are likely outcomes, with girls as the most probable sufferers. He adds how children see themselves impacts on every aspect of their lives positively and negatively, affecting their long- and short-term choices, including their ability to meet and make friends, and can prevent them from trying new things or seek higher education. 'These consequences often last a lifetime and have health consequences. Those who have low self-esteem are more likely to be depressed and have anxiety,' he says.

Psychologist Peace Amadi at the Hope International University in California says that 'a slight edit can spiral into obsessive-compulsive tendencies around body image. This alteration divorces you from reality-nobody glows, sparkles and has perfect abs 24/7 in real life,' he says.

A recent report by Wall Street Journal indicates that Instagram, with photos as the app's focus and filters that make it easy to edit the images, is having a negative impact on one in three teenage girls using it. One teenage girl said from her experience on Instagram, 'I feel like I am too big and not pretty enough.' Another user shared, 'It makes me feel insecure about my body even though I know I am skinny enough.' 72% of teens use Instagram; 50.8% of all Instagram users are female; 49.2% are male.

In that report, 32% of teenage girls said that when they felt bad about their bodies, Instagram made them feel worse. Angela Guarda, Associate Professor of Psychiatry at the John Hopkins Hospital and Director of the Eating Disorders Program commented that Instagram could escalate an eating disorder that is developing in Instagram users. 'She estimates Instagram and other social media apps play a role in the disorders of about half her patients.' How disturbing is that, especially when teenage girls tend to compare their own attractiveness to the images they see on Instagram that are often touched up and filtered.

Society teaches us about our bodies: families; friends; social media like Facebook, Instagram, Twitter, WhatsApp, TikTok and QQ; and traditional media. We learn about body image – what is considered beautiful and not from these sources. And the media often shows us unrealistic images of what is considered as beautiful bodies: 'perfect skin, tiny waists, ample breasts, fashionably protruding behinds of celebrities (like) Kardashian and Beyonce.' These images then shape our perceptions of beauty: the positive and negative. And it is not uncommon for the viewer of these images then to feel bad about how they like if not matching those pictures.

'Body image is both internal (personal) and external (society). This includes how we perceive our bodies visually; how we feel about our physical appearance; how we think and (perhaps) talk to our bodies and our own sense of how other people view our bodies. How we look has never held as much societal importance so significantly on our perceived self-worth.' And as the above studies indicate, girls' self-worth is not healthy when they see those unrealistic images of beauty and their skin is not clear, and/or they are not thin with a perfectly proportioned waist, good-sized breasts and a shaped bottom. Clinical psychologist Rachel Cohen observes how 'we have grown up - that our worth is tied to how we look.'

Phillippa Diedrichs, Associate Professor from the Centre for Appearance Research, University West of England sensibly says that we need to help girls to develop resilience to overcome beauty pressures and change the socio-cultural environment so that girls are not judged on their looks.

I agree. All these studies indicate that we need to help girls build self-esteem, not by valuing and chasing beauty as their ideal to achieve it but by reframing what beauty is in a more positive, constructed way. It's by helping them to develop their inner selves. That's not to say girls must not partake in girlie things like clothes shopping or having nails done with their mums or other girlie stuff but for enjoyment and fun, not to measure up to some ideal beauty image that they feel pressured to achieve and feel like failures if they don't.

It's not only young girls who have internalised Western society's value placed on a woman's looks. A current study of 7000 Australians dating online aged 18–65 confirms that men across all ages prioritise attractiveness and physical build as desirable traits they seek in women. In contrast, women valued intelligence, trust and emotional connection in men more than their looks.

This study was conducted in 2021 and is most disconcerting to see that men value external appearance so highly in women when they are so much more than the sum of body parts or a pretty face. What is it going to take to shift this mindset of men?

The second motivator for writing *Reframing Beauty* was the birth of my granddaughters, born ten weeks apart. Each was born aesthetically beautiful, one with piercing blue eyes, the other with lovely slanted eyes and both with heart-shaped faces and perfectly fine features, like handcrafted little diamonds.

But I don't want them to be lauded for their beauty. I want them to be valued for something deeper than their looks. I want their inner selves to be what is valued and how they live their lives.

I want them to be valued because they are human beings: kind, loving, thoughtful, fair, caring, considerate, courageous, charitable and capable in whatever they are naturally or by choice or effort. Hopefully they can perform acts of beauty by helping others and working for humanity, making our world a better place in some way, whether big or small. These are the meanings I want beauty to have for them and other girls. This is how we can rethink, redefine and reframe the idea of beauty, not focusing on the outer shell.

Psychologist Renee Engeln suggests telling your daughter that she is 'smart, resilient or funny' rather than beautiful. Let's add these traits to the list of the new beauty we should strive to develop and promote for young girls and women of today and tomorrow. And with all these traits to encourage and applaud, and help our girls to build self-esteem.

External beauty as a value is so empty and shallow and can never be fully satisfied or sustainable in life. Internalising it as an ideal to strive for can be detrimental to the physical and mental health of young girls and women as Dr Daron suggested. So individually and collectively, let's abandon the dominant idea of outward beauty as a powerful social value in Western culture. Let's replace it with how a person lives their life and what they do with it. We can critique our culture and teach young girls about the pressures to conform to a narrow ideal of external beauty and counteract the pervasive media and beauty business' bombardment of its dominant value.

THE EXPERIENCE OF BEAUTY

I don't consider myself outwardly beautiful but rather average. Recently, I read about what it feels like to be a woman who is beautiful in appearance. In New York magazine *The Cut,* an unnamed woman was interviewed about what life was like for her being beautiful in her youth. At the time of the interview, this woman was in her fifties.

She described her physical appearance as 'intimidating' when wearing 'make up, eyelashes and high heels.' Pretty, tall and willowy, the woman was thin, never weighing more than 54.4 kilograms throughout her twenties. She was convinced that her good looks, her brown eyes and long brown hair worn down to her waist had landed her work in public relations, acting, producing, writing, reporting, doing television commercials and working as a talk-show host. 'I never interviewed for a job I didn't get.'

A string of boyfriends kept her busy in her thirties. 'I never had any trouble getting guys, but I got bored easily and moved on. I should have taken the good ones more seriously. I can see now they would have made good husbands, fathers and providers but I'd just drift away on to the next and stop returning their calls.'

The woman eventually married at 35 and has two children with her husband. She says that he had had a drinking problem but overcame it. She considered leaving him but had no idea how to find someone new. Never before had she needed to pursue a man and could not deal with a possible rejection. She shared that other women had been mean to her and behaved very badly towards her because of her good looks.

Now in her fifties, the woman has aged, no longer wears makeup and concludes that to men under 40, 'I am invisible. They do not see me. I could walk across the street naked – it's that bad... As far as the world is concerned? I've lost all my value.'

In an interview with American media personality Oprah

Winfrey, actress Cybill Shepherd disclosed that she feared growing older, having no value (like the unnamed woman above) and being 'disposable.' Winfrey said in the podcast that you are treated differently if you are beautiful, a reward for beauty, discussed later in this book.

Winfrey reminds us that 'if beauty is your calling card, it will fade.' She advocates that we not attach to our external outer selves because as we age our bodies change and I add, so do our faces. 'Your inner life is your real life. I'm more than what I look like or what I do,' she shares. And of course, Oprah is right in what she is saying. The person we are inside – our character – is much more important than the person we see on the outside: a kind, considerate, caring, loving, honest person, for example; that's real beauty.

Nevertheless, what you *do* can also be beautiful: the kind of work you *do* if it is helping others and society at large or it is artistic, creative, uplifting and inspiring others. And the work you do says something about who you are as a person. It is a statement on part of your character. We shall see women and young girls around the globe *performing beauty*, *doing* beauty in this book. Nevertheless, I would still like to know why the external is so valued?

Over 30 years ago, Namoi Wolf, in *The Beauty Myth* aptly raised this issue of a woman's value. 'What is a woman? Is she what she is made of? Do a woman's life and experience have value? If so, should she be ashamed for them to show? What is *so* great about looking young?'

These questions continue to be relevant today with women still valued for their appearance and their physical, youthful beauty, even though they have made seismic strides in the public sphere, including the paid workforce. Perhaps, this is partly because the value of women's external beauty had been rooted in history, in early 18th century Britain, America and Australia, for example, when women were largely depended on marriage for financial security.

The Victorian feminine ideal for white upper-middle-class women at that time was to marry and become a wife, mother and homemaker. To attract a man who could give her that meant a woman needed to look attractive and groom herself to gain his attention and affection. And the man was expected to provide for this woman and family.

Fashion writer Robin Givhan brings us up to speed in today's Western world and informs that 'on a powerfully emotional level, being perceived as attractive means being welcomed into the cultural conversation. You are part of the audience for advertising and marketing. You are desired. You are seen and accepted. When questions arise about someone's looks that's just another way of asking: How acceptable is she? How relevant is she? Does she matter?'

This really sucks because we are ALL very relevant and matter regardless of how we look. But how we look is big business, involving big bucks. It's about money, profits and commercialism. And external beauty for most of us requires the spending of those big bucks and ongoing financial maintenance. It's up to the beauty industry to constantly bring out new products and fashion looks, and advertise them through mass and social media to keep our spending and beauty maintenance going, so the money and profits keep spinning.

Former First Lady of the United States Michelle Obama shares what she had to do in order to get her look, her appearance right, in her book *Becoming*. Why the hell should appearance matter if you are the First Lady of the United States?

She says the media kept reporting on her clothes that then led fashion bloggers to follow her. 'It seemed that my clothes mattered more than anything I had to say. When I wore flats instead of heels, it got reported in the news. I wore a sleeveless aubergine dress to Barack's address to the joint session of Congress and a sleeveless black sheath dress for my official White House photo, and suddenly my arms were making headlines.'

Obama could see that the great focus of public attention was on her appearance and fashion sense rather than what mattered to her. She wanted to change that so hired a fashion saleswoman she knew to help her get the right look. Obama persuaded her to move from Chicago to Washington and work with her as a personal aide and wardrobe stylist.

'When I came to my choices, I tried to be somewhat unpredictable to prevent anyone from ascribing any sort of message to what I wore. It was a thin line to walk. I was supposed to stand out without overshadowing others, to blend in but not fade away. As a black woman too, I knew I'd be criticized if I was perceived as being showy and high end, and I'd be criticized also if I was too casual. So I mixed it up.'

Not only did Obama have a personal stylist but she also had a hairdresser and makeup artist. She dubbed her team as 'the trifecta' who she says gave her the 'confidence needed to step out in public each day, knowing that a slip up would lead to a flurry of ridicule and nasty comment. I never expected to be someone who hired others to maintain my image.'

Who would think the First Lady of the United States, a woman like Michelle Obama who was a smart, educated lawyer, needed a team of beautifiers to make her feel confident that she had the right look – the right visual image? Why should she need to feel confident to look right?

I am not a famous public figure like Obama but recently experienced a smack in the face that for some time deprived me of the right look. And what should that matter? It made me feel like shit. And I am just an ordinary person. I'd like to share my story.

CHAPTER ONE: FACE SURGERY

The scar stares at me in my mirror, surrounded by redness, raging.

Riled up. I didn't expect to see this. *Ever.*

Screaming sunshine, shimmering, seductive is the skin I hoped to see in the morning: this stare, unblemished, unmarked, unimpaired. Flawless, except for the natural aging process that I *choose* to accept.

The super skin look is ubiquitous amongst the images that jump out at us of beautiful young women. Everywhere you look – on the Internet, in the cinema, magazines and books, on trams and billboards and shop windows where business is conducted. It represents a facet of a modern Westernised beauty ideal, also popularised in parts of the East. This ideal can and does have a powerful effect on various women, physically, emotionally, mentally and/or psychologically.

The other day, I was hit by this image of beauty, strolling down a main suburban street close by to my home, where there are retail shops, restaurants and food outlets. I don't know what compelled me that day but I paid more attention to my surroundings and these visual images leapt out at me from shop windows: beautiful young women with asymmetrical faces and perfectly unwrinkled tight skin; glossy long hair; luscious lips coated in shiny lip colour; supple bodies, toned and tanned;

pearly white teeth. And what was the purpose of this whole look, I asked myself?

It was to advertise beauty treatments, how to make us look good externally, focusing on visual appearance: lip and cheek fillers, teeth whitening, non-surgical body sculpting and contouring achieved by non-invasive techniques to reduce or remove stubborn fat while tightening, firming up and remodelling the skin.

I was struck like lightning, almost dumbfounded by the intensity of these visual images: beautifully constructed young women and the services offered to create them to look this way. In my youth, beautifying was far less simple: the use of good skincare products, makeup, freshly washed hair followed by a blow-wave and foils perhaps if the hair was coloured, a sense of fashion style, and a good, healthy diet and exercise was the way to go.

Today, cosmetic surgery and non-surgical beautifying treatments and procedures have made seismic inroads into the process of beautifying and are increasingly sought after by more women, perhaps even considered a norm.

It is a sign of our modern age with new technological and scientific breakthroughs and the action and practice of a big business – the beauty industry, a money spinner, a commercial paradise, promoted by social and mainstream media.

Amidst this socio-cultural practice, there was me with my freshly cut face. I had gone to my dermatologist for an annual routine shin check. My skin is olive and I was told at very low risk for skin cancer. I loved being in the sunshine from childhood. For many years, I wore no sunscreen, luxuriating in having olive skin that tanned readily, although could burn if exposed to too great heat or sun exposure for too long. I avoided that. However, my olive skin did not save me from my fate and I contracted skin cancer. It was a jolt, a bold, rude awakening.

My doctor asked me in the check-up whether I had noticed any changes in my skin since the last consultation. Yes, I did. I had observed a cluster of what were seemingly pimples on my left cheek under my eye that didn't disappear. I pointed them out to her. 'It looks a little untoward,' I said.

'Hmm,' she mumbled, after examining the area. 'You could be right. I'd like to do a biopsy now to check but I suspect it is a skin cancer – basal cell carcinoma, most likely. If so, I suggest to surgically remove it. Don't worry, basal cell carcinoma is the best form of skin cancer to get if you are going to get it,' the doctor tried to comfort me.

But the big C word hit me like a ton of bricks – the probability that *I have skin cancer?* Me, with my olive skin who had been assured so many times that I was safe from getting skin cancer. Shock and disbelief was my immediate reaction. And then fear struck me, fear of whether the surgery would go well and the cancer be totally removed and out of my body forever. Fear that I would look different afterwards. Fear that I may look disfigured from the surgery. I was truly scared and freaking out.

This was an emotional reaction. Yet, cognitively, I thought why should it be important how I look if the surgery will save my life? These two parts of me were conflicted. I realised that the currency of external appearance and its strong cultural value in the Western world and now parts of the East underscored my emotional reaction. And the conflict was the tension I felt between the expectation of following the beauty ideal, achieving flawless skin and understanding the medical procedure needed for my health may impede this achievement.

Was retaining good skin my expectation or a cultural expectation? I suspect both, the latter informing the former. Is that what the woman discussing beauty in the Prologue meant? Was she no longer seen or valued because her youthful beauty had vanished in the eyes of men and the world? Is that our cultural norm, our cultural prescription and expectation? Are we invisible as we age and blemish? Is that what we are teaching our daughters, our future generations?

Returning to the skin cancer – I had been naïve to think I'd be exempt from getting it. My father, also olive-skinned, had a couple of skin cancers removed so I don't know why I thought to be exempt. Why should I be so special? Why should I be different to all those who are afflicted by skin cancer? I'm no stand out. And according to the Cancer Council, Australia's leading cancer charity that focuses on research, prevention and support, 'it is expected one in two Australians will be diagnosed with cancer by the age of 85.'

So, I was one of the two to get it. A week after my initial consultation, the biopsy result confirmed the diagnosis and I agreed to have the cancer surgically removed. A day procedure with local anaesthetic was the way to go, the dermatologist advised me and she recommended that her colleague who was trained in the MOHS surgical technique, the gold standard for treating basal cell carcinoma, (according to the American College of MOHS surgery) perform the surgery.

He was very pleasant, understood and validated *exactly* how I felt. I was surprised and dumbfounded. The specialist looked at me gently, sympathetically and said softly, *'It is very confronting to be told you have a skin cancer on your face.'*

But why should it be confronting?

Perhaps, because as plastic surgeon Bryan Mendelson notes, the 'human face is a psychological and physical space bearing our identity to ourselves and others.' 'Outward appearance is a signifier of each person's individuality. Our face contributes to the person we are.'

And that's what I was frightened of losing – my visual identity that was with me all my life, the visual statement that this is me. It is who I am. This is the face I wear and that others see. It is mine and signifies me. And then, the images of those glowing, perfect-looking women in the suburban shop windows flashed before my eyes and I was struck by the flawlessness of their skin, confronting the possibility of me losing my hitherto good skin. The real and the cultural – these images juxtaposed.

They were spinning inside my head after I was trying to process the information that the doctor was imparting to me. He explained the MOHS surgical technique he'd perform, named after founder and surgeon, Frederic Mohs. A micrographic form of surgery, the cancerous skin is progressively removed and tissue cells examined microscopically while the surgery is taking place and has a very high success rate, the doctor tried to reassure me.

However, going into the hospital for the procedure, all those initial fears that hit me when I was informed that I had the skin cancer had returned. In my mind, the medical and cultural dichotomy confronted me again: a life-saving procedure and possible facial disfigurement – my face, the visual window to the world. How could I be so split in the middle? At the time, it made no sense. It felt jumbled in my head and was emotionally distressing to me.

In the surgical room, the specialist marked the area of the cancer on my face with a pen for reference. He then took a photograph of it and inserted a local anaesthetic in the cancerous area. When I was numbed by the anaesthetic that really hurt, the doctor surgically removed a layer of visible cancerous tissue. No roots or extensions of the cancer were visible on the surface. The sample was then to the pathology laboratory for analysis. My wound was dressed and I was ushered into the waiting room with the other patients who were having the same surgery.

I sat for a couple of hours waiting, wondering whether the specialist would have to cut me again. I was fortunate and grateful on the day of my surgery, as the specialist was able to remove all the cancer in one go. What I had learned on the day of my surgery was that the doctor needed to perform surgery more than once for some patients once he removed the first layer of cancerous tissue. Patients then had to wait bandaged in a waiting room for the analysis before the doctor removes more cancerous tissue. And for those patients, it can therefore be a lengthy procedure if the specialist has to remove the unhealthy tissue that penetrates the various layers of skin. One patient told me the doctor had to surgically cut her nose three times to successfully remove the cancerous tissue. I really felt empathy for that woman sitting in the waiting room whose nose was all bandaged.

When I re-entered the surgery room, the doctor gave me another anaesthetic before carving ten stitches into my face and suturing me up. The nurse then handed me a mirror to see my face, what Psychology Professor Renee Engeln coins 'the tyranny of the mirror,' the hard reality, the visual truth in *Beauty Sick*. Again, I freaked out internally and silently. I looked battered, blue and red as if I had been badly bashed. Engeln shares that generally, 'We don't see unvarnished reality when we look in the mirror. Instead, what we see is shaped by years of cultural input, comments from friends and family members, and inner worries.'

Not only did I see cultural imperfection in that moment, I also saw reality in that mirror. My reality. It was far from a pretty sight. I looked like I was a victim of domestic or other violence. My battered face really bothered me and made me very self-conscious. I needed to think about all this and ultimately counsel myself, realising that my face does not *totally define* me as a *person*, even though to the outside world it does visually represent me. It is an outward identity but not an inward one. It doesn't showcase the person, the human being that I am.

Engeln informs that a 'beauty-sick culture (like our Western one) never lets a woman forget their looks are always up for evaluation by others.' On YouTube, she instructs that we are living in a culture bombarded by the message that being beautiful is the most important and powerful thing a woman and girl can be.

Perhaps, that was lurking in the back of my mind. How will others judge me? How will they respond to me? What would they think? And how long would I look like this?

The day following the surgery, I looked like a shining rainbow. I was actually stopped in the street and in the supermarket by strangers to ask me if I was all right. Perhaps, those strangers had thought that someone hit me. They appeared to be most concerned about me. I looked so outside our cultural norm that perhaps they questioned it. I really don't know the answer but felt shaken by their response. I obviously looked really bad and my former inner thoughts raced back, reaffirmed.

It is now five months post-surgery and while the scar is minute, the redness is still there, visible to the naked eye. I see a thickening on that surgical spot, a thickened pink skin, not smooth and flat. Every morning when I brush my teeth and look in the mirror, I hope that it has disappeared and grimace to see that it hasn't. And yet, the fragility of life faces me in that redness and is a reminder of my mortality. The conflict still ensues, even though I know that my face does not define who I am.

The specialist said it should take nine months for the redness to disappear. Australian former model and television presenter Deborah Hutton also experienced a basal cell carcinoma on her face soon after I did. She has had two develop in the same spot on her face within nine years. And her surgery was more extensive than mine with her needing a skin flap. Hutton said that if she had left the cancer, there was a good chance it would enter the bloodstream.

Like me, Hutton shared her emotional reaction, 'I had cried

when I came out of surgery because it was so much bigger than I thought. And then after the stitches came out and I looked at it… Wow! I shed more tears.'

Reading her story and going through this medical and surgical experience with both of us reacting so emotionally to the scarring of our faces made me think about why women's looks are important to them? Why does our external appearance and women's beauty matter? Not to all women but to those who want to look beautiful. And it prompted me to look at and consider some ideas about beauty, so let's turn the page and explore.

CHAPTER TWO: IDEAS ABOUT WOMEN'S BEAUTY

'Beauty is a concept, not a fact.'
– Autumn Whitefield-Madrano, *Face Value*

I agree with this view that women's beauty is an idea rather than a fact because over time what is considered to be beautiful changes. It is not static and it is also specific to a particular culture.

The subject of women's physical beauty is vast and has been written about extensively. In this chapter, I discuss some ideas about women's beauty that have been influential and made me think. Some may strike a chord with you, perhaps prompting further thought, some questioning and even fruitful chatter.

NAOMI WOLF: *THE BEAUTY MYTH*

Feminist scholar Naomi Wolf's impassioned book *The Beauty Myth* ignited great conversation, divided responses and sparked what her publisher coined 'a cultural grenade for the 1990s.'

'No other work has so forcefully confronted the anti-feminism that emerged during the conservative, yuppified 1980s, or so honestly depicted the confusion of accomplished women who feel emotionally and physically tortured by the need to look like movie stars,' Caryn James reported in *The New York Times* after publication of the book.

In *The Beauty Myth,* Wolf argued that men in Western culture hold the power and created 'the beauty myth,' an idealised perfection of women's physical beauty as young, thin and beautiful. Years later, she added being tall, white and blonde with huge breasts. Beauty is a 'currency system like a gold standard… the last best belief system that keeps male dominance intact.'

Wolf suggests that female beauty is a weapon used against women to socially control them so they focus their time and energy on beautifying rather than their continued advances in the public workplace. And effectively, this pressure undermines the women's self-esteem who often internalise this myth, she said.

How is this achieved? Wolf says largely due to the visual images of beautiful thin women everywhere; the advertising of beauty products and tips to embody the beauty ideal, filling women's magazines. Wolf discusses the functioning of the beauty myth in different areas of life: in the media, at work, religion, sex and sexual relations, violence, in women's eating disorders and their quest for cosmetic surgery. 'About ninety per cent of cosmetic patients are female.'

I don't agree with Wolf that there is this male conspiracy against women to imprison them in beautification, side-tracking them from pursuing work dreams and opportunities to achieving them. I think that this view is extreme. The idea of women wanting to look beautiful has been around in different forms for centuries. It is not new to the time that Wolf is writing about. Perhaps, it has been heightened during that time but I think that's partly a reflection of rising commercialism of the beauty industry and commodity consumption of the consumer.

Rather than a male conspiracy, I see it as more of a business enterprise. It's where the beauty industry is catering to a mass-market of cosmetics, skincare, haircare and fashion. It is creating beauty looks, responding to consumer demand and initiating new products and ways of beautifying. As Business History Professor Geoffrey Jones explains, the growth of a mass market for beauty products was 'facilitated by new developments in media and advertising which (further) drove the creation of a mass market for consumer goods.'

Wolf did acknowledge that the place of the beauty myth in magazines is primarily economic, with advertisers selling beauty products to the female consumer, but the thrust of her book is about male culture keeping women in their beautifying place with beauty as the measure of their social value.

In 2020, during the COVID-19 pandemic when many women globally were in lockdowns in private homes, the beauty market value worldwide (beauty, personal care, haircare and colour cosmetics) was an astonishing $US742 billion. It rose from 2019 valued then at $US532 billion. At the time Wolf wrote *The Beauty Myth*, she reported a revenue of $US20 billion worldwide in skincare.

The statistics of today illustrate what a huge business the beauty industry is, intent to make money, largely through women buying their beauty products and services, and/or cosmetic surgeries. In 2018, Australia's beauty products and services were worth $6.5 billion.

Patrick Tansley, President of the Australasian College of Cosmetic Surgery informs that, 'it is estimated Australians spend $1billion on cosmetic procedures a year, excluding the "underground" black market, making Australia one of the "cosmetic surgical capitals" of the world. The country now spends more per capita in this area than the US.'

In 2019, it was reported that woman account for 92% of all cosmetic surgeries. The most popular surgeries included breast augmentation, breast reduction, liposuction, tummy tucks and eyelid surgery.

Getting back to Wolf's thesis, I question how many women globally have actually fully internalised the beauty ideal? And what does this really mean in practice? Do they then act on this internalisation by trying to achieve the ideal or measure themselves by it? Can we quantify this and what about women exercising their own agency, making choices whether to follow the whole ideal, some of it or whether to reject it entirely? Where do these variables factor into her contention? Surely, not every woman alive actively pursued all elements of the feminine beauty ideals she espoused during her time of writing? I admit that I like to have my hair foiled regularly and wear eye makeup, lipstick and blusher because it makes me feel more attractive but I am not prepared to have fillers and botox in my face to achieve that result.

There are women out there who actually enjoy the process of beautification and feel empowered by it, like exercising and following a healthy lean diet because it makes them feel good. And the result is that they usually are slim or thin because of these processes, not because they are starving their wondrous bodies and/or because of good genetics and/or good metabolisms. Feminist and Co-founder of *Ms. Magazine*, Gloria Steinem, was accused of being anorexic, to which she replied, 'Anorexia is young well-to-do women who starve themselves. That's not me. I feel better when I'm thinner.'

Undoubtedly, there are those women who do take it to an extreme, denying themselves nutrition to get there. But again, can we quantify this in numbers? How many women are there in entire populations? Wolf's sweeping assertion is also stretching, that women want this beauty ideal so much that 'At a certain point inside the cult of "beauty," dieting becomes anorexia or compulsion eating or bulimia.' Surely, not every dieter develops an eating disorder. While dieting to look like the ideal body may be a precursor to contracting an eating disorder, it is unlikely to be the one and only root cause of such a disturbing mental illness.

The highly regarded medical Mayo Clinic in the United States informs that there are a 'myriad of causes of eating disorders like anorexia or bulimia: genetic and biological ones such as changes in brain chemicals. Psychological and emotional problems contribute to the disorder such as low self-esteem, perfectionism, impulsive behaviour and troubled relationships. Dieting and starvation can affect brain chemicals; influence mood changes, anxiety, rigid thinking and reduce appetite. Stress can also increase the risk of contracting an eating disorder, the clinic reports.' Family and cultural factors can also contribute, author Autumn-Whitefield Madrano adds in *Face Value*.

My eating pattern changed when I was around 20 years old. I used to love watching the television series *Charlie's Angels* about crime-fighting detectives enacted by three beautiful white actresses: Farah Fawcett, Jaclyn Smith and Kate Jackson. They were all very slim. Jackson was thin and impeccably groomed, and Fawcett's feathered layered hairstyle was copied by women worldwide who loved the look. I copied it too.

I wanted to look like them. At primary school, I was called 'fatty' a couple of times, as my figure was fuller then. I wasn't fat. But the memory of being called fat in a derogatory way and the image of the three *Charlie's Angels* did have some impact on me, influencing me in my future appearance. I wanted to look very slim at least. At that point in my life, I was probably not so confident in myself as a person but that changed positively in time.

When the television show aired in 1976, I didn't eat well nor did I exercise except for going for walks. I lost weight and became very slim but didn't approach it in the healthiest way. During the late 1970s, a friend told me about aerobics classes – exercise to music with a cardio component. I tried it and loved it but was so unfit that I had to lie down on the bed afterwards to recuperate. I realised how unfit I was and decided to go more often to become fit. The exercise made me hungry and over time, I needed to learn how to eat well, healthily and find a balance so I could attain the desired look I wanted to. That includes having a little chocolate daily which makes me feel good. A few years ago, I became ill and realised the importance of good nutrition even more. Starving one's body does damage, depriving the body and brain of nutrients they need to function healthily.

When I did achieve my desired look, I'll never forget how one of the fitness instructors reacted when he saw me. 'Wow! You did it. You look great!' he praised me.

This reaction shocked me quite frankly. But he made me feel exactly how Robin Givhan described in the prologue: 'welcomed into the cultural conversation... seen and accepted...relevant and I matter(ed).'

Why should it matter whether I lost weight or not? It shouldn't. I was no different as a person, fuller or thinner.

AN UPSIDE OF BEAUTY

While Wolf touches upon an upside of beauty, Law Professor Deborah Rhode shifts the beauty discussion and suggests that 'For some women, our cultural preoccupation with appearance is a source of wasted effort and expense. For other women, the pursuit of beauty is a source of pleasure and agency, and a showcase for cultural identity... Time spent shopping or in spas and salons provides pleasure and opportunities for female bonding. (And) appearance is an opportunity for self-expression and self-determination.'

Hannah McCann, Lecturer in Cultural Studies adds to this positive view of women's beauty. She argues that there is an emotional component in beauty to consider. There are women who feel good by accessing beauty treatments and frequenting beauty salons. It's not just the aesthetic result they feel good about but through their emotional and social human connection to their hair and beauty therapists.

McCann has interviewed hair and beauty workers in Melbourne to learn that they hear about many aspects of these women's lives – their mental health issues, illness, personal grief, family woes, and gender and sexuality struggles, for example.

McCann indicates the physical intimacy of salon visits that women experience in the process. 'In the salon, social and physical proximity collide with surface improvement. That the line between identity and appearance is slippery means that the change process in the salon feels deeply personal. Not only are you spilling the details of your life to someone who is massaging your head, you are also letting them style your identity.' I have also engaged in chatter with my hairdresser on occasion when I felt emotional like when my mother had passed away. I just let it all out.

She cites the example of Rosa, a CBD hairdresser, to illustrate her case: 'People come in sometimes really depressed and when they walk out … they are just so happy. You are talking to them, you are giving them something that makes them feel good. You are like their psychologist … Some of them don't really know you that well and they love to pour out their heart to you.'

McCann concludes that beauty treatments can transform a person's outside as well as inside.

AUTUMN WHITEFIELD-MADRANO: *FACE VALUE*

Based on scholarly research and interviews with nearly a hundred women from all walks of life (fashion models; photographers, bodybuilders, morticians, sex workers and nuns, for example)

Madrano's *Face Value* goes a step further to discuss contradictions in how women feel about beauty. She finds women's relationship with beauty and self-image is not clear-cut, not black and white. She states, 'contradiction is the marker of how so many women regard beauty.'

She cites an example of herself looking in the mirror and thinking she looks good some days and rotten on others. Frankly, I think that would be a common response among many women. It applies to me. Recently, I went to a person's private home for dinner and thought I looked pretty ordinary. The hostess's mother who was there said to me in the course of the evening 'Gee, you look good.'

But Madrano wonders whether the outside world sees her the same way as she sees herself or if it is just her who sees her like that. And she raises an interesting, valid question about contradictions: 'Do we keep buying women's magazines because they make us feel bad or good, or both?' I actually subscribe to *Marie Claire Australia* and *Vogue Australia* for the value of reading the interesting articles in the former and looking at fashion and beauty in the latter – not for either reason Madrano asks.

Through her research and interviews, Madrano dispels the myth that the media is universally harmful to women and that most women feel bad about themselves because of the media's visual images. 'There is a more nuanced story of our response to media,' says Madrano.

Interestingly, Madrano found fluctuations in how women saw themselves compared with the visual images in the media. Typically, she found in her interviews that those women had a richer relationship with how they saw themselves, one that was actually uplifting. I find this extraordinary, particularly because we don't generally hear this in the media. Why isn't it publicised more? How often do we hear that women feel good about how they look – that they are actually satisfied?

Admittedly, Madrano's interviews were conducted at a later time than when Wolf's book was written. And since then, there has been some public persuasion urging the media to represent more realistic images of women that better reflect our society with some small success so far, discussed further on in the chapter on diversity.

In *Face Value,* Madrano was surprised to find women who identified with the images of women in the media and actually viewed themselves more positively afterwards. She cites three studies, two of which were conducted around the time of Wolf's publication. In one study, dieters who looked at pictures of slender women said they did not want to be thinner. Those women believed they were slimmer than the women in the visual images and this belief increased their evaluation of their overall appearance. In a second study, she looked at women who viewed idealised images of other women and found that they 'experienced a mild euphoria and reported *lower* levels of depression, an effect echoed by participants in yet another study whose self-esteem rose after looking at pictures of moderately thin models.'

Through her findings, Madrano concluded that women who have good self-esteem and a positive sense of their own body image are less likely to respond negatively to the visual body images in the media. 'So despite talk of the damage that beauties on billboards can do, it's not that images *globally* hurt women, but rather that women with shaky self-esteem are susceptible to their potential damage.' This is an important finding that looks at the chicken and the egg situation – what comes first? It should be publicised so that women are aware of the connection between feeling good about oneself and self-esteem.

Rhode concludes with some useful pointers that we could follow: 'Appearance should be a source of pleasure, not of shame. Individuals should be able to make decisions about whether to enhance their attractiveness without being judged politically incorrect or professionally unacceptable. Our ideals of appearance should reflect diversity across race, ethnicity, age and body size. The media needs to offer more diverse and natural images of beauty and avoid promoting fraudulent appearance-related advertisements. In order for appearance to be a source of enjoyment rather than anxiety, it cannot dictate women's self worth.' Rhodes' comments make a lot of sense.

HEATHER WIDDOWS: *PERFECT ME*

Perfect Me by philosopher Heather Widdows is based on academic research and the author's personal view about women's beauty. She claims that beauty is an ethical, moral ideal and value framework.

Sweepingly, she says that 'Many people judge themselves according to their success and failure in beauty terms... We are "good" when we do all kind of beauty-related actions: when we say "no thanks" to cake, chocolate, cheese, or carbs: force ourselves to go for a run.' She extends this 'good' to mean 'morally good.'

'Beauty failure results in explicit judgments of culpability and responsibility and as such, beauty failures, for some, are effectively equivalent to moral vices. Beauty failure is not a local or partial failure, but a failure of the self.'

This is the crux of her book – that beauty is a moral ideal.

I see a number of problems with this claim. I agree with philosopher Steven Ross who says that Widdows offers 'no systematic or even casual account of "the moral"... what is characteristic of the moral, and how much of it might be found intact in contemporary beauty practice?'

Ross adds that 'There is no wrongfully injured party when one fails with respect to beauty.'

I think rather than 'moral', perhaps what Widdows is getting at is that there is a belief system in place where certain women believe that their behaviour is good if they follow the beauty practices like dieting, saying no to that tempting piece of yummy cake or chocolate, for example, or exercising to shape their bodies into the current feminine ideal or following any other prescriptive kind of behaviour that achieves the beauty look of the moment. And consequently, they pat themselves on the back and feel good about themselves for acquiescing.

This has happened to me. I have said no to a slice of cake, thinking it will show outwardly on my tummy, feeling proud of my decision. Then, I became angry with myself for thinking this way and not really wishing to behave like that. It is years of conditioning – denial of that pleasure of eating the cake to look good. That's what we have been taught in our Western culture.

There are problems with some of Widdows' other claims: for example, *Perfect Me* is laden with descriptions of 'many' or 'some' in her assertions. I would like to know how many? The majority, or? And what does 'some' mean? Two or three or?

I find it hard to believe that 'many' judge themselves a total failure if they don't achieve the feminine beauty ideal. Our identity and subjectivity are not singular. Rather, we are made up of multiple selves. First and foremost, we are a person, a human being – perhaps a daughter, granddaughter, mother, grandmother, paid worker, friend etc. Each position has its own meanings.

We all have character and are not one-dimensional. We can be kind, generous considerate and hot-headed and have many other character traits, for example. How we look is merely an outward representation. It is not the sum of who we are as people. As Steven Ross says, 'There is no one self with one set of desires, but a series of selves across time with different concerns.'

I also find Widdows' claim that beauty is a 'value framework' limited. It excludes other worthy values in life. What about relationships with family, friends, work, good health, philanthropy, appreciation of the arts and sciences, love of animals, care of our environment and so on? Don't they count as aspiring values in life? Why should external physical beauty be a value? What is so worthy about that?

So what is the current feminine ideal according to Widdows? 'Being thin is primary in being perfect.' With global variation, beautiful bodies must be thin, perhaps with curves, and bodies with breasts and butt curves and faces must be firm, smooth and young, (with) luminous, glowing skin, with smallish-straight noses, large eyes and plump lips.

Before Widdows published her book in 2018, the body positivity movement and campaign for diversity and inclusivity had begun and yet she excludes any major discussion of these changes other than a sentence on the body-positive movement. I would have liked to see more discussion here. She does say, however, that 'thinness remains a key feature of the beauty ideal, one that is becoming more dominant.' In women's magazines like *Marie Claire Australia* and *Vogue Australia*, most of the models are thin. However, some diversity is seeping in and *Vogue Australia* is making a concerted effort to address this issue.

I agree with Widdows when she says that we can 'choose the extent' to which we comply with and endorse the beauty ideal and there is not only individual choice but (also) social and communal pressure. I have bought into this one before but it also made me question whether I was compromising my health to do it. However, I disagree with her claim 'to choose not to conform is regarded as abnormal'.

For whom is it abnormal? There are women who are not interested in beautifying and prefer to stay natural. For those women, it is not an important value at all even if they may be a minority.

We do have choices in life, whether to follow a beauty ideal, some aspects of it or reject it entirely. But these choices are contextual and historical, located in time and place and are constrained by these circumstances. Widdows rightly says, 'We are constrained, but not coerced, and we make agential and active choices in contexts that are extremely limited and prescribed.'

But ultimately, we are the ones who make that choice.

Overall, *Perfect Me* is an interesting read and offers insight into the technical, surgical and chemical ways to create the perfect feminine ideal, perhaps something to learn about, even though I may not agree with some of her claims.

EVOLUTIONARY PERSPECTIVE

An evolutionary perspective explains women's physical beauty differently to the previous views. Evolutionists see women's value as a mate, providing genetic success based on their physical beauty. Evolutionist Jack da Silva says our urbanised world has inherited our roots as hunters and gatherers.

In this hunting and gathering world, it was important to the male that the female could bear and rear lots of children. The male's job was to hunt for food and protect the women and children. 'For the vast majority of our history, that's how we lived.'

In this perspective, women's beauty has been associated with their potential to procreate and extend the gene pool. 'The theory is that beauty reflects a person's genetic quality,' da Silva says.

Da Silva explains that even though a man wants a fertile mate when making his choice in partner, for evolutionary reasons, this is not a conscious decision. He informs that human beings judge beauty based on symmetry, so symmetry of the face is a quality sought after in choosing a mate because possibly that reflects (a good) genetic quality of the person.

Evolutionary biologist, Jeanne Bovet adds that youth and health to reproduce are determining factors of women's beauty in this evolutionary perspective. Men use the cues of aging present in the face to judge a woman's attractiveness. And they tend to prefer partners with a lower waist-to-hip ratio (although this can vary in rural areas) because it is correlated to hormone levels and fertility.

Da Silva notes features that attract men to a female mate include a face with average features – not too big or small a nose or ears, eyes not too wide apart or too close together.

The colour and texture of the skin is also factored into what is considered to be genetically attractive and a feature of the feminine beauty ideal. 'Skin quality is an important element. Homogenous, smooth skin is judged as healthier, younger and more attractive. Reddish skin is linked to health and fertility.'

Da Silva claims that even though 'there are a lot of variations, people generally agree on who's beautiful and who's not. Everybody tends to think (celebrity) Angelina Jolie is beautiful.'

Molecular biologist Daniel Yarosh claims that 'the preference for symmetry is culturally universal suggesting that is hard-wired into brain judgments by natural selection and not derived from culture.'

But how can we really know this?

And what about men choosing female partners who don't have the attributes considered as evolutionary attractive? How can evolution theory explain that?

Those women are likely to be attractive in some other way/s to the men who have partnered with them.

What about cultural and geographical variations of the evolutionary feminine ideal across time and place? How does evolution account for those differences?

History also illustrates that feminine beauty ideals change

over time and place; they are not static.

Perhaps evolution has played a role in our considered ideal of feminine beauty but the theory also leaves me with those unanswered questions. Socio-cultural influences are very likely to shape our perceptions of what constitutes a woman's beauty. And it is likely that there has been some interplay between evolutionary, economic and socio-cultural forces that accounts for feminine beauty ideals.

Or could it be that human beings derive pleasure from looking at a beautiful face? Could it simply be an appreciation of the aesthetic? Is that why we value women's beauty in Western society today and have for some time?

Psychologist Olga Chelnokova from Oslo University says the brain reward system creates feelings of pleasure when we look at a pretty face.

And perhaps there is. But how can we really know?

SUSIE ORBACH: *BODIES*

I think *Bodies* by psychotherapist Susie Orbach is a valuable contribution to the discussion on women's physical beauty. She says that our bodies 'are no longer seen or experienced simply as things to be washed, deodorized, dressed and performed before getting on with our day.'

So, what then are bodies?

According to Orbach, 'bodies are and have become a form of work. *The body is turning from being the means of production to the production itself.*'

Orbach means that we *do* bodies. Doing bodies is beauty labour. The end achieved is a product. And I agree with her. We do beauty. Most of us are not naturally beautiful according to the cultural yardstick of beauty at the time. But we can make ourselves look like a version of what the current standard of beauty is in that moment through current beauty practices.

We do our hair or the hairdresser does. We dress. We perform our exercise. We do our makeup. It's all an act, a 'doing' action. In the end, we give and deliver a performance, a 'doing' action. We present ourselves outwardly as a woman. I elaborate on this idea of beauty as a performance in chapters 5–7 of *Reframing Beauty*.

Orbach alerts us to the extent that Western culture is focused on transforming our bodies to fit a physical feminine beauty ideal. I was horrified at what she wrote about cosmetic surgery app games marketed to girls as young as six, where bodies are carved up into parts – 'eyes, hairline, from breast to waists, then hips, bums, leg shapes and feet' – that can be transformed to achieve this beauty ideal.

There is something very wrong with a culture and society that creates, markets and sells apps like these to little girls. And to their mothers if they are the ones buying them – what are we teaching our daughters and granddaughters? That we, as women, are merely made up of body parts and our bodies are to be manipulated, dismantled and reconstructed as a norm?

So who is to blame for the focus on doing bodies?

Orbach credits highly profitable business under the umbrella of the beauty and style industries – fashion, cosmetics, diet, wellness, fitness, surgical and pharmaceutical industries all promoting the 'body beautiful.'

And she says that our visual culture promotes the body beautiful globally. The images become 'identity markers, framing our streets, our magazines, Facebook and Instagram. We engage with these images, using them as a means to belong and to show our belonging. We want to be inside not outside.'

This wanting to belong would particularly apply to the younger generation who are very engaged with social media. And this argument about wanting to belong inside a group of people is a human need, a need to connect with other human beings. It makes sense to me as I think back on my youth. When I was around 15, I wanted to be accepted by, feel connected to and be part of my peer group. So what did I do?

I remember consciously observing what they wore. Collectively, they looked like a uniform – blue Levi jeans, a white or black Bonds t-shirt and Adidas sneakers.

I went out and bought this look – the uniform to feel a belonging and be accepted by the group, even though I knew they had already accepted me for who I was. I suppose I wanted to be identified as one of them.

Orbach's *Bodies* was originally published in 2009, written before the body positivity movement emerged in 2012 that challenges unrealistic feminine beauty standards and send the message that 'all bodies are beautiful,' advocating greater acceptance of all body shapes and colours. *Bodies* was also written before the campaign for diversity and inclusivity of feminine beauty hit the runway – the fashion and cosmetics industries, discussed more fully in chapter four.

Her point, however, is still valid that the 'new grammar of visual culture' – 'the photographic image, the moving image on television, film and the selfie – have created this new visual grammar ... almost worldwide dissemination of common imagery. Its effects should not be underestimated ... The very quantity of these images make it impossible not to be affected by them ...what we see in London is not so different from what the billboards display in Rio, Shanghai or Accra.'

This grammar of visual culture was not around 70 years ago or so. It has really taken off big time with the advent and power of the Internet and social media enabling and promoting human connection over the last 30 years. And has impacted with its bombardment of messages about women's external almost as a norm to be followed.

PERFORMANCE OF BEAUTY

Extending the notion of Orbach's *doing* beauty, I invite the reader to consider the idea of beauty as a performance. An act of beauty, an act of 'doing', as Susie Orbach has referred to about bodies. This idea of beauty as a performance can be applied widely in different contexts. I look at it in terms of how women are living their lives and what they are doing with their lives personally and/or professionally. It is about the inner self rather than the visual, outer and external self. Chapters six and seven address this issue in more detail but for now, let's explore what others have seen as a beauty performance.

HISTORICALLY

Historian Christine Adams discusses the idea of beauty as a performance, executed by the mistresses of French Kings, for example. She suggests that Madame de Montespan, mistress of King Louis XIV of France (late 1660–70s) deployed her beauty – her 'blonde hair, blue eyes and dazzling white skin' – to ignite the Kings' passion and favour. This mistress used her beauty that also encompassed charm, wit, intelligence and self-confidence to become a power broker at the French court, when few women had economic power or political sway.

Similarly, historian Linda Kiernan has found that Madame Pompadour, mistress of King Louis XV of France (1745) also deployed beauty as a performance to assert political influence in his court. In this case, Pompadour, with her 'fiery, sparkling, blue eyes, magnificent skin and good figure, performed her beautification at her toilette', a morning ritual introduced by the King who relied upon her opinion, mediating between him and court members.

The 'toilette' was her private yet public space where she would groom and dress for the day, establishing or cementing political ties with 'courtiers, brilliant men of letters and diplomats, as she held audience in her de facto court.'

It was where she fashioned a beauty performance in her appearance on public display.

Christine Adams also examined the beauty performance of Madame Tallien, the wife of French politician and revolutionary Jean-Lambert Tallien. Adams notes how Madame Tallien deployed her 'dazzling' beauty – her perfect features, silky black hair, enchanting smile and charming voice – for political ends to help end the political terror engulfing France.

She used her beauty, sense of fashion and trend-setting style to shape political outcomes, working as a power broker, saving lives from arrest and the guillotine during the Directory in France 1795–1799 in the hands of a French revolutionary government, amidst corruption and political unrest. Her 'beauty gave her access to powerful men.'

Of course, there have been women before these French mistresses who have used their outward appearance and beauty as a means of getting what they wanted, politically or otherwise. Those cited here are just a few examples.

CONTEMPORARY: MODELS

This idea of beauty as a performance is evident in today's world too, not just historically. Sociologist Patricia Soley-Beltran notes that 'Models are performers.' Apart from their outward attractiveness, runway, billboard or magazine models perform beauty. It can be in the application of makeup, hair styling and/ or strutting the catwalk runway. It's all a performance, a 'doing' action. 'Strutting the catwalk may require a model to have runway lessons with a professional catwalk coach to learn how to walk the exaggerated walk that's expected, lifting the legs, planting one foot directly in front of the other rather than in front of its own hip socket. The overall effect generates a very distinct bounce that is an over-blown parody of a walk,' according to Joanne Entwhistle (reader in cultural studies) and Ashley Mears (former model and sociologist).

The model has to care for her body, manage her shape and weight. To achieve this goal, the model may need to perform workouts at the gym or undertake some sort of exercise program, consume a low-calorie count intake of food or follow a specific diet. She also needs to perform a sense of style when dressing for a casting. Sometimes, brokers guide models, take them shopping to a store like Topshop or suggest they look at *Vogue* magazine for ideas on style.

And the model has also to create and cultivate a personality. She needs to give a performance of 'self'. She needs to do this to sell herself to 'brokers who broker the trade' or at a casting audition for a modelling job. This performance is executed through smiling, 'solid eye contact and manufacturing the persona of *genuine* niceness, (even) flirting.'

'Self confidence is an emotion models constantly perform,' says sociologist Patricia Soley-Beltran.

I extend this idea of beauty as a performance and see how it can be applied in other ways of seeing beauty further on in the book. It seems, however, that external appearance or beauty is somewhat rewarded. Oh, please!

REWARDS OF BEAUTY: 'THE BEAUTY PREMIUM'

Journalist Roe McDermott describes the rewards of beauty as 'the beauty premium.'

She highlights some of these economic and social rewards. According to research findings, she informs that those considered conventionally attractive earn more money with a starting salary higher than those deemed less attractive and are more privy to professional advancement. Real estate brokers, for example, who are considered attractive, bring in more money than their less attractive peers.

More attractive congressional mid-term candidates are more likely to become elected than those less attractive. She says that 'assumptions are made about attractive people like they are more sociable, dominant, sexually warm and socially skilled than unattractive people.'

Reading someone's character based on their appearance is coined the 'halo effect' – the assumption that a beautiful person has positive character traits too because of their physical attractiveness.

McDermott cites a Harvard study that illustrated how women who wore makeup to work were thought to be more competent, likeable and trustworthy than those women who wore none. She says another UK study found that women classified as overweight or obese are more likely to be paid a lower salary than men of the same weight.

Allana Akhtar, Reporter, and Drake Baer, Deputy Editor of *Business Insider,* add to McDermott's list, citing other global research. They inform that one finding indicated teachers favoured good-looking children, perceiving them to have greater potential, and their subsequent preferential treatment of these students leads to building greater confidence, social and communication skills that 'translates into academic success and professional success.'

Another study found that more attractive female and male political candidates were found to be more successful than their less attractive competitors. And yet, another discovered that attractive women were invited for call-back interviews 54% of the time compared to 47% of attractive men and the average call back placed at 30%.

Are we surprised to learn that other research discovered that 92% of males wanted someone good-looking in a long-term partner, a trait they deemed essential or desirable? 80% of these men wanted a good-looking woman who was also slender.

These findings bear out how a woman's physical beauty has been socially valued and how it can be a 'powerful tool of persuasion.' But it's time that we dismantle that value.

We don't really think about beauty as an idea but these pages have explored and offered ways of seeing it in this light. The ideas of beauty discussed here have been influential, impactful and gained contextual currency in the time they were espoused and continue to be considered today, like Naomi Wolf's. For me, Susie Orbach's views expressed here are a takeaway because she articulates a concept of *doing* beauty in terms of bodies. But this notion can be extended in a number of ways and I extend it to examine how girls and women are doing beauty in the ways they live their lives in the later chapters of this book.

Now, let's take a look at beauty ideals of the past to see what they were and how they have changed in time.

CHAPTER THREE: CHANGES IN BEAUTY OVER TIME

*'History shows that standards of beauty
are constantly changing.'*
– Sharon Romm, *Beauty Through History*, Washington Post

This chapter offers a glimpse at and sample of dominant ideals of women's beauty to illustrate some variation or changes in the ideal. The beauty ideal incorporates several components – the face, body, fashion, skincare, cosmetics and hairstyles – and the chapter highlights some at different points in time. The components are all a visual part of our culture produced in a social context, time and place and can vary culturally and geographically.

The beauty ideal is part of society – the inside part, not outside, external to it. We need to bear in mind what Charlotte Fiell, design historian, and Emmanuelle Dirix, fashion historian, say: 'Fashion is bound to the imaginary with its fixation with the perfect body and its obsession with ever-changing ideals of beauty.'

WAY BACK

Let's go back in time and start with the ancient Greeks. Going back 2,400 years ago where physical beauty was considered a virtue like honesty and bravery.

Beautiful, according to the ancient Greeks, equalled harmonious proportioned facial features. According to Plato, the Greek philosopher, 'the perfect face was a system of triads. It was divided into three sections: from the hairline to the eyes, from the eyes to the upper lip and from the upper lip to the chin. The ideal face was two-thirds as wide as it was high.'

Other features seen as physical beauty for the ancient Greeks was a straight nose and a low forehead to look youthful. Perfect eyebrows forming an arch, a reddish mouth, lower lip slightly fuller than the upper. But the most important trait was something that has long been treasured as a contemporary feminine beauty ideal – blonde hair, flax colour. The blonde hair was also an ideal feminine beauty trait in the Middle Ages from the 13th to the 15th centuries.

This may surprise, but a fuller, plump body shape was perceived as beautiful for the ideal ancient Greek woman and light skin. In contrast, the ancient Egyptian feminine ideal (500–300 BC) was slender with a high waist, narrow shoulders and a symmetrical face.

In the Han dynasty (second imperial dynasty of China, 206 BC–220AD) the ideal feminine beauty had large eyes, red lips, white teeth, a slim waist, pale skin and small feet.

The Italian Renaissance (C1400-1700) favoured the ample bosom, rounded stomach, full hips and fair skin as the feminine beauty ideal. The paintings of 16th-century artist Peter Paul Rubens were of female subjects, pale and plump, with 'rounded thighs and swelling busts.'

The look for the Victorian feminine ideal was a pale face

with rosy cheeks, big dark eyes, a plump face and a body with a cinched waist created by the corset.

THE MODERN BEAUTY LOOK

The 1890s witnessed a period of change with the world moving away from the moralistic, stuffy Victorian era. In America, there was the growth of urbanisation and new technology like electricity introduced into manufacturing, creating a ready-to-wear clothing market.

At this time, middle-class women were enjoying new levels of independence working outside the home and sought the right to vote and other rights. They were intellectual, young, cycled and played sport. 'This woman was personified in the Gibson Girl, the archetype of American middle-class womanhood.'

The Gibson Girl was youthful looking, ephemerally beautiful, sexy but respectable and graceful, with ample bosom, hips and buttocks, sporting an athletic figure. Her hair was worn up. Her makeup routine would comprise putting on moisturiser; powder; foundation; rouge; grey, brown and lemon eye shadow on her eyelids and lightly stained lips.

She wore a new kind of corset, bell-shaped skirt with a nipped-waist effect: shirtwaist; tailored dresses high in the neck with fitted sleeves. Women of all classes wanted to wear the fashion of the Gibson Girl. She set the standard of beauty and fashion. And 'was widely imitated abroad.'

This image, a feminine ideal created by Charles Dana Gibson, a popular illustrator, and his 'Gibson Girl' was stamped into the pages of popular women's magazines that women bought. 'Illustrators and advertisers defined beauty and marketed to a mass audience of young American girls who wanted to emulate the fashionable woman in their favourite magazines.'

20TH CENTURY: WORLD WAR ONE (1914–1918)

For most of the 20th century, Western ideals of feminine beauty meant a Eurocentric, Caucasian face with blonde hair as the dominant and most highly valued look. Going back in time, we can see the changes made along the way as we travel forward.

World War One (1914–1918) emboldened women as they stepped into performing men's jobs like munitions, factories, railways, guards, ticket collectors, bus and tram conductors, postal workers, bank tellers and clerks, police, firefighters, engineering, on farms, in the public service and they also worked for the Red Cross while the men fought for their countries.

These changes had ramifications in beauty. By the end of the war, women were more daring, more confident rejecting the 'Gibson Girl' image of their mother's generation, wanting more, particularly when the roaring 1920s hit.

Caucasian models in advertisements were the feminine ideal early on in the war, when colour cosmetics were deemed socially unacceptable, although there was a double standard with beauty advertisements enticing women to beautify. There were women who defied societal standards and women painted their lips, not in quite the bright red lipstick worn by prostitutes or the suffragettes, to signify power and strength 'as a defiant symbol of their right to make choices as women.'

Ordinary women did wear colour on their lips during the war in deeper colours (pink, pale and soft red and auburn like autumn leaves) more-so than the Gibson Girl wore as many online visual fashion images indicate. Lip salves were sold, portable and affordable to many and so was a metal push-up lipstick, even though at this time, society objected to women applying colour cosmetics.

During the war, women did wear face powder and rouge even if they were discouraged by the broader society. 'During

World War 1, an enameled compact (of powder, puff and mirror) symbolized just how quickly women changed their place in society in the span of four years. It hinted at freedom and being seen and heard.'

Ironically, while society expected women not to indulge in cosmetics, they were encouraged by beauty advertisers like cosmetics mogul Helena Rubinstein to buy beauty products in the name of patriotism and there was an uptick in makeup ads to reinforce (women's) duty to stay feminine.

The sales of Rubinstein's face cream soared while she lectured to women in advertisements: 'your patriotism demands that you keep your face bright and attractive so that you radiate optimism.'

In 1916, there were women who wore eyeliner and mascara, although it was in the 1920s when these products were more heavily used. And it was not until after the war that the beauty industry in America took off big time, making millions of dollars in the sale of cosmetics, and New York became a new fashion player that rivalled Paris, hitherto the fashion leader of the world, says Geoffrey Jones, Professor of Business History.

At this time, 'Tastes in clothing fashion changed as did taste in women's faces.'

Women's fashion became simpler during the war. Jackets were worn longer over hips and belted dresses no longer emphasised the waist as they had been in earlier corseted dresses. Skirts became shorter as the war progressed.

In the last year of the war, 1918, midi dresses were worn; the waistline sat above the natural waist. Belted skirts were popular along with blouses and knitted cardigans with matching scarves, mittens and hats. In the home, percale striped cotton and chambray gingham checked dresses were popular. Taffeta, velvet, silk and crepe were worn by those who could afford the fabric for going out. Brown or black-laced boots were seen as a necessity and pointed and round-toe shoes, on small heels one to two and a half inches were enjoyed.

A slightly hourglass figure seems to have been the ideal body image even though a range of bodies can be seen in the advertisements for corsets that were improved since the 'Gibson Girl' days. The corset at this time was intended to minimise the abdomen and hips. The Designer Magazine advertised the Gossard corset for ideal tall and short heavy figures; ideal tall, slender figures; ideal large women above and below the waistline; ideal arched back and a short waist figure.

The feminine ideal hairstyle during the war was a soft-curled bob that women sported.

THE ROARING 1920s: THE FLAPPER

Out of the following socio-cultural, political and technological developments, a new feminine ideal was born in the 1920s: the flapper in the United States of America and Europe. In the 1920s, women did not want to surrender their independence gained during World War One through their increased participation in paid employment. In 1920, in the United States, women were granted the right to vote, giving them some political power. Alcohol was sold and consumed by young women in this time of prohibition when it was banned from consumption and purchase. Technology was advancing and the automobile became available at cheap prices increasing the flapper's mobility. And birth control allowed women to explore their sexuality without facing the consequence of unwanted pregnancies.

So who was this flapper? A cultural symbol of the 1920s, she was young, free-spirited, 'fast-moving-fast-talking, reckless and unfazed by previous social conventions and taboos. She smoked cigarettes, drank alcohol, rode in and drove fast cars and kissed and "petted" with different men.'

The flapper was the feminine ideal that appealed to young women – her ideal look, a boyish figure, emphasised a lack of hips, breasts and a defined waist. Flappers generally wore no corset although at this time, a girdle or elasticated corset replaced the former stiff restricted whalebone version (for those who wore it). The flapper ideal embraced an androgynous look. This young woman wore bras or fabric bands to flatten her breasts and clothing that gave a curve-less look.

'The fashion look was about the whole look and how the body itself was fashioned. The simple lines and androgynous shapes of fashion looked best on bodies free of curves. Through exercise and diet and various shaping undergarments women attempted to achieve this look.'

So what did the flapper wear? Silk or rayon sheer stockings were worn on the legs, sometimes rolled below the knee, with high-heeled shoes or pointed low-heeled ones that were easier to dance in. Flappers wore their dresses at calf length, waistless and straight. Evening dresses with long necklines tended to be beaded or embroidered or trimmed with fine lace, epitomised by French designer Jean Patou. Coco Chanel's influence was also asserted in the 1920s with her design of the long chain necklace and multiple strands of pearls that flappers adopted as a look.

The narrow, close-fitting cloche hat decorated with feathers, beads or artificial flowers was an accessory worn by flappers during the day. Flappers wore their hair cut into a bob, usually with waves or curls and a flashy headband. Their eyes were heavily made up with kohl eyeliner and mascara, lips painted red, powder and rouge dabbed on cheeks and thinly plucked arched eyebrows.

The movie industry impacted on and influenced the beauty ideal, further popularising the 1920s look and it continues to influence beauty ideals today. Great Garbo, Marlene Dietrich and Clara Bow embodied the 1920s look. Dietrich with her 'plucked eyebrows, etched lips and rouge painted beneath the cheekbones typified the elegant face.'

'And Clara Bow embodied the flapper, exemplifying the iconic image of the 1920s,' says her biographer Judith Mackrell in *Flappers: Six Women of a Dangerous Generation.*

THE 1930s

While the 1920s marked a decade of liberation for women in terms of economic, social and political gains, it manifested in the flapper fashion ideal. But this freer look changed by the end of 1929 after the Wall Street crash and the collapse of the stock market that plunged America into a Great Depression with global ramifications. Subsequently, fashion lost its youthful free-spirited look from the ebullient 1920s and became more conservative and elegant in the 1930s.

The 1930s feminine ideal was influenced by the Hollywood Golden Age and talkie movies that replaced the former silent ones. 'Thanks to Hollywood, the ideal of the "blue-eyed blonde" female with pronounced cheekbones was born.' Movies popularised the peroxide blonde look sported by 1930s movie stars Jean Harlow, June Lang, Carole Lombard, Ginger Rogers and Mae West, for example.

There was a shift in eye makeup style from the 1920s vamp look to one that was softer in the 1930s. The dark kohl on the eyes was replaced by softer hues: pearl; blue; violet; green; brown or grey. Blue or black mascara or curled false eyelashes complete the eye look. And dark, heavily tweezed arched eyebrows framed the ideal face.

Matte ruby red lipstick was the stand-out colour worn on lips. The ideal look was to have nail fingertips matching the lipstick. 'The polish was only applied in the centre of the nail with a half-moon above the cuticle and tip left bare.'

The movie stars of the time embodied the feminine ideal in the 1930s, inspiring women to emulate their style by copying their makeup and hairstyle at an affordable cost. The ideal face was made up to look like a light complexion with a pink undertone, followed by powder in white or ivory. Cream rouge was then applied to the cheekbones in apricot or rose or raspberry then patted with translucent powder. Hair was worn short with a wave or curl. *The 1930s Fashion: The Definitive Sourcebook* offers a wonderful visual representation of hair, makeup and fashion of that period.

'By the mid 1930s, the ideal female figure sported a small waist (belted) and slim hips to accentuate the elegant form fitting clothing styles.' Suits accentuated by exaggerated shoulders presented a popular look and dresses cut on the bias against the weave. Day dresses in floral, plaid, dots and abstract prints were worn at mid-calf length. Casual clothing was another look – high-waist pants, jumpers and shirts. Pointed and closed-back shoes were the ideal footwear on a heel and hats were a must-have accessory.

The look for evening was a soft silhouette – satin dresses with a low back, glamorous shining dresses, silk fabric, fur and feathers were fashionable. Germany did not follow these fashion and beauty ideals under the rule of Adolf Hitler. While he promoted a natural look for women: 'healthy skin free of make-up and natural hair worn in buns or plaits... the majority of German women continued to dye their hair and paint their lips throughout the decade.'

THE 1940s: WORLD WAR TWO (1939–1945)

Women's beauty was considered important during World War Two to boost the morale of soldiers. It was encouraged by the

American and British governments, a reminder to the men of what they were fighting for and grew out of the demarcated gender roles of the period.

The effort in maintaining appearance was also to remind women they could retain femininity during war, boosting their morale, when they were working the men's jobs while they were away fighting the battles. 'Make up was seen as a patriotic duty.'

A more natural facial look was favoured now, given that this was wartime, achieved by a foundation darker than one's skin tone followed by powder lighter than skin tone as the ideal look with pink cheeks. Red lipstick was a must-have item and symbolised 'the precious right of women to be feminine and lovely, under any circumstance,' Tangee, one of the biggest lipstick makers of the time, advertised. That included war. Cosmetics mogul Helena Rubinstein created red lipstick with military names: 'Fighting red'; 'Commando' and 'Jeep Red', for example. These lipsticks assumed a 'nationalist meaning, gave women a chance to fight the war from home... and (a sense of) normalcy that was ripped away with war.'

Eyes were brushed with eye shadow in brown or grey tones, eyeliner and mascara darkened at night, and an eyebrow pencil defining arched thicker eyebrows.

The hourglass silhouette was the feminine bodily ideal created in the 1940s, largely achieved by the undergarment: an uncomfortable girdle, usually with a slip on top. Nylon stockings to the thigh fastened by a garter graced the legs, a shade darker for fair-skinned ladies and lighter for dark-skinned tones.

A military look characterised women's clothing, influenced by the war, shoulder pads in dresses, blouses and jackets, a key feature. The look was a nipped-in high waist, A-line skirts and dresses, knee length. Two-piece suits were worn and pants with high waists, buttons or zips down the side.

Shoes came in velvet, reptile skins in peep-toe, as leather was needed for the war. Heels were short and thick during the early 1940s but thinner by the end of the decade. The wedge assumed a popular look in the 1940s and loafers were also worn.

The ideal hairstyle was parted on the side with soft curls falling over the shoulder or hair was worn pulled back in a silk snood, particularly at work. More mature women would wear their hair up.

Hats continued to be popular from the 1930s as daywear, the beret, turban and snood being frontrunners. Small hats with brims, 'fedora' felt hats and veils were also worn. Gloves were worn at mid-arm-length in the day and long opera gloves at night with ball dresses.

THE 1950s

The ideal feminine beauty of the 1950s grew out of the post-war period where the focus was now on women's role as wife, mother and homemaker. 'Dainty and ladylike was the ideal.' A woman's appearance became important because it was linked to her husband's success and there were women who had money to spend on new fashion styles post-war.

The ideal silhouette was hourglass with a 'wasp's waist' – a narrow or tightly corseted waist with accentuated bust and hips. To maintain a tiny waist, girdles were worn, some extending to the thighs. They were worn under dresses, skirts and pants 'to create a slim, smooth look.'

Femininity and formality characterised the look of the 1950s. So what was the look? Softened shoulder lines and tiny waists shown off in swirling full skirts called 'poodle skirts' or fitted pencil skirts. And tailored suits were in vogue. Twinset cardigans and sweaters were a look and dresses were a must-have for social events: V neckline dresses and tight waistlines; dresses with full skirts and pleated skirts; structured satin dresses; halter neck dresses with structured bodices and wide straps. Shirt-dresses were a popular design buttoned up at the front with a collar and matching fabric belt. By the mid-1950s, sheath dresses made of silk, taffeta, lace or velvet were an ideal look worn when hosting a dinner or a black cocktail dress.

Belts, gloves, hats and handbags were must-have accessories for daywear. Pearls and sweater clips were popularised. Shoes became an understated accessory in the 1950s. A variety was worn depending on with what clothing and for which occasion: pumps (a shoe on a thicker heel), wedges, loafers, saddle shoes, thin kitten heel shoes, stiletto heels, sandals and flat ballet shoes.

The looks of Hollywood actresses continued to influence hair and makeup trends. Makeup artist Allison Barbera identifies the major looks of the decade: the girl-next-door look like actresses Debbie Reynolds and Doris Day; elegant glamour-like actress Grace Kelly and the sultry glamorous look of actresses Ava Gardner and Gina Lollobrigida.

And there was the 'raw, sensual' actress, Marilyn Monroe with her peroxided hair, described as 'an icon of American beauty from the 1950s.'

The ideal makeup look was a pale complexion with rouge on the cheeks in soft peach or pink. Lipstick was bold in pinks, reds and corals. Women tended to match their nail polish to their lipstick. Fingernails were kept long and oval-shaped. Eye shadow was applied to the eyelids in pastel hues of blues and greens. Brown or black eyeliner was worn winged at the top lash line and no eyeliner preferred on the bottom. Mascara was applied to the top lashes. Eyebrows were thick to medium thick, highly arched and a brow pencil was used to darken and thicken the brows.

The Italian actresses Sophia Loren and Gina Lollobrigida inspired a short haircut with soft curls that women wore chin length or shorter. The pixie cut, also a short hairstyle, was worn, short and the back and sides of the head and slightly longer on top, like actress Audrey Hepburn wore in the movie *Roman Holiday* (1953). Chemical relaxers available in the 1950s popularised a straight hair look for African American women.

THE 1960s

In the early 1960s, Jackie Kennedy, First Lady of the United States represented the iconic 'look' until her husband President John Kennedy was assassinated. She wore dresses without collars, jackets with one button, low-heeled shoes, pillbox hats, pearls and perfectly matching accessories.

The 1960s witnessed a period of social, cultural and political change in the west and fashion responded to the events and movements of the time. In the 1960s, the prescribed ideal of the 1950s role for women as homemaker, wife and mother was challenged by feminism and Betty Friedan's influential book *The Feminine Mystique* (1963) in the United States. Friedan identified an independent fulfilling life possibility outside the home for women.

The advent of the birth control pill gave women more life choices in how to live and plan families, live more freely sexually and work in the paid workforce. In this period, women fought for various rights and reforms in America, parts of Europe and Australia. 'Feminism was embodied in the mini skirt.' And the mini marked a new era in fashion; it 'represented a shift in societal dynamics, a rebellion born out of a youth culture, wanting out of a repressed post war fashion.'

The mini skirt, coloured tights, low-heeled shoes and knee-length boots in white, silver or brown were the ideal 'look' geared towards the young, initiated in London as the 'mod look.' Mary Quant, 'the most iconic fashion designer of the 1960s', took the lead and popularised the mini in 1964, setting the trend globally. Quant 'molded street fashion style and culture' with her bold colours and introduced PVC fabric in this 'mod' fashion look.

And fashion designer Prue Acton followed this mini-trend in Australia. Demographically, a high percentage of people living in America, Australia and Europe during these years were young, under 25, with a youth culture emerging and demanding their own fashion style.

British supermodel 'Twiggy was the poster girl for the 1960s mini skirt' and epitomised the thin, willowy body ideal of that time. And British supermodel Jean Shrimpton internationalised the mini look when she dared to wear a white mini shift dress at the Derby races in Melbourne with no hat, stockings or gloves that were usually worn to accessorise them.

Twiggy's makeup was 'the look', trendsetting in the mid-1960s with brown or black or grey liner drawn exaggeratedly in the socket of the eye, pale eye shadow, winged eyeliner, false eyelashes on the top and bottom lashes coated in liquid eyeliner painted downwards over them finished with black mascara on top and bottom. Eyebrows were groomed and natural. Her face had light beige foundation with a 'fluff' of rouge and nude lips.

In the 1960s, hair was worn either in a big bouffant, long hippie waves or pixie-cut like Twiggy's. Jewellery was influenced by pop art and worn in bright geometric shapes.

In the 1960s, the United States civil rights movement, a social justice movement fighting for the end of racial segregation, discrimination and equal rights under the law gained ground, impacted on fashion. Many African American women sported the Afro natural look with their natural hair, as a symbol or rebellion against white dominance, 'pride and empowerment, an assertion of black identity.'

By 1968, an androgynous hippie look was another new 'look' with men and women wearing frayed bell-bottomed jeans; tie-dye shirts; peasant shirts; kaftans in psychedelic prints, inspired by an African American influence; sandals; bangles and flowery headbands; flower patches adorning jeans and skirts, representing peace and love; beaded necklaces and embracing the grunge rock generation.

This fashion statement and expression of identity was a rejection of social norms through dress that grew out of opposition to American involvement in the Vietnam War and a belief in 'politics of no politics.'

Shift dresses were a 'signature '60s style' shapeless A-line dresses. Prints were colourful, seen in stripes, checks and floral patterns. The geometric dress design of the 1960s was influenced by optical art at the time that focused on optical illusions in largely black and white. Capri pants, black turtlenecks and berets were a popular look too. Older women tended to wear a mid-calf skirt, white blouse and cardigan.

THE 1970s

Farah Fawcett, *Charlie's Angels* movie star, embodied the 1970s beauty ideal – young, Caucasian, slim, toned and athletic-looking with flowing feathered hair and a natural makeup look. I remember wanting to look like Fawcett. She was the golden girl movie star pin-up at the time. I wanted my hair to be like hers, have a tan and her body. I think I was not the only one who wanted to emulate her.

Light liquid foundation makeup was worn if at all, with bronze powder brushed all over the face to exude a suntanned look and berry rouge over cheekbones, clear, nude or light pink gloss or lipstick. Light blue, brown, lilac purple, and green eye shadow were popular with black/brown mascara.

Flared pants, pantsuits, jumpsuits and denim dresses, skirts, jeans and jackets were the '70s trend worn with chunky platforms shoes or wedges in the early '70s. I was a teenager at this time and

I wore it all. The chunky platform shoes were a favourite fashion item of mine because they were so comfortable and created the illusion that I was tall. I am petite and always wanted to be taller. Aged 14, I wore a soft silky leopard-printed jumpsuit to my older cousin's engagement party held in her parents' private home. I had my hair blow-waved and wore a little eye makeup, looking about 18 and feeling very chic, I recall. On weekends, my friends and I were clad in denim jeans and denim jackets if the weather was cooler.

Actress Diane Keaton in the movie *Annie Hall* 'inspired women to wear baggy pantsuits, men's ties and hats.' Women wore mini-skirts, men's suits and whatever they chose, roused by the sense of freedom imbued in the women's movement. The kaftan inspired by African American and Eastern styles continued on from the 1960s, ignited further by singer/songwriter Joni Mitchell. Punk music also influenced fans to wear torn clothing, black leather and anti-establishment styles.

Following the 1960s trend, increased sexual freedom was expressed in '70s fashion designer Diane von Furstenberg's wrap dress that 'could be swiftly and silently pulled back on in a dark bedroom without waking last night's sexual conquest.'

The 'hippie look' of the 1960s extended into the 1970s, refined by more embroidery and patchwork that was influenced by homemade craft.

I remember wearing black vinyl hot pants (short shorts) and high boots in the 1970s. This was a 'look' during the decade, popularised on the dance floor, a 'fad that took young women by storm, (worn) in bright colours of satin, cotton, nylon, denim and velvet with high boots and bright tights.' The maxi skirt and jumpsuit were also popular.

THE 1980s

The ideal feminine body in the '80s was tall, thin and tanned, slightly athletic with big breasts. To achieve the thin athletic look, exercise became important in the lives of many Australian and American women: aerobics classes, gym workouts, jogging, tennis and yoga. And they were dressed in the appropriate sporty gear – the aerobics workout look was Lycra leotards, bright leggings and leg warmers, headband around the hair, inspired by actress Jane Fonda's video workouts and the movie *Flashdance* starring Jennifer Beale. Neon colours were 'in'. And Nike athletic wear really took off.

I recall wearing this athletics gear in the '80s, watching and doing the Jane Fonda workout in my home if I was not able to attend an aerobics class I enjoyed. Today, I still watch the repeats of the movie *Flashdance* and love the songs in it. I also wanted to be like the movie star Jennifer Beale, dance like her and have her taut, fit body.

There were a few iconic fashion looks in the '80s. Dresses and suit jackets with shoulder pads were one of them, inspired by the television soap *Dynasty*, worn by its stars, Joan Collins and Linda Evans. And power suits for professional women were a big hit, with a button-down blouse, pantyhose and pumps. In Australia, women were granted equal pay in 1972 and by the 1980s, 'wearing a masculine, wide shouldered suit was a way of expressing women's new found sense of power and asserting their equality with men.' The power look was completed by wearing costume jewellery like a pearl necklace, gold earrings and clothing covered in sequins for evening and pump-heeled shoes, a look promoted by the television soap *Dallas*.

Denim was a 'cool' look in the '80s and designer jeans were the rage: high waist and snug hips. Denim jackets, shirts and overalls were also popular. Stirrup pants and leggings were another trendy look worn with oversized jumpers or windcheaters. I loved wearing these for their comfort; I was a young mother at home with small children so it was a practical set of clothes to wear. It has come back today in more attractive versions. I have returned to wearing this gear daily when looking after my very young grandchildren. Knits varied from cable to textures to pastels. Belts were worn to create a cinched waist over jumpers, shirt dresses and A-line skirts.

Punk fashion, a non-conformist, rebellious style, emerged in the 1970s gained momentum in the '80s, a 'reaction against idealistic peace-loving hippie era and rejection of consumerist, money-obsessed culture of the 1980s.' Punk fashion intended to shock, was aggressive, angry and loud inspired by rebellious English bands like the Sex Pistols.

The punk look included 'tight black jeans, a ripped tattered T-shirt held together with safety pins and heavy Doc Martens boots.' Punk hair was short, often dyed in a vibrant colour and silver metal jewellery was popularised as were studded belts, spiked collars and studs in the ear or nose.

I remember wearing my hair crimped at a gala event at Chadstone Shopping Centre in Melbourne one evening, dressed in a simple black dress. A photographer approached me to have my photo taken in his studio with this crimped hairstyle. And I did. He then placed a huge version of it in his window. The crimped look was really 'in' during the '80s, as was the volume look, curls or perms.

Bold makeup was the 'look' of the '80s. Smoky eyes – multiple layers of thick black eyeliner and mascara on the top and bottom and in the waterline; eyeliners in green, blue and purple; eye shadows in electric blue; deep purple; bright orange and applying more than one shadow at a time; eyebrows natural or darkened slightly; a thick layer of foundation followed by bronzing powder; red or pink blush; lips lined with liner in scarlet; fuchsia; bright pink; orange or mauve lipstick. I loved experimenting with the colours in the '80s and enjoyed the fun of the variety.

THE 1990s

The 1990s witnessed more change in the definition of what was considered by the fashion industry as feminine beauty. Fashion critic Robin Givhan notes that the definition of beauty as it applied to women loosened in the 1990s 'thanks to the arrival of Kate Moss with her slight figure and vaguely ragamuffin aesthetic... five feet seven inches, short for a runway model... Moss was disruptive to the beauty system, but she was well within the industry's comfort zone of defining beauty as a white, European conceit. Even the early black models who broke barriers were relatively safe: women such as Beverly Johnson, the first African American model to appear on the cover of American Vogue, the Somali-born Iman, Naomi Campbell and Tyra Banks. They had keen features and flowing hair.'

Moss set the bar for the feminine body ideal of the '90s: waifish, extremely thin.'

In 2009, she reportedly said, 'Nothing tastes as good as skinny feels,' a mantra she retracted in 2018. I wonder how many young girls or women may have followed her lead and starved or dieted excessively to achieve that waif look.

Sudanese model Alek Wek graced the cover of American *Elle* magazine in 1997 and like Moss, 'her beauty was something entirely different... Wek was abruptly and urgently transformative... Everything about her was the opposite of what had come before.'

Wek's beauty, her dark skin, natural corkscrew hair, full lips and wide nose were considered as atypical in fashion or American culture.

So Alek Wek signalled the idea that what constitutes

conventional beauty was changing in the fashion and beauty industry, paving the way for the diversity to follow in the 21st century.

In the '90s, models Naomi Campbell, Christy Turlington, Cindy Crawford and Kate Moss were the fashion style icons. And so were the musical celebrities – Spice Girls, Madonna, Britney Spears and Gwen Stefani – who pioneered grunge clothing for women with plaid pants, neon colours, leather boots, chokers, studded belts and midriff tank tops.'

Spears sported midriffs, tube tops and low-waist pants that became fashionable in the '90s. And American rapper Missy Elliot oversized jumpsuits, baggy bomber jackets and loose leather suits, with the leather jacket being a 'must have' fashion item in the '90s.

Denim was a big look in the '90s – a crop top worn with jeans, jackets and pencil skirts. I loved wearing the pencil skirt and thought it chic at the time. I remember wearing it with a silk blouse or jumper thrown on top and boots. And overalls were also in with a variety of pants and jackets, a much softer look than the '80s. Leather was a look – skirts, dresses and jackets along with plaid blazers and skirts; cardigans and leopard 'the rage' in coats, dresses and hats. A classic leather jacket was a must-have in the 90s.' Nylon futuristic clothing was also popular. And Birkenstocks, platform shoes and heavy-duty boots were the go.

Hair was worn as either a short bob or long loose tresses either straight or curly. I wore my hair short in a bob then or long and straight during that decade.

The tanned look was in – foundation, followed by translucent powder, pink rose or coral blush and matching lipstick. Popular eye shadows were purple, grey, maroon and orange followed by black, brown or burgundy mascara, heavily applied to the top lashes and lightly to the bottom. Lip liners were in two shades darker than the lipstick on top in pink – rose, brick, red, nude, berry, plum, scarlet red and red-orange. The 'in' nail polishes were blue, green, silver or clear coated over natural nails.

2000–2010

During the early 2000s, the ideal feminine body was very skinny to curvy skinny and then a full hourglass and booty were favoured, influenced by the Kardashian women who were thin with hips and bottoms: a sporty athletic body, sexy and lithe, fashionable.

The first decade of the millennium focused on looking presentable and camera-ready at all times impacted by celebrity and influencer culture. Celebrities, Nicole Ritchie and Paris Hilton epitomised 'the look' that young women wanted to emulate in her Juicy Couture tracksuits and tightly cropped t-shirts. As did Sienna Miller in a coin-studded leather belt and ugg boots and Kate Moss, in a black waistcoat and silver micro hot pants, the face of Topshop, both 'blonde, skinny and white conforming to the entrenched Eurocentric beauty standard of the time.'

Celebrity and fashion blended in this wish to get the fashionable look largely thanks to the Internet (fashion blogs, social media), paparazzi and weekly women's magazines. Shows like *Sex and the City, Friends* and movies – *The Devil Wears Prada* – also impacted on fashion. Influencers in fashion then included Stella McCartney, Zara and H&M.

During the early 2000s, denim, cargo pants and t-shirts, activewear, glitter, paisley patterns and maxi skirts, oversized silhouettes and knitted fabrics were in. I loved wearing the maxi skirt, then with an oversized jumper in cold weather, with boots. Designer logos on bags, scarves, belts, caps and clothes and bags were a status symbol in the mid-2000s. A belt worn on the hip to accessorise was a look. Office-wear included pinstripes, pantsuits, colourful tops and jumpers with shiny pumps. In 2008, fashionable looks included skirts, blouses, blazers, laced, print or dotty tights, skinny jeans, flannel shirts, cardigans, a leather jacket or trench and a scarf, colours toning down to navy, black and beige.

Celebrity Tyra Banks represented the ideal makeup look with her smoky eyes. Thin eyebrows were in along with lots of bronzer and pink blush as were highlights that contrasted natural hair and coloured hair. Shiny and sleek dominated around 2008. I loved her smoky eye look and replicated it when I had functions to attend during that period.

The celebrity Kardashian women have been a seismic influence on women's beauty and fashion. Being at the 'forefront of pop culture', they have amassed millions of followers who want to look like them. 'Throughout the 2010s, the Kardashian-Jenner influence has become ingrained in the fabric of the fashion industry, their most enduring contribution has been to the rise of athleisure.'

2010–2020

Apart from the pervasive influence of the Kardashian women, this decade witnessed great change in ideas about beauty by women who were hitherto largely ignored or sidelined by the beauty world: black women, plus-size older women and transgendered persons, for example. These groups wanted to see themselves represented in the beauty and fashion world and advocated for change from seeing largely thin, white women represented, largely via social media and their platforms. This change has also been part of a larger external conversation about fairness, social justice, political correctness and cultural enlightenment that the beauty and fashion industries should reflect real people in life, represent them and make fashion available and accessible to them.

In the past, women wanted to look like models and celebrities. Now, they are influenced by what social media defines as beauty and that is, women of all shapes and sizes.

In this time, the consumer base had widened to include these minority groups; a more expansive retail network; social media like Hot Spot, and Instagram; and watchdogs pressuring the fashion industry into greater accountability regarding how it depicts beauty.

This decade has witnessed many changing feminine ideals when it comes to beauty and the body. At the beginning of this decade, the Kardashian body shape was a dominant body ideal: thin with curves, a bust and a butt. By around 2012, a new idea about beauty emerged with the emerging body positivity movement emerged, a movement where followers would accept their body, feeling positive about it, not conforming to the societal ideal of thin beauty. It intended to promote strong self-esteem but copped the flak for encouraging an obese culture that was said to be damaging to health.

In 2015, the body neutrality movement emerged, focusing on the body as a vessel rather than an aesthetic. This movement was more about being, embracing women of all sizes and those with physical disabilities, the celebration of feminine beauty in all lovely varieties. I think it would be healthier for us not to focus on the body at all and shift the mindset to doing beauty, in thinking of others, trying to action that to make our world better through the work we do. This is discussed further in chapters 5–7 of the book.

In 2016, a fuller figure was welcomed with a further cultural shift, expanding the definition of women's beauty, when plus-size model Ashley Graham was acknowledged and valued, gracing the cover of the Swimsuit Edition of Sports Illustrated and curvy, tall and petite Barbie dolls were introduced into the toy market. Diversity in beauty ideals was making inroads into the beauty and fashion world, discussed in the following chapter.

'In 2017, the Council of Fashion Designers of America (a non profit organization of America's foremost women's and men's wear, jewellery and accessory designers) reminded designers ahead of New York Fashion Week that health was one of the utmost concerns when it came to the models (and that year) "a healthy body was (idealized) a perfect body."'

However, in 2019, Instagram through its influencers, celebrities, advertisements and content played a huge role in defining the feminine body ideal one with a 'flat stomach, not muscular, with boobs and an hourglass figure.' It is a Rihanna body type – 'slim thick' prominent butt and thighs included.

During this decade, millennial women emerged as a prominent force with their distinctive style. This 'selfie' generation have been defining beauty as 'self- awareness, personal swagger, individuality... chiselled arms and false eyelashes and a lineless forehead... rounded bellies, shimmering silver hair and mundane imperfections. Beauty is a millennial strutting around town in leggings, a crop top, and her belly protruding over her waistband.'

Millennials tend to want to accept others for who they are including diverse models.

Cosmetic and fashion shopping for the millennial has been and continues to be very influenced by social media and what others are buying. Spanning the decade 2010–2020, the Millennial wore skinny and high-waist (mum) jeans, crop tops, a high-low dress, chokers, ath-leisurewear, slip dresses, bike shorts, leopard prints and midi skirts.

In this decade, big, bold and bushy eyebrows were idealised, achieved through threading, waxing, micro blading or laminating. Either layers of foundation or a natural look of makeup was in. Full lips were the go, a dark berry colour favoured in 2010. The smoky eye was popular in 2012 and so was bronzer contouring epitomised by Kim Kardashian West. Skincare was important with Korean beauty masks and creams trending to create glossy, glowing, radiant skin in 2017. Nails were painted as experimental art.

Ideal hair was worn bouncy with a body like Kate Middleton, Princess of Wales, or beachy waves. Balayage with a darker colour at the top of the head graduating to lighter at the ends was popular. Rainbow and pastel hair were also worn.

There were a number of looks trending in this decade: athleisure inspired by the Kardashian women; the wellness movement and 24/7 access on Instagram and Snapchat for more fashionable workout clothes. The royal effect of Kate Middleton, Princess of Wales and Meghan Markle, Duchess of Sussex also influenced fashion. The former preferred English designers like Alexander McQueen and wore structured knee-length coats, long-sleeved dresses, high-waist trousers and closed-toe pumps; the latter championed smaller and emerging designers and supported American designers. While having individual styles, both Middleton and Markle like the fashion labels Sentaler, Boden and Alemdara. When reported wearing an item in these labels, it has sold out or increased sales across all products in Alemdara, for example, when Markle wore a particular necklace. 'The royal effect has the ability to transform a company and the way it is viewed on the world stage.'

I must admit that I have been interested to see what they wear and how they seem to set fashion trends after.

Street-style fashion was also favoured during this period by budding influencers on fashion blogs, websites and Instagram, with sub-cultures like Gen Z Internet culture using video-sharing apps and other technology to access the fashion look. Sneakers were big in this decade. So it was a varied fashion look apart from the diversity of models that were beginning to be represented.

And this last decade has particularly illustrated that it is not only thin white women who wish to be included and part of the beauty conversation whether it be the body, skin or fashion. It has largely been outsiders speaking up, demanding their inclusion and this change. And the beauty/fashion industry is listening and starting to change in response to become more inclusive and represent diversity. There are some inside the industries also championing this change as the following chapter highlights.

Today, 'Beauty is about respect and value and the right to exist without having to alter who you fundamentally are... Modern beauty asks us to come (to the table) presuming that everyone in attendance has the right to be there.'

And today, we are also seeing something else that is refreshing in the beauty/fashion industry. British designer of menswear, Bethany Williams, works in fashion, combatting social and environmental crises side by side. She is into helping others, protecting the environment and embracing sustainability by repurposing discarded materials like rejected children's books, using them for her satchel, for example. She is about helping those located in 'society's fringes'. I describe this as performing beauty. It's not just about her making money selling her designs. She considers others and the environment.

'Her ethos is collaboration where social and environmental concerns go hand in hand, she embeds herself within communities from charities to prisons, to provide meaningful employment, create engaging and empowering opportunities to create positive changes.'

Her jersey fabric, for instance, is manufactured by women prisoners in London, who are learning fashion and manufacturing in a special program 'Making for Change' to increase their wellbeing and reduce reoffending. Williams is all about social consciousness and looks after the underdog as she employs those who are rehabilitating from drug addiction, for example, to weave book waste into fabric for her 2019 spring/summer 2019 where those who are disabled physically and mentally adorn her fabrics.

She collaborated with Spires (a south London-based association open to vulnerable, socially isolated women, women in sex work, homeless and disadvantaged, offering them food, clothing, support, showers and health care) for her spring summer 2020 collection. Spires' weekly run sessions named 'The Butterfly Café' enables its female participants to partake in creative activities like learning to knit and making jewellery and cards, having a transformative effect on their lives. It was this that inspired Williams' collection and she named it 'The Butterfly Effect,' with growth and transformation as underlying themes.

Unsurprisingly, Williams is the 2019 recipient of Queen Elizabeth's Award for British Design, an honour that recognises community values and sustainability practices. And generously, Williams always donates 20% of her proceeds to the charity with whom she collaborates. She is a star – a great role model for girls to emulate.

Alongside Williams' social consciousness underlying her work, there are other positive signs of change within the beauty/fashion industry. We are witnessing a movement for social justice, encapsulated in the issue of diversity and inclusivity that has captured the attention of the beauty/fashion industry during the last few years.

In these pages you can see that the idea of beauty has not been static but has changed over time with the rise of big business in the beauty industry influenced by historical context and what was happening in the Western world. You have learnt about beauty trends that have come and gone and those of us living today see some re-emerging like the bold red lipstick, a symbol of power, assertiveness, female beauty and sexuality.

Now let's take a peek at the current trends in beauty – a subject area that could warrant a whole book.

CHAPTER FOUR: A GLANCE AT DIVERSITY

A beauty writer comments that 'diversity is not a trend, it's real life.'

Yes, it is real life as the global population is diverse in age, gender, sexuality, ethnicity, body size and shape and age. And one would expect that the beauty and fashion industries embedded in our culture would reflect that. Yet, it has not been the case until recently where signs of change are surfacing with inclusivity and diversity making inroads.

And yes, it is also trending but Casting Director James Scully doesn't see the 'pendulum swinging back. Fashion is represented by a lot of different people and now that they're in the door, they're going to keep that door open.'

Scully has been an outspoken critic of the lack of diversity on the runway but says he has seen improvement in 2017, in the fashion capitals of New York, London and Milan. He has seen an exotic African girl emerge in Paris represented by Gucci and Prada and represented in the American Vogue magazine. And, he has observed that the American Allure magazine has showcased diversity on its covers.

Scully credits the young: Millennials and their values, who are now working in the fashion business driving diversity. For them, 'it's important that everyone be represented, the norm,' he says.

Ivan Bart, President of IMG Models, a leading international agency representing more than half of the highest-paid supermodels, has been championing diversity. He has implemented it in practice by signing up models who are Sudanese: Alek Wek, for example, and plus-sized like model Ashley Graham. His agency hires plus-sized male and female models. Bart says, 'I hope that we're leading the conversation and the industry is changing with us.'

He adds, 'if people are resistant (to showcase diversity) they will change if you stay the course.'

On March 17, 2017, Bart and his team wrote a fabulous letter on Instagram, urging American designers to make diversity casting decisions before the '17 New York Fashion Show in the fall. 'Through the thread of the fabric, there is connectivity in building a dress. And through this human experience is the thread that connects us all. As we celebrate your vision and design, we ask you to celebrate our diverse talent by considering all of our models regardless of their size and backgrounds. Fashion designers are aspirational, and every consumer wants to experience the beauty and joy of well-designed clothes. Diverse women connect the dream to become your consumer. Everyone deserves the opportunity and privilege to wear your clothes.'

Venezuelan fashion designer Carolina Herrera, whose name is splashed on billboards at international airports, has said that 'culture, fashion, music and film has to be a place where it starts to happen. That's the responsibility of culture, including fashion to move the cultural zeitgeist in that direction. That white and skinny isn't the definition of beautiful and to change it.'

In the last decade, brands have begun to shift this image as the primary definition of beauty. In 2017, singer Rihanna launched her makeup line 'Fenty', offering 40 shades of foundation (now 50) to include those customers who have dark and black skin. Her Fenty line has had a huge success and impacted on other brands to diversify their products to include darker skin. The Fenty Beauty trailer is amazing in that it includes beautiful, young, ethnic and exotic women – Asian, Black and Caucasian rather than just the white skinny models only, in an attempt to redefine what beauty is.

Sandy Saputo, Fenty's Chief Marketing Officer, said that the trailer 'was the first time underrepresented, underserved women and cultures were featured on a global prestige beauty campaign. There was no precedent to our radical approach to inclusivity. We had to break and disrupt all the traditional marketing rules and carve a new path. In our first year of business, Fenty Beauty became the biggest beauty brand launched in YouTube history.'

Saputo shared that Rihanna's vision was to enable many women to find themselves in her brand and feel included. The Fenty line was made available to women around the globe simultaneously so they could all access the products. 'What resulted is a movement that shifted the beauty industry,' Saputo reports. Fenty's 'Beauty For All' marketing strategy redefined beauty ideals and started a conversation about foundation shades for all women. The darkest shades sold out first. 'Fenty Beauty connected emotionally with women who had long been treated like they didn't exist by the beauty industry.'

However, the Fenty Beauty trailer does exclude larger-sized bodies and disabled bodies. But Rihanna improved this in her second Fenty lingerie show where her models included disabled, larger transgender women along with models of mixed races and ethnic diversity to try to embrace everyone, showing the message of inclusivity. Other brands – MAC, NARS, L'Oréal Paris and Maybelline, for example – also offer a wide range of foundation to cater for diverse complexions. And there are brands like 'Aerie, H&M, Dove, ASOS Beauty challenging stereotypes and celebrating individuality.'

Brands are responding to the zeitgeist and consumer, rejecting past unattainable beauty ideals. Many consumers know they can't achieve them and the body positivity movement has had significant impact in empowering women to rebel against the hitherto dominant thin ideal. 'As a result, brands casting only young, thin, white flawless models no longer feel relevant in the modern age.'

In the last decade, we have seen the transgender community demanding greater representation and inclusivity in the beauty industry with leading transgender celebrities advocating change like mega-influencers Nikkie de Jager, Dutch makeup artist; Nikita Dragun and Revlon ambassador Gigi Gorgeous who are all transgender women.

With a following of millions, de Jager has been supporting diversity and inclusivity in beauty, via her influential platform on social media. Nikita Dragun is one of the 'most influential voices of and for the transgender community in the world' who has created her own makeup brand 'Dragun Beauty' that sold every product within 24 hours. And Gigi Gorgeous is 'one of the most visible trans women in the world', a prominent voice for the trans community who earns six figures monthly. *Time* magazine named her one of the most influential people on the Internet in 2017. As Revlon Ambassador, this social media star can help broaden the social reach to include Generation Z consumers.

Gorgeous says that she wanted makeup that would make anyone feel beautiful and so developed her own genderless makeup line in 2019. She wanted to create makeup that could be worn before and after transitioning.

Luxury brand Chanel Beauty hired its first trans model, Teddy Quinlan, to advertise Chanel beauty products. Quinlan said she was proud and humbled to work for the luxury brand representing her community. Designer Marc Jacobs publicly gave his support to Quinlan saying that 'Now more than ever it is vital that we pledge our allegiance to the LGBT community and use our voices to encourage and inspire acceptance, equality, understanding and love.'

In the last few years, trans models have become more visible, increasingly included in the modelling industry and creating some firsts. And they are using their visibility and voices to relay socio-cultural messages about wider representation and instigate change in the industry. Valentina Sampaio is Victoria Secret's first transgender model, gracing the Paris, Brazil and Germany Vogue covers in 2017. She says 'the fashion industry is an instrument to raise flags and promote diversity, where things are more fluid and beauty evolves.'

However, the Victoria's Secret brand was initially not on board to embrace diversity of models, only showcasing white, thin models, the norm then and dominant beauty ideal. Consequently, sales plunged as consumers withdrew support for the label not keeping up with the zeitgeist. Former Victoria Secret's white model Bridget Malcolm recently shared on 60 Minutes (Australia) how the brand encouraged her as a minor to become skinnier by using drugs and having lots of sex. She was told if she became skinnier she'd be an Angel and world-famous. Angels were the icons of the brand and their spokespeople, enjoying high status and prestige, strutted the runway in the celebrated annual televised fashion show event.

Size and fashion are addressed productively by Bond's first trans model, Andreja Pejic, who advertised its lingerie line. 'Fashion reflects what surrounds it and changes when the world does... Someone beautiful should be somebody who walks into a room and you think, "Oh this person is special. I don't think it should always be a person that's a size zero or size two or size 11. There's a million ways of being special.' How true!

Leyna Bloom is the first trans woman of colour to grace the cover of Vogue India.

In 2017, she walked the fashion runway during New York's

Fashion Week, 'the first time the event welcomed such diversity.' Bloom adds another spin, one that is understandable: 'We are in a world where we don't fit in, so we need to create one where we do. That's our responsibility, the gift we need to pass on.'

Hari Nef is the first trans model to sign with IMG Worldwide modelling agency and Mimi Tao, the first trans model on Project Runway in 2019. Tao shares her ambition, 'I want to change the industry. I want to inspire all the transgender young generation who have a dream. Keep knocking the door. If they don't open, the door is going to break one day.'

Lea T is the first transgender woman to be the face of luxury brand Givenchy. She was the first trans woman to be the face of Redken (hair products) before joining Givenchy. Lea T is optimistic: 'We live in a new era where societies are starting to believe in us. I think this will happen more frequently... this fills my heart with joy.'

Times are a-changing, evident in the call for diversity from trans models and their impact. The US beauty company Sephora offers in-store makeup lessons for the trans community and how to remove unwanted hair. And there are trans focus groups of customers providing feedback about which products work for them.

Apart from beginning to include the transgender community in beauty/fashion, there have been other moves in the industry to address and include other dimensions like age, race, ethnicity and ability of models advertising products. The online shopping site Babor is featuring people of all ages, races and sizes, publishing photos that are unedited, reflecting real-life humans. Dove is representing women from various backgrounds and ages, from 11–71. Helen Mirren, in her mid-seventies, was the face of *Allure* magazine in 2017 and the magazine banned the term anti-aging, preferring to focus rather on healthy aging. CoverGirl Cosmetics signed up Maye Musk, 69, as the brand's oldest representative in 2017.

Amy Deanna was CoverGirl's first black model with vitiligo in 2017. Aerie intimate apparel featured women with Down syndrome and amputees in a wheelchair to promote inclusivity. Target brought out its swimwear range in 2019 showcasing diverse models including black model Kiara Washington who has a prosthetic leg.

Over the last 20 years, the fashion industry has been somewhat slow to represent or cater for the disabled. However, this is changing due to technology, enabling designers to expand the landscape of fashion and design and get their names out via social media: Instagram, YouTube and Facebook, with a greater understanding of tapping into a huge consumer market, and the 'realisation of fashion and style is fundamental in redefining the notion of beauty and ultimately the social identity of persons with disability.'

We can see that fashion and beauty brands are starting to represent and cater for the disabled the world's largest minority community – 15% of the world's population, over a billion people. And there are some loud voices like disability advocates Xian Horn, Sinéad Burke, Stephanie Thomas and Jillian Mercado (among others) who are using their varied platforms to try to instigate this change within these industries.

Horn, who was born with cerebral palsy at birth, is mobile thanks to her hot pink electric ski poles. She is an educator and disability advocate championing change in the fashion and beauty industry. Horn is critical of disability inclusion where a disabled person is blended into an advertisement or only represented in a wheelchair. 'It is important to represent a full range of disabilities. The general public is otherwise ignorant to the vast spectrum of disability,' she said.

She is also critical of the beauty industry for not making packaging accessible or innovating with the disabled in mind.

Horn praised Grace Beauty and Guide Beauty for actively thinking of the disabled consumer in their product designs. Grace, for example, has honed in on dexterity, designing mascara with different grips.

Other brands are making inroads to cater for disabled consumers: Estee Lauder, L'Oréal and Unilever. Kohl Kreative offer flexible brushes with an easy grip base. Skincare brands L'Occitane and Bioderma are adding braille to their external product packaging. Model Ellie Goldstein, an 18-year-old girl with Down syndrome, is the new face representing Gucci beauty, a real change from the conventional beauty image.

Not only are beauty products starting to address disability but some fashion labels are too. Fashion designer Tommy Hilfiger was inspired by his autistic daughter to create and lead in adaptive fashion, designing ranges for the disabled, children and adults. Horn loves her Tommy Hilfiger adaptive jeans and shares that 'the jeans fit like they were made for me and flattened my behind.' She also loves the white button-down business shirt Zappos designed that has magnets instead of buttons.

Zappos, Target, FFORA and Izzy Camilleri are other brands designing for the disabled. Reset by Monika and Usha Dugar offer Velcro closures on their jackets and easy shoulder fastenings to cater for the disabled. LVMH brands are looking towards developing adaptive clothing in the near future.

Shirts that are put on over the head, buttons and closures have been challenging for disabled people, Horn informs.

In 2016, Horn contributed to the field of adaptive fashion where garments are adapted to the needs of the disabled wearer. She worked with the Open Style Lab at Parsons School of Design in New York City where they designed an adaptive accessible raincoat for her, one that would not get caught on the back of chairs as her other coats had done. The Lab focuses on the creation of wearable items for people with disabilities.

The following year, Horn modelled in Cerebral Palsy Foundation's Design for Disability Program that partnered with fashion designer Derek Lam and six young designers from Parsons, Pratt and FIT, the three top New York fashion schools, to create six amazing collections of accessible outfits. In 2020, she modelled for Zappos in the New York Fashion Show 'Runway of Dreams' virtual format.

Sinéad Burke is another amazing disability advocate, teacher and Director of consulting organisation 'Tilting the Lens' working to improve access in design.

She asks questions of companies like 'When you bring somebody for an interview, are you asking if they have any access requirements? Are you ensuring that businesses and the headquarters of various global brands are happening in accessible buildings?'

She asks other questions too: 'Who isn't graduating from fashion schools? Who gets the opportunities? Are companies hiring practices disability- inclusive?'

3'5" in height, Burke has a big voice and is influencing the fashion world. She delivered a TED Talk in 2017 entitled 'why design should include everyone' that has over 1.5 million views and explains how basic design is not accessible to a little person like her, for example, public toilets, hand basins, soap dispensers and the lock on cubicle doors are all too high and unreachable. But accessibility in fashion is also an issue for her and other little people too.

Burke became interested in fashion at the age of 16 but has not always been able to enjoy its offerings because designs have not catered for little people. She often had to shop in the children's department. At 19, she started a fashion blog while studying to be a teacher. Her TED Talk, however, opened doors in the fashion world to her where she is exerting influence regarding disability. '*TED* changed Sinéad's life. She was getting calls from movers and shakers in the fashion world who wanted to collaborate.'

Burke has persuaded Salvatore Ferragamo to design shoes for little people and is dressed by Ferragamo, Gucci, Prada, Burberry and Christopher Kane adapting for her proportions as well as Australian designers Camilla and Marc, Gail Sorronda and Bassike. She is working on a project to create opportunities for disabled people at Gucci.

And recently in Australia, Burke was on a panel with Brisbane's most influential change-makers and stakeholders delivering messages about disability inclusivity. Firstly, 'It's possible for brands to be more adaptable with their designs for this group,' she said. Secondly, 'Who is not in the room when decisions about inclusivity are made?' She implored all designers, guests and business leaders to ask themselves.

Burke had the first little person's mannequin designed when the National Museum of Scotland asked to borrow her clothing for its exhibition in 2019. And she has landed an appointment by British Vogue Editor-in-Chief Edward Enninful as contributing editor to advise on 'fashion through a disability lens.'

'I'm working with brands to make a difference. What I really want is systemic change... if we can change who gets to study fashion, that will help change the system and the types of clothes we make,' Burke said.

Burke together with disabled designer Liz Jackson founded the Inclusive Fashion and Design Collective, which gives the disabled a voice in the design of products from which they require greater functionality and aims to incorporate design into disability. Jackson says 'it isn't enough to hire disabled models for an Adaptive campaign. Using the face and body of a disabled person to sell a product designed without their input is exactly the problem.'

Disability styling expert Stephanie Thomas is championing disability diversity. She is a black woman, a congenital amputee, born without a thumb and no toes. 'I was created this and this is my normal. I have one thumb on my left hand.'

Thomas is known as the go-to stylist in Hollywood for disabled actors and influencers. She says that the disabled are erased from our collective visual audience. 'You can't market to or design for someone you don't value, and you can't value someone you don't see as a fashion customer.'

Thomas has created a Disability Fashion Styling Guide for the disabled and their dressers to navigate dressing with confidence. She is the author of 'Fitting In: The Social Importance of Fashion and Dressing with Disabilities' and founder of the platform Cur8able. 'Its pillars are to empower and educate. She wants to empower the disabled to have fun shopping and dressing with dignity and independence and educating the fashion industry on how to meet the design and styling needs of people with disabilities.'

Successful highly visible disabled model Jill Mercado is another loud voice working for disabled inclusivity, hoping that over the next ten years, 'the work brands put out reflects the world that we see.' Mercado feels, because of her opportunity and privilege as this highly visible disabled model, that she needs to make the industry a fairer place for other members of the disabled community and helps others in her community.

Egypt's first disabled model in a wheelchair, Rania Roushdy, does not share the high profile that Mercado has. This young woman started as a hijab and makeup model. 'I have been working (as a model) for two and a half years... I have a team of friends who are helping me such as photographers and makeup artists.'

She is designing and modelling dresses while fashion houses have yet to agree to her modelling dresses. For Roushdy, modelling is a means through which to send her message that 'to reject people merely from being different is the epitome of ignorance. I will quit modelling when I see people who are considered different walking side by side with the standard models...models who are deaf or have artificial limbs, or who are sitting on wheelchairs on the runway.'

These examples are just but a few that showcase the work and thoughts of some working to help create a diverse fashion/beauty world. And there are more like the two young Melbournian women who are trying to instigate change in fashion, stamping diversity and inclusion as the pillar of their brand. Lifelong friends Carly Warson and Stephanie Korn created swimwear 'Form and Fold' for women with large breasts. In 2014, they were swimming in Europe together on vacation after completing university studies in Melbourne, when they started talking about how uncomfortable and unsupported they felt in their bathers. Carly is an E cup and Stephanie a DD, and they wear sizes 8 and 10 bottoms.

At that time, there was not a single product on the market for big-busted women, the girls inform. This group of women had been excluded as potential consumers. 'Imagine if we could fit into swimwear that supported us in the bust and we felt comfortable in,' one said to the other. That's when their idea to create that kind of swimwear was born. The girls effectively identified the gap in the fashion market and decided to fill it. It took them three years to develop a high-quality fit and fashionable look. And then the brand hit the market in 2017.

With no business fashion experience, the girls dived in and through a friend found a lingerie technician, an expert who helped them design patterns and structure the bra top that would support consumers' large breasts. 'We wanted women to feel good in the bodies they had and not feel they had to change their bust size, but rather feel comfortable and look great. Swimwear is the most vulnerable purchase for a female as their bodies are totally exposed,' the girls commented.

Form and Fold was right in the zeitgeist internationally. 'The body positivity movement was already trending internationally and Form and Fold followed,' Warson says. If you look at their website, you can see images of women in different shapes and sized bodies, modelling the brand's swimwear. There is a wonderful image of a woman in a bikini breastfeeding her baby. I love that – mothers are represented. And refreshingly, the look is not the skinny white model that hitherto has been dominant for many years, a standard where women's bodies have been measured and valued, promulgated by the fashion and beauty industries and media. Size 12 DD and 12 E are the brand's best-selling sizes.

'We don't photo-shop and want real women to be at the core of our brand. We represent real women who buy the product and are authentically representing diversity in our business model. We get the most engagement from older women who like our product on older unique unconventional looking models and think it would therefore look good on them. Diversity needs to be part of brands and authentically integrated from the beginning of the business model,' Warson says.

She adds, 'We need to change the aspiration of beauty from the size 8 image to a woman's intelligence. That's sexy.'

Korn hopes 'to see more diversity in fashion magazines, pop culture and film and can't wait to see what happens with this over the next ten years.'

These are not the only examples but indicate that change in beauty/fashion has actually begun in the representation and inclusion of its advertising models. But how far will it go? And is it here to stay permanently or is it merely a ploy of political correctness, a sign of the zeitgeist and/or a realisation that there is a potential larger consumer base out there?

There are some concerned that it is not enough for the beauty industry (including fashion, cosmetics and skincare) to represent diverse models in their advertising. They argue it should not stop with the models. Real difference, they suggest, includes the difference being behind desks and part of the decision-making process that influences outcomes. It's about diverse voices being included, valued and listened to in the making of these decisions. Janelle Hickman, Beauty Editor of 'Well and Good', a lifestyle publication, affirms that 'without a broad array of voices, life-experiences, and diverse perspectives in both junior-level and executive roles, it's hard to truly bring authentic change across the board.'

Ofunne Amaka, a black beauty brand entrepreneur and founder of the Cocoa Swatches app (offering the latest makeup swatches for darker skin) affirms that 'true diversity needs to be present in every facet of a company: from the hiring practices to their marketing efforts, to their product development, to their communications, to their influence relations.' Stephanie Thomas echoes this view and adds supply chains to the mix. She suggests bringing a 'disabled person into boardrooms, design houses and on sets to help educate on disability.'

Bringing lived experience to the table makes sense here in the quest to diversify the beauty industry. However, people also need the skills required for specific positions they may hold. It's great if a diverse pool have those skills but what if they don't? If a company is committed to implementing diversity, it may need to train staff so that they do have the skills to occupy their position. One could ask whether it would be like implementing quotas for women. Is that what companies would or should be doing with diversity? This practical issue would need to be addressed to achieve diversity across every area of a company or brand.

New Zealand transgender model Manahou Mackay sees the fashion industry as 'a pillar of cultural change that shapes how people navigate their lives. As an industry, it's important that we're diverse and inclusive so we cultivate a culture that is rich in perspectives and inspiration.'

The Australian fashion industry is trying to do that now. Australian Fashion Week 2021 has included Indigenous representation in the designers chosen: Indii, Liandra Swim, MAARA Collective, Jirrikin, Ngali and Native Swimwear. Perina Drummond Founder of Indigenous modelling agency Jira Models said that 'such recognition marks a milestone and offers a much needed springboard to indigenous designers', crediting the fashion industry for moving in the right direction.

Fashion designer Lizzie Renkert, who co-founded fashion label We Are Kindred, has embraced diversity and includes sizes 4–20, catering for all ages. She has cast older models Lucy Kemp and Kate Bell (52) to model her clothes during Australian Fashion Week 2021 (AAFW).

Bell commented 'if you don't see yourself out there, it's like you don't exist.' Imagine, then, how many women have felt excluded from the world of fashion?

Maria Thattil, Miss Universe Australia, discusses how the lack of representation of culturally diverse Australians in the modelling industry adversely impacted on her, feeling she was an outsider, on the fringe. As a daughter of Indian migrants, she shares, 'I didn't feel as if I had options because I didn't see people like me doing it. There was an image of what it was to be Australian and I didn't fit.' As Ambassador for the Shein Bella unsigned model search run by Bella Management Modeling Agency, she leads an industry campaign to change perceptions of Australian identity and beauty. And change is on its way.

During Australian Fashion Week 2021, there are panels of discussion conversing about the issues of diversity and inclusion and how to drive them forward in the Australian fashion industry. Plus-size model Mahalia Handley, representing Black, Indigenous and people of colour, first-generation plus-size women of Australia Indigenous is on a panel, talks about guiding 'businesses on responsible inclusion, how to reflect diversity meaningfully and connect authentically with their new and current audiences.'

Another panel featuring Yatu-Widders Hunt, Director at a Sydney PR and research agency and Indigenous fashion advocate, is hosting a discussion about driving change and representation across the fashion industry. A Dunghutti and Anaiwan person, she sees the Indigenous fashion industry, which is more than 60,000 years old, as 'an anchor of the Australian fashion industry – an unbroken tradition. Fashion is one of the ways broader Australia can start to embrace and celebrate indigenous history and peoples. It has a purpose beyond the aesthetic. Buying an indigenous design and wearing it contributes to positive social change because it helps start conversations that would otherwise not be had. It shows we are proud – indigenous history is part of who we are as a nation,' she said.

Panellists in her session include Lisa Cox (Media Diversity Australia's Disability Affairs Officer) who is 'excited to help Australian Fashion Week navigate the nuances of visibility for disability. Making the events more inclusive is recognition that disabled people are consumers of fashion too,' she said. 'I'm optimistic this will be the catalyst for further permanent changes. I'm delighted to be one of the people challenging and changing the fashion landscape in Australia.' Model Manahou MacKay, IMG model Bree McCann and Meghan Kapor, Creative Director from Imprint Magazine are the other panellists in this *Wonder Women* session.

Australian plus size model Kate Wasley praised Australian fashion week for showcasing 'some exceptional diversity this year,' filling her with 'hope and excitement' about the future. While she acknowledged that First Nations designers ran and created shows with Indigenous models, trans and older models were included, size diversity was an issue for her. Seeing 'three 'plus size' and a sprinkle of models above a size 8 was not what she expected.

Wasley drew attention to social and economic implications of this minimal representation. She felt unwelcome and didn't see herself represented, feeling discriminated against. 'There is an entire group of people that want to be represented, that are missing out on fashion and we have money to spend. Money we want to spend on expensive clothes to make ourselves feel fabulous. And with 'average' size women in Australia being a size 16+, there's a huge market that the majority of brands are missing out on.'

Fashion is big business and designers could tap into the 'plus size' market where money is to be made and spent. The value of Australia's fashion industry in 2021 has been priced at '$27.2 billion with exports valued at 7.2 billion, an "economic powerhouse" dubbed by Fashion Editor of *The Australian* newspaper and a "national driver of employment, creativity and innovation", according to former Australian Foreign Minister Julie Bishop.' As an economic driver, it has the power of effecting change in the fashion industry. That includes catering for the various dimensions of diversity.

The international label Prada has deepened its commitment to diversity, equity and inclusion in its company and the fashion industry as a whole, investing in talent and educational advancement programs. To increase representation in the industry, Prada has partnered with the Fashion Institute of Technology to develop scholarships. One will go to a top-performing diverse American student and another to one from Ghana or Kenya. An internship will be offered for diverse talent to work in Prada's corporate and retail teams. Talented designers of colour will be recruited for Prada from Chicago, New York and Los Angeles. In Paris, 2021, L'Oréal, in support of diversity, championed models of all ages on their runway – Helen Mirren,

Aishwarya Rai Bachchan, Amber Heard and Liya Kebede – using their platform to convey 'a strong message of self-worth.'

Teen Vogue writer Gianluca Russo makes an apt point about the future. She advocates for inclusivity to be a global value, not just a New York trend. 'We must continue to uplift marginalized voices in fashion and in society as a whole – who long to be heard, valued and represented.' For diversity and inclusion to work in the beauty and fashion industries, it needs normalisation rather than something to think about. And it starts at the inception of design with design schools admitting and encouraging diverse students as the new designers of today and tomorrow.

The autumn-winter haute couture collections in Paris Fashion Week 2021 were a mixed bag when it comes to diversity and inclusion. Kerby Jean Raymond, founder of his label Pyer Moss, is the first black designer to be invited to the Haute Couture Paris Fashion Week, where only elite designers are invited to show their luxurious creations. 'As a Black American, he was included in a historically exclusive space. The designer is a formidable voice in American fashion.'

'Much of Jean Raymond's work focuses on social justice and commentary, as it pertains to the Black experience.'

His brand is his platform for making political statements and his (2021) 'show's message is about everyday racism, servitude and of wearing your culture (and clothes) as armor.' Jean Raymond recruited Elaine Brown, former Black Panther chairwoman to make a speech before his show, on the fight for racial equality and black empowerment.

'I'm trying to lead by example. I know there's been a changing of the guard. We've been passed the baton. It's up to us to make the change that we wanna see. I just wanna see a complete rethinking of what it means to be diverse, which in my mind is just accepting the multitudes of existence. Every kind of person should see themselves in fashion I want to create a sustainable system where new brands helmed by people that looks like us can get a shot at being sustainable,' he said.

Yet his show was not showcasing diversity. It was reverse discrimination where all his female models were black. Quite the opposite of what has been – white dominance – for some time. That was a political statement in itself and just as confronting as an all-white model cast.

I watched a few of the autumn-winter Paris fashion shows of 2021 that were accessible. Ellie Saab's models were all white and thin, as were Vaishali S and Dior's. Armani's models were predominantly white with few Asian and black models. Balenciaga and Gaultier had greater diverse representation. However, most models were thin in all brands. Until there is an even spread of diverse representation across all axes in all the brands, they cannot claim to be totally inclusive. The disabled and plus size models were markedly missing in the shows I had seen, for example.

German-American supermodel Heidi Klum sees a positive future for the fashion industry, a 'direction where everyone is accepted.' We will have to watch this space to see if she is right.

BARBIE AND DIVERSITY

In recent years, Mattel has developed a range of diverse Barbie dolls apart from the thin, blue-eyed, blonde hair one that was hugely popular in the past and continues to be today. The diverse range was created to boost sales that plummeted and keep up with our changing times and cultural milieu. 'Barbie is (currently) the most diverse fashion doll ever produced and the No. 1 fashion doll in the U.S. More than 100 dolls are sold every minute with a total of 58 million sold annually in 150 countries worldwide.' Before discussing this issue of diversity, let's take a look at the creation of Barbie first.

ORIGINAL CONCEPT OF BARBIE

When Barbie was created, her 'shape typified what the feminine ideal was in the late 1950s and Ruth Handler's figure was (then) a popular media image.' Since inception, over time, her body shape and size has been heavily criticized, discussed further on.

But the doll as conceived by creator Ruth Handler was intended to be autonomous, reflecting women's ability to work at a time when their role was primarily seen as homemakers but on the cusp of change as the 1960s approached with women's liberation looming on the horizon. 'My whole philosophy of Barbie was that through the doll, the little girl could be anything she wanted to be. Barbie always represented the fact that a woman has choices.'

Central to Barbie was the 'idea that girls could play with their future selves, whatever that may be.' Editor of Quartz, Annaliese Griffin, recalls playing with Barbie as a child and sees Barbie positively as 'a blank slate for children's hopes, ambitions, imagination and aspirations. This blankness is her greatest asset... (providing girls with) immeasurable power to imagine many different ways of being. I don't remember ever wishing I looked like her.'

Like Griffin, psychology lecturer Dr Stacey Bedwell does not recall wanting to look like her either, nor did her friends, according to her, who she says became 'successful surgeons, physicists, psychologists and chemists. Playing with Barbie dolls as a child does not necessarily result in lower career aspirations and poor body image. I do not agree that media suggestions of a negative impact of Barbie on girls' development is true.'

I also played with Barbie dolls as a young girl, just enjoying changing her outfits and engaging in fantasy stories about her and imaginative play. I never gave her body shape or size a single thought.

Over the years, Barbie has represented many occupations like, changing with the times and what was considered as acceptable work for women and as such aspirational for many girls. She has been an astronaut, vet, scientist, teacher, babysitter, medic, bee-keeper, air-hostess, pilot, sportswoman, political candidate, entrepreneur, CEO, firefighter, journalist, computer and robotics engineer, video game developer, Mars explorer and 'had over 200 inspirational careers' over the years.

Barbie is just a toy. She is not real as creator Ruth Handler intended her to be for imaginative play. She has and continues to entertain girls globally. Barbie represents independence in the Western world where men have largely had the power and control in the public sphere. She is a working role model for both girls and boys to see that women have the ability like men to succeed in multitude work possibilities. Barbie has also represented iconic American beauty, femininity and heterosexuality yet her external appearance has been a focus of concern among some researchers.

IMPACT OF BARBIE ON GIRLS

The iconic Barbie doll that has been so popular amongst girls has also been considered controversial as a play item largely because of her body shape and size. The Barbie doll has been criticised by some researchers for contributing to unrealistic and unhealthy beauty ideals, with dangerous consequences for the mental and physical health of the girls playing with the doll, although not all researchers agree.

Some have criticised the doll suggesting it harms the girls' self-esteem, although research on this question is scarce.' Others conclude Barbie engenders body dissatisfaction in young girls who play with her.

This particular study was conducted with predominantly 162 white girls, aged 5–8, in southern England to determine the effect on their body dissatisfaction. A variety of tests were given to the girls ranging from showing them a picture book with images of US size two Barbie dolls and size 16 Emme dolls, and a questionnaire asking them their reaction to their actual bodies compared to their ideal bodies. The researchers concluded that the younger girls aged 5.5–7.5 had higher levels of body dissatisfaction after exposure to Barbie.

However, I don't think that there is a definite Barbie cause-effect relationship to explain this. The Barbie doll can't be blamed as the reason these girls may have reacted in that way. It is unlikely the Barbie doll had a sole direct negative impact on the girls' body image but rather that it may have reinforced the wider cultural message about thinness as the favoured body type espoused in the media, talked about by mothers and peers around the girls. 'Children observe their parents' body experience, therefore parents can become role models in developing body dissatisfaction in their children…The way in which parents react to media messages about appearance, body shape and behaviors towards the body informs children on how they are supposed to behave towards their own body.' Also, as the 2006 study did not employ real dolls for the girls to interact with, only images of them instead, I am not sure whether this fact could have skewed the results.

Another study of Dutch girls aged 6–10 found no body dissatisfaction among them when they played with a thin Barbie doll or the Emme doll. They found no support for the assumption that playing with dolls influences body image. Instead, they found that the girls exposed to the thin dolls ate less of the chocolate-coated peanuts snack provided by the researchers than the girls who played with Emme, the average size doll. Perhaps, the girls were given the food when they first played with the Emme doll and were full, not needing any more food when playing with Barbie. This is not specified in the study; therefore, no definitive conclusion can be drawn from the food intake.

What is troubling is that child development expert Jacqueline Harding informs 'by the age of 3 or 4, some children have already made up their minds (and even hold strong views) about how bodies should look.' Some studies indicate that three-year-olds display a preference for thinness, attributing positive attributes to it and negative attributes to larger figures.

A study of 84 3–10-year-old girls in southern California found that 39.3% of them preferred to play with the petite Barbie who is thin like the original and 39% did not want to play with the curvy fuller figure Barbie doll. Moreover, they attributed negative attributes to the curvy Barbie, like being mean, having no friends and not being pretty. The researchers concluded that 'results question the degree to which children will choose to interact with dolls that represent larger (and more realistic) body sizes and shapes. The simple availability of body-diverse dolls may be insufficient to fully combat pervasive cultural messages about body size.'

The problem is that messages about an ideal body shape and size are disseminated in wider society through agents of socialisation like parents, media and peers, for example.

In an earlier study, 55 girls aged 3–5 were given a choice of a thin, average or fat game piece to play with in a board game. 69.1% chose the thin body piece. 52.6% were unwilling to swap it for another. Most disconcerting, the researchers found that three-year-olds were internalising the thin body ideal, displaying body stereotyping. Internalisation of the thin body ideal is a known risk factor for eating pathology and body dissatisfaction, they add. But how do we know whether this internalisation is permanent or whether it will actually lead to eating disorders in those girls?

As writer Kat Armstrong says, 'When people focus on Barbie's body, they're subtly telling their kids that they should be concerned with women's bodies over their achievements and abilities.' Writer Natalie Reilly affirms and adds, 'Rather than focus on children's appearance, compliment or acknowledge children for their actions and behaviors.' This would be a positive step forward in trying to combat the internalisation of body shape or sized ideals. And parents can always tell their children that the Barbie doll is not real but can be what they want her to be, again moving away from her body image and give them the many examples of her multitude of occupations to date.

Reilly adds something important: 'Research has shown that the more we are exposed to one particular body type, the faster we normalize this body type in our minds, rendering other bodies not just uninspiring, but distasteful.' Perhaps this finding had been unconsciously present in some of the findings reported in the research studies cited here. It should be part of the educative process of us as a society trying to instigate change, shifting away from seeing beauty as external and aesthetically physical. And that's no easy task when we are bombarded by messages about what is considered physical beauty and the emphasis on it by the beauty and fashion industries, digital and mass media.

However, we need to fight against all that, dismantle the social value placed on outer beauty and focus on inner beauty of people, what they do for each other and how they live their lives rather than dwelling on body shapes, size and facial attractiveness. We need to educate very young children from preschool through to high school on the roles played by the beauty and fashion industries as big businesses, digital and mass media in perpetuating the social value of women's beauty with a team of professionals like psychologists and educators working out how best to do this for the appropriate age groups. We need to reinforce that diversity of people is a fact of life, including shapes and sizes of bodies, skin colour and pigment, ethnicity, disability, gender and sexuality, and that as a society, we need to accept and embrace all people and not judge them upon appearance.

MATTEL'S DIVERSE BARBIE DOLLS

Since 2015, Mattel has created ranges of diverse Barbie dolls, trying to shift Barbie's image as the thin, white icon. Body shapes include a petite, tall and curvy Barbie in addition to the original. The petite and tall Barbies retain an hourglass figure like the original while curvy Barbie is a fuller figure. Recently, Mattel has added ethnically diverse dolls to the Barbie range, including black Barbies with Afro hairstyles, dolls with various skin tones, hair and eye colour and hair texture. In 2020, there were a variety of 176 Fashionista Barbie dolls: nine body types, 35 skin tones and 94 hairstyles.

And now there are more diverse Barbie dolls like one with a prosthetic leg, one in a wheelchair, one wearing a hijab, one who is bald and one who has vitiligo, a loss of pigment in the skin resulting in white blotches.

Since the diverse range was introduced, sales of Barbie have soared. Barbie in a wheelchair and black Barbie with Afro hair have been best sellers.

As psychologist Gemma Witcomb says, 'these additions are a welcome step in the right direction in allowing girls to play with Barbie dolls that provide more diversity.' 'Mattel said they want to showcase a multi-dimensional view of beauty and fashion.' Lisa McKnight, Senior Vice President and Global Head of Barbie and its dolls portfolio, said, 'We are proud that Barbie is the most diverse line on the market that continues to evolve to better reflect the world girls see around them.'

In 2020, Mattel created a team of Campaign Barbie dolls to work as a political team in public life and encourage girls to imagine their role in public leadership and raise their voices. There is a black candidate, campaign manager, fundraiser and voter in the team. Mattel also introduced a diverse female athlete range honouring European sportswomen including British black world champion sprinter Dina Asher-Smith, French football captain Amandine Henry, Turkish Paralympic swimmer Sümeyye Boyaci, Ukraine world champion sabre fencer Olga Kharlan and German world champion long jumper Malaika Mihambo.

If we are going to change our conception of beauty, we need to embrace diversity as a norm – not to be thought about, rather as automatic. But external appearance should not be the focus of beauty because it eventually fades and if that's how a woman measures her self-worth, she will go through a lot of grief as she ages and eventually loses her looks. For others who feel pressured to look a certain way to fit society's beauty ideal, it is often unachievable or unsustainable, causing distress, and can be detrimental to their sense of well-being. This want or expectation should be dismantled and replaced with seeing beauty as the focus on developing our inner selves and what we do to make the world a better place and to help those in need.

As a society, we need to engineer this and combat the messages about appearance coming from the media, beauty and fashion industries, focusing on seeing beauty as internal. The Enlighten Education program that offers workshops to more than 20,000 girls aged 11–18 in schools around Australia, New Zealand, Singapore and Malaysia is trying to help girls discover their own inner beauty. The workshops don't tell the girls what to do but rather inform, inspire and empower them to find their own voice.

In one of their workshops, the girls learn to decode and critically evaluate media and social messages about having a 'perfect' body and being flawless externally. The girls are also taught to develop self-worth and resilience. Dannielle Miller, CEO of Enlighten Education, informs that it is 'important for young women to be given the skills to understand what's real and what's artificial and the skills to understand they can choose to define themselves in many ways and not conform to an ideal that's thin and limiting.'

This is the sort of program that needs to be taught globally and begin as early as possible designed by educators, psychologists and a team of the right professional people so that girls can be informed and empowered as early as possible growing up.

Looking back, we can see how narrow the fashion and beauty industry has been in favouring a white, thin European model. It is refreshing to see that change has begun by people inside and out of the industry, pushing for diversity that reflects our broader society even though the former model is still quite dominant. With time, however, we will hopefully see a plurality of models in terms of race, ethnicity, colour, size and disability and in beauty products that has already begun, reflecting and catering to members of our society.

Now let's see a different kind of beauty: how some young girls are doing and performing beauty.

CHAPTER FIVE: EXAMPLES OF BEAUTY AS A PERFORMANCE BY YOUNG GIRLS

Girls and young women need to see female role models growing up so that they learn that others have forged positive paths in life before them. Performing beauty is one such path and this chapter highlights examples of young girls doing it in different ways. I hope you feel as excited as I do when you read about these young girls and how they are performing beauty through their ideas and actions, to make our world and/or society a better place in some way, improving or enriching the lives of others largely out of kindness and inclusion.

I chose them because their life stories touched me – seeing how they think and taking action to help others and make our world a better, fairer and cleaner place. They ignited a fire in my belly, a feeling of excitement about what they were doing with their lives and what drives them to do it. Female education activist Malala Yousafzai and climate activist Greta Thunberg are not included here because hitherto there has been a lot written about them and they are already well-known globally for their work. Some of the girls mentioned are better known than others. I thought that they were a good mix – caring, loving, thoughtful girls who share a warm, open heart and who will make and are already making a difference. And they were all very young when they started their own journeys with performing beauty.

MARLEY DIAS: CHANGE-MAKER AND ACTIVIST FOR SOCIAL AND RACIAL JUSTICE

Articulate teenager Marley Dias blew me away. She is an amazing person: so driven from a very young age, passionate about what she believes in – that's justice and equity. She performs beauty by instigating both. Dias is a high achiever as a child-teen. She is an inspiration to me and hopefully to others who learn about her.

As a young girl aged ten who loved to read books, Dias was given books at home to read that had black female characters in them. However, at school she repeatedly saw a white boy featuring as the central character in the books she was assigned to read. In 2015, less than ten percent of children's books published featured a black character in them. This disparity bothered her and not being able to see a character like her in the books. Instead of doing nothing about it, she took social action.

In 2015, with her mother's help, Dias launched the platform #1000BlackGirlBooks with the goal to collect, donate and disseminate books to schools and libraries featuring black girls as the main character. She wanted black girls to see black female characters in books, represented in this literary, cultural space so they could relate and perhaps identify with them. Since 2015, she has donated books with black female characters in them to schools in the United States, Greece, Ghana, Singapore and Jamaica where she was born and raised. Today, her #1000BlackGirlBooks has skyrocketed to 13,000. This is an act of beauty, borne out of the desire to effect positive change, as a matter of racial and social justice, fairness and equity. And I agree.

Dias says she drew her inspiration from her parents, 'whether it's through reposting on social media or helping me develop an idea or showing me a documentary about representation.' Her parents raise her together, mindfully bringing their backgrounds and experiences into that, teaching her the need to look back in order to move and pay it forward in everyday practice. Dias applied this principle in the creation of her #1000BlackGirlBooks. They are helpful and fully supportive of her cause.

Her mother Dr Janice Johnson-Dias has a PhD in sociology and founded and is President of GrassROOTS Community Foundation, which helped Marley start her work. It is a public health and social action organisation focused on creating a world for all girls to grow to be healthy women. And its philosophy focuses on African Maat principles of harmony, utilising four of the core principles – truth, order, balance and reciprocity – so Marley has been exposed to working for social justice in her childhood. Her mother says that Marley has been trained to make a difference to her community and the world. And that lies at the core of #1000BlackGirlBooks.

Nevertheless, it wasn't so easy for Dias to reach the 1000 book target. But when word spread about what #1000BlackGirlBooks was all about, author and blogger Kelly Jensen at Stacked Books and bookseller Barnes and Noble raised money and donated books to her cause. Television host Ellen DeGeneres donated $10,000 to Dias' cause.

Barnes and Noble said, 'some books introduce us to characters who are different from us, allowing us to see the world from a different perspective. But for children in the process of figuring out who they are, and who they want to be, it is just as important to also read stories about characters they can relate to and see themselves in.'

'Girls need the power of example in the books they read as they may not see it anywhere else in their world. Without representation, they risk losing their sense of identity,' Dias adds.

She elaborates on this point and speaks out to say why representation and diversity is important in books. 'It allows kids to relate to characters and feel motivated to read. When you read a book, you enjoy it because of the storyline, plot and ideas. If ideas don't connect to your story or experiences it can frustrate you and demotivate you to want to read. I wanted black girls to be able to see themselves because of the power, confidence and motivation it gives them to want to read their stories more, to live more experiences and be confident and excited about their own identities.'

'I want people to imagine black girls as leaders and accept that we can be and are the main characters of our lives. Achieving equity and open spaces for black girls and others to learn are the core reasons for my campaign. My work is about education and acceptance. I want people to develop the patience and tolerance to know that there are other ways of being – to make space for other thoughts, ideas and possibilities.'

In 2016, #1000BlackGirlBooks had become digital, providing a resource guide for parents, educators and students, a place and space for them to find books with Black girls as characters in them.

Dias is campaigning for curricula to represent diverse characters, particularly black girls. She is talking to teachers and lawmakers about how to include books in schools that have black characters and represent diversity. Teachers have given her positive feedback about including stories of Black girls in their school libraries.

The teenager wants to see adults ensuring that the curriculum includes the study of African and Black people throughout history, providing contextual examination of 'today's monumental current events.' She believes it is important that kids are able to find and identify with Black women they admire and who represent who they want to be across the board. And she wants kids to learn about today's creative women and achievers, like US Vice-President Kamala Harris of the 21st century. It is 'through the work of people that fought during the enslavement period and Civil Rights Movement, we can celebrate some of the women that have done amazing things today.'

In 2019, when only 13 years old, Dias published her own non-fiction book *Marley Dias Gets It Done: And So Can You*, a children's book about inclusion, social justice and activism with tips on how to become an activist. It is well worth reading for girls and adults.

In 2020, Marley achieved another huge milestone in representing and promoting Black voices in *Bookmarks: Celebrating Black Voices*, a Netflix series she hosted and executively produced. It is a preschool series featuring prominent celebrities and artists reading children's books from black authors. She says the series aims to value, understand and show respect for all Black experiences.

She hopes it will encourage kids and families to 'watch, read and learn together and to hopefully create movements and create campaigns that can change the world and really shift conversations about Black identities, Black Lives and Black people.'

Dias advocates for children to be given a seat at the table with producers and broadcasters and involve them in the content because she says that today's tweens and teens are rejecting outdated stereotypes they see in movies and series.

In 2021, Dias hosted *Rebel Girls Fest: Adventure Awaits* on YouTube, a free and virtual event where high-achieving women talk and illustrate what they have done in their lives, encouraging girls to see that they can become leaders in various fields of endeavour. She clearly wants girls to believe they can do wonderful things with their lives and is encouraging them to do so. She is performing beauty by thinking of the future of others and wanting the best for them.

Dias won the American Ingenuity Award for youth awarded by the Smithsonian in 2017. She was named in the *Time* magazine list of 'Top 25 Most Influential Teens of 2018', recognised for her 2015 #1000BlackGirlBooks initiative. That year she was recognised as the youngest member of the Forbes 30 Under 30 award winners.

Marley Dias is a person to watch as I am sure that she will perform other acts of beauty in the future in the name of social justice and improving what is not right.

She shares: 'When we give back we reciprocate, we share the best within ourselves with the rest of the world. We're making the world a better place. And when the world is a better place, everybody's happier-including me and you.'

KHLOE THOMPSON: LIFE CHANGER

I fell in love with Khloe Thompson, a young girl with a very big heart. She performs beauty through her thinking of others and the kindness of her deeds. Let's take a look.

When she was only 8, Khloe passed a homeless woman called Michelle in Skid Row, Los Angeles. She asked her mother why the woman was homeless and her mother explained the possible reasons. Seeing Michelle made a huge impact on Khloe. She knew that she wanted to help her.

As she kept seeing Michelle, she asked her why she was on the street and the black-haired woman told Khloe how she had been kicked out of her apartment and did not have enough money for another.

Khloe has learnt to be kind from her Papa, she says. 'He taught me what kindness is and how to show it, the meaning of kindness. I live my life being kind to people.' Khloe shares.

So how does Khloe show her kindness?

Khloe's mum and Khloe came up with the idea of sewing toiletries bags for homeless women filled with a three-month supply of necessities like soap, a toothbrush and toothpaste, lotion, deodorant, wipes, hand sanitiser, socks, feminine hygiene, beanies, gloves and scarves in winter, and sunscreen in summer. Khloe's mum also helps with the sewing. And her dad packs the bags. Khloe's family is on board and supportive of this 'giving' work.

Her grandmother is a really 'amazing seamstress,' Khloe says. She taught her how to sew toiletries and shoulder bags. 'It's our bonding time,' says Khloe. It's her favourite part of making the bags – spending time with her grandma. And her favourite part of distributing them is seeing the smile on someone's face.

The toiletries bag gave rise to the idea of 'Khloe Kares', a non-profit charity organisation created by Khloe and her mum that has now distributed more than 6000 toiletries bags to homeless women. She works with companies, churches and other organisations in Southern California to co-host Kare Bag Day, where they distribute bags filled with the necessities to homeless communities, engaging youth in the process. On KhloeKaresDays, 100 bags are made and people informed about when and where they can come together for them via social media.

In 2016, Khloe was a guest on *The Real* daytime show and given a new sewing machine in support of her cause. The show announced that Dove also donated 1000 bottles of hair intensive shampoo as well as conditioner and 1000 white beauty bars to her cause as well.

With the help of her mum Alisha Thompson, Khloe Kares also runs workshops to train youth to become leaders and teach them business planning and public speaking. Khloe wants to help others to set and achieve goals and help young people to discover and realise their passions.

Khloe took a trip with her grandma to Ghana where she saw there was a need for water pumps and toilet facilities. She learnt that people were squatting to go to the toilet in small spaces so Khloe raised $12,000 to build a borehole and toilet facilities for a school in the village Abidjan Nkwanta. Khloe says 'a borehole is technically like a water pump.'

Khloe has partnered with philanthropist Dawn Sutherland (her grandma's friend) who is based in Ghana. Sutherland explained, 'To get water, you have to pay to dig a borehole and it is not cheap, or buy the government water. Not everyone can afford it, that's why you have to fetch water every day. You can only buy what you can afford at the time. This is the first time anyone has done a borehole and toilet facility with a flushing toilet in a rural school. This really sets the stage for something great. The water is for the school but the community can come in and buy water.'

Sutherland mentors 12 girls in The Sunday Morning Club, which motivates, encourages and empowers them to be what they want to be. The club heard about what Khloe does in Los Angeles and invited her to come to talk to them. Khloe delivered the same message to these girls: 'you can be what you want to be' and gave them a workshop with a vision board that included setting goals. Some had high hopes to become a fashion designer, doctor, great leader, pilot and soldier, all doing something for their country.

The girls were excited to see Khloe, a young girl like them, being so articulate and confident in public speaking. And she was blown away to see how differently they live to her – how a family lives in one room. The girls need to fetch water, cook dinner and possibly marry at 14, expecting to be cared for by a husband. She saw such a different life to hers.

In 2019, Khloe led a youth initiative #GivingTuesdayKids to encourage young people to take action about the causes close to their hearts and give to the community through acts of kindness.

She wants to show that everyone has the power to make change and give something.

That year Khloe was awarded the International Young Eco-Hero Award, given to 8–12-year-olds. She donated the money to install more water pumps in Ghana. She also won the George H.W. Bush Points of Light Award for her human spirit to create positive change and demonstrating empathy in her giving of Khloe Kares. 'I can't imagine my life without Khloe Kares because it changed my life completely,' said Khloe.

In 2020, Khloe sent school supplies and hygiene items to Ghana.

She also worked on a community project, 'Community Fridges', that sprang up in Los Angeles to feed the community who are food insecure. Khloe has a fridge donated to her and has collected money to stock it.

Khloe was asked what skills she has used so far on her giving journey, and acts of beauty, I add. Compassion is the first. 'Since I was little, I've always had a heart to help others.' Curiosity is the second. 'My curiosity made me ask questions.' And the third: Social Responsibility. 'I am very selfless and always think of others before myself.'

She forgot to add a skilled author. Khloe has written two books for children about helping the homeless, kindness and community service: *Girl Blazer, The Girl Who Became the Change* and *Marisol's Helping Hand*.

She hopes to inspire other kids. 'We have the power to change the world,' says the positive-thinking young girl with a big heart.

Khloe also hopes to feature a collection at New York Fashion Week and do a TED Talk. And she wants to grow Khloe Kares and establish a community centre in Ghana and Los Angeles, travel the world and teach kids to create their own projects, continuing her work for the homeless.

Khloe Thompson fervently believes her generation can change

the world. And I am sure she has a lot more to give in her acts of beauty.

RUBY KATE CHITSEY: COMMUNITY WORKER AND ACTIVIST

Ruby Kate Chitsey hadn't found her shtick until recently. She would accompany her mother Amanda, a geriatric nurse practitioner, to nursing homes and meet the elderly living there. One day, Ruby noticed a resident, Pearl, looking forlorn after her dog had left her. Pearl did not know when she'd see it again. The cost of the doggy visit was $12 and Pearl couldn't afford it. Patients were given $40 a month by the government to cover their expenses apart from a room and board. The money didn't go very far. Ruby was sad to see Pearl fretting about her dog and decided to do something about it.

Taking on Pearl's plight, ten-year-old Ruby wanted to help her and other elderly residents. 'They deserve more than the $40 stipend a month. I help these people that have very little,' Ruby shared. She took out a notebook and asked residents for their three wishes and has raised over $300,000 so far to make them happen. Ruby was ten when she started to take action and perform acts of beauty to give the vulnerable in our society some happiness and improve their quality of life.

Initially, Ruby and her mother held local fundraisers and then Amanda Chitsey opened a GoFundMe (an American platform to raise money) entitled 'Three Wishes for Ruby's Residents' one. Once it circulated on social media, it drew in tens of thousands of dollars.

Residents' wishes were very basic: well-fitting clothing, a haircut, fast food, a pillow for neck support. Some residents just wanted prayers.

'With the money we've raised through GoFundMe, we've been

able to provided pet food, clothing, shoes, phones, corrective learning devices. My ultimate goal is to make the elderly people happy,' Ruby said.

Ruby and her mother are helping to change people's lives. Shannon, a patient, suffered a stroke in her fifties on the right side of her body wished for an electric wheelchair. Amanda shares that 'Ruby sat in the chair and drove it to her. It was beautiful.' Ruby discloses that Shannon was 'really happy, happy-emotional.'

Another resident needed an assessment by a physiotherapist to determine whether she could use a wheelchair. Amanda found her a physiotherapist and the lady cried like a baby when she and Ruby told her that one would come to assess her.

'It's big life-changing things,' Amanda notes. 'Something about her (Ruby) is making people really want to give and donate – not just give money, but give their time and their services to really improve people's lives.'

This community work is 'so perfect for Ruby and her personality and she is so good at it. She's so rewarded for it, much more self-confident than she was because she realizes that she does have value, that she does bring something to the table, that she contributes. And she's grown so much as a person.'

Since 2019, Ruby Chitsey has raised over $300,000 for her cause to help brighten up the lives of the elderly and fulfilled over 8000 of their wishes. Ruby's organisation has a KID BOARD of young activists, a non-voting group who want to make a difference in the lives of nursing home seniors. 'We believe it is crucial to the vision, mission and trajectory of the organization to have a "KID BOARD" to continually remind the adults of their perspective, to offer ideas and creativity and help us think outside the box.'

Ruby's community service helping the elderly and acts of beauty has not gone unnoticed. She has received multiple local, regional and national awards for this work. Ruby was named among the 'Ten Girls Changing the World in 2020' by People's Magazine. She is the Arkansas 2021 winner of the Prudential Spirit of Service Award, named a CNN hero and Fox News Midnight Hero.

With Ruby's kind big heart, I am sure that she will continue to do wonderful things and engage in acts of beauty to help others and she is someone to watch down the track.

ISABEL AND MELATI WIJSEN: ENVIRONMENTAL ACTIVISTS

By the tender age of ten, Isabel and her older sister Melati Wijsen, 12, had already developed a social conscience. The year was 2013. They were appalled at seeing the build-up of plastic bags harming their environment: the beachside and rice paddy fields in Bali where they were born and bred. 'Who is going to do something about this?' they asked themselves.

They did. In 2013, the young girls became activists and founded a campaign and movement to ban plastic bags in Bali: 'Bye Bye Plastic Bags' and remove plastic pollution there. Their goal was to 'stop those plastic bags from wrapping and suffocating our beautiful home.'

'We launched the idea of Bye Bye Plastic Bags at the Global Initiative Network Youth Conference in Bali (and) chose plastic bags not plastic bottles or straws, for example, because they were something we saw given away every day and are not necessary. Plastic bags are something that the consumer has control over saying no to. They can refuse a bag. It seemed like a good place to start.' But what influenced them to do something like that to protect their environment and perform an act of beauty in thinking of others around them and their future?

It seems that the school they attended played a pivotal role in their developing this social conscience. The Green School they attended in Bali was ecological and 'built to train green leaders (where) students are encouraged to take initiatives for the future.'

'Its program promotes independent thinking and innovation. Its mission is teaching children to be change makers.' And that's what Melati and Isabel are.

The school's attitude was that the girls were learning a lot in their campaigning for a clean future and so enabled their school time to be flexible.

The girls say that when at school, they were inspired by a few people who came before them: Nelson Mandela (activist, former President of South Africa) who helped to negotiate the end of apartheid in South Africa; Diana, Princess of Wales, philanthropist and humanitarian and Mahatma Gandhi, social activist who led the successful campaign for India's independence from Britain. Confidently and articulately, the girls shared in a TED Talk in London in 2015, how they wished to also be significant like these three model figures and discussed their mission and journey of banning plastic bags in Bali.

After visiting Mahatma Gandhi's house, the girls were motivated by his non-violent practices and embarked on a hunger strike (a tactic that had been used by Gandhi to reach his goals) to attract the government's attention. It evoked a huge reaction on social media and earned the government's support to ban plastic bags in Bali. The governor was 'proud Indonesian youth are trying to do something about the environment,' shared Isabel. In 2019, thanks to their hard work, single-use plastic bans have been banned in Bali. The girls had become change-makers.

Initially, they were also inspired by the efforts made by other countries like Rwanda or cities like Oakland and Dublin in saying 'no' to plastic bags.

And they are lucky to have supportive parents: their Dutch mother, Elvira, and Javanese father Elko Riyanto, drove them where they needed to go, providing moral and practical support.

Back in 2013, when they began, the girls did some research and discovered that 'Indonesia was the world's second largest source of marine plastic pollution after China.' Then they started up their campaign Bye Bye Plastic Bags educating and persuading people to say no to using plastic bags. In their TED Talk, they refer to Bali as 'a dream paradise or a paradise lost' because '600 cubic meters of plastic garbage' is generated there daily, the size of a 14 storied building and less than 5% get recycled. Almost all plastic bags end up in drains, rivers and the ocean, Isabel said.

The girls recruited others to help them with their plastic ban campaign so they worked as a team with volunteers from the island and around the world helping them. They cleaned up the beaches, rivers and streets with thousands of people coming to help them, collecting trash at 115 sites in Seminyak, Indonesia.

Since 2013, Melati, Isabel and their team have been working hard to spread awareness and educate people about the pollution of plastics. They produce educational booklets on the harm of plastic that is distributed to primary students across Indonesia.

In 2014, the sisters and their team also worked to create an example of a plastic-free village: Pererenan Village in Bali with local government and community support. While the village is not 100% plastic free, it has dramatically reduced its amount of plastic bag use. The group established 'One Island One Voice', a sticker campaign, giving stickers to, publicising and promoting the shops, restaurants and hotels that were plastic bag free.

In 2017, the Bye Bye Plastic Bags group had a huge beach clean-up with 12,000 people from around Bali clearing 43 tons of trash in one day.

The same year they recruited a community of women, 'Mountain Mamas', to make reusable shopping bags from recycled material as an alternative to single-use plastic, creating jobs for women and built a network of more than 36 Bye Bye Plastic Bag chapters around the world. Bye Bye Plastic Bags has partnered with other agencies to track river boons collecting trash and be guided on where to clean them.

Melati and Isabel Wisjen say the ban on plastic bags will be good for the economy, stimulating new business and innovation in making alternative bags; it will positively affect global warming if bags are no longer littered or burned and the animals living in the sea will stop dying because of less trash in the ocean.

Their takeaway message is: 'We believe very strongly in education (as) the key to change.'

In their TED Talk, which is well worth watching, they encourage kids to make things happen. 'Make that difference,' the girls advise. They certainly have.

Watch this space, as I have no doubt that these activist sisters will continue to perform beauty in their activism to protect our environment and world.

KATIE STAGLIANO: VEGETABLE GARDEN GROWER/COMMUNITY WORKER

Katie Stagliano is another girl performing beauty, making a positive difference in others' lives. 'I am proud to grow healthy food, prevent hunger, empower kids to grow a healthy end to hunger in their communities,' Stagliano said.

So what's her story?

In 2008, when Katie was nine and in the third grade, she grew a seedling into a cabbage in her back garden for a school project. That cabbage weighed 40 pounds. Katie donated it to a local soup kitchen in North Charleston, South Caroline and the cabbage fed 275 people.

'I wanted to share it with families struggling with hunger. That one day changed my life. Until I went to the soup kitchen I didn't realize how big of an issue hunger is and how it affects so many people. I thought if I can feed 175 people with a cabbage, then imagine how many people an entire garden can feed,' she said.

Katie developed her flagship second garden in Summerville, South Carolina after growing the cabbage in her own back one.

After that, she says kids across the United States reached out to her and she offered them grants through her non-profit organisation, Katie's Krops, that helps other youth to become growers and start gardens in their own communities where proceeds are donated to feed those in need. In 2018, 40,000 pounds of fresh produce was donated to those in need across the United States of America.

'So far, thousands of kilos of food has been grown under Katie's Krops initiative, feeding many thousands of homeless and vulnerable people able to eat because of the vision and hard work of one girl.' And she has successfully drawn in others to help and grow 100 gardens growing produce across 31 states in America.

Katie has written and published an award-winning book, *Katie's Cabbage* (2014), that shares her journey of growing her first cabbage, developing Katies Krops and how we can make a powerful difference in people's lives.

Thanks to WP Rawl, leafy greens sponsor, Katie's Krops has been able to offer an annual summer camp for the Katie's Krops growers where they learn creative growing techniques, as well as lessons on food safety and develop friendships with fellow growers.

Stagliano's flagship garden now has an outdoor classroom where children can learn the fundamentals of gardening and how to cook the produce.

Other educational programs planned in the garden include story time with Katie, exploring what is growing in the garden; family cooking; and a science and photography class that explores the garden through the lens of a camera.

During the Covid pandemic, Katie's Krops is stepping up

further in providing free meals distributed via drive-through: pasta with a heart meat sauce, tossed green salad, fresh bread and dessert.

During the pandemic, Stagliano has shipped seed to families interested in starting their own backyard gardens to help feed themselves and their neighbours. 2100 seed packets have been shipped to more than 270 families across 23 states in America since the start of the pandemic.

Stagliano has deserved the various awards bestowed upon her: America's Top 10 Youth Volunteers by the Presidential Spirit of Community Awards, Global Teen Leader for Three Dot Dash – a global initiative recognising and supporting the efforts of global teen leaders. In 2012, she became the youngest recipient ever of the Clinton Global Citizen Award for leadership in Civil Society and is a 2010 Sodexo STOP Hunger Scholar granted a $5000 scholarship. The business company Sodexo recognises those who made a significant impact in the fight against hunger. In 2016, Stagliano was awarded their new 'Growing Together' award and described as a person who has 'grown a movement.'

Katie Stagliano has achieved a lot since she was nine, having grown her cabbage in the back garden. I am sure she will continue to perform beauty by doing more to help others in need.

DANIELLE BOYER: STEAM INVENTOR AND ACTIVIST

Entrepreneurial Danielle Boyer who comes from the Ojibwe tribe (American Indian) wants to help children around the world actualise their potential by having easy access to a good STEAM (Science, Technology, Engineering, Art and Mathematics) education. Her concern is to reach those particularly from lower socio-economic brackets: girls and minorities who may not have this access and be disadvantaged. She wants to address this gap in society and help improve employment access and career opportunities.

'When not exposed to quintessential programming, focusing on robotics, digital design and coding, it is near impossible to break into the most influential (work) fields,' Boyer says.

Boyer is performing beauty in having her goal, leveling the playing field from a very young age and carrying it through to adulthood. She is now spending her life working towards achieving it. 'I wake up looking forward to using my technical skills in robotics and technology to better the education of those in the community and the world,' Boyer shares.

At ten, Boyer loved STEAM and wanted others to learn in this area. One day on a shopping spree with her mum, Boyer saw some animal puppets and realised that she could teach other youngsters about them. With the support of her mother who is an artist, she taught a kindergarten animal science class. She utilised artistry in her teaching apart from researching the animals. This early in her life, Danielle realised that resources are not so accessible or diverse and she felt the need to change this.

Her animal curriculum was helping kids learn specifically about STEAM concepts. 'I made the colouring sheets myself, I taught the kids, I read to them, I had activities planned.

Wanting others, particularly the disadvantaged, to learn STEAM and her home life certainly paved the way forward in shaping her future direction. Boyer was home-schooled with her father being an electrical engineer, enabling her to learn 2D drawing and CAD software early. That's where computers are used to assist in the design process.

From childhood through to young adulthood, Boyer has spent her young life dedicated to providing educational accessibility, affordability and ensuring diversity as a STEAM promoter. She has been multi-tasking to achieve this goal and has done a lot since the age of ten. Boyer is now around 21.

She has worked on robotics since the age of 11. In 2019, Boyer invented a robotics kit that children can access for free. 'The robots teach project-based learning in electrical and mechanical engineering and computer science.' Her robotics kits are made of recycled and biodegradable materials. And she composts and reuses old robot parts to make new ones for kids to use. They are available from her non-profit organisation THE STEAM CONNECTION (steamconnection.org), which she founded in 2019, run by students and minorities.

Her first designed robot EKGAR: Every Kid Gets a Robot consists of four 3D printed pieces made of bio-plastic (sustainable), using low-cost WFI and Bluetooth-compatible technology. Since 2019, she and her team have distributed more than 4500 robots for free to more than 12 countries globally. There are more than 20,000 educators and students on her 'Make-A-Robot Platform'.

Her second-designed robot TWENTY is a creative robotics kit that can be assembled for free at home and she has two more forthcoming: Auto Oscar and EKGAR: Bio Botz.

Boyer has written a series of Earth Books for her mentees and other teams to equip them to deal with environmental issues around them. Boyer and her team have also created five free books for children in grades K-3. The series showcases and promotes diversity through featuring children of different ethnicities, religions and those with disabilities. 'Children's books shouldn't be isolating or unrelatable.' Boyer creates posters featuring diversity so that girls can see themselves represented in STEAM and feel they belong. She is working on a photo series featuring minorities in STEAM and their projects. 'I know it makes a difference when you can see someone in your culture doing interesting work in science and robotics,' Boyer informs. The STEAM entrepreneur has also has written activity books for the robotics teams she mentors to handle environmental issues and is developing more books for girls.

Boyer and her team use SOLIDWORKS software. At 17, she met a SOLIDWORKS representative at a world robotics conference and since has established a relationship with the software company, invited to be a keynote speaker at a national conference, speak on podcasts and panels, for example, and using their software in her work. 'They are the reason I am able to do what I do now,' she says.

Boyer is currently studying electrical and mechanical engineering but during her gap year, the entrepreneur had taught students in their homes and volunteered at robotics competitions, setting up, organising and judging events. 'I love working with kids,' she says. She proved that by visiting children in hospitals, playing video games with them and giving them her created colouring books. 'I feel it's important to help everyone I can.' Another example of her performing beauty.

Helping is channelled into classes that she teaches to students 18 or under who are interested in developing their technical skills and social change projects. She has taught thousands of youngsters.

Not surprising is that Boyer has received kudos and won awards for her work: she was named one of PEOPLE Magazine's Girls Changing the World in her endeavours to use technology to create positive change globally and for our Earth. Boyer was nominated L'Oréal Paris Women of Worth Class, 2020, honoured for making a difference in the community through volunteering. Danielle performed an act of beauty when she donated the moneyed prize to the American Indian Science and Engineering Society that supports Indigenous students on North America in Science, Technology, Engineering and Mathematics.

She was named 2020 Brower Youth Awards winner for 'promoting a tangible love for our Earth through her STEAM education – she is making engineering and environmental education more widely available.' And showing learners how engineering can help to innovate solutions to problems, says Aishwarya Arvind, STEAM Changemaker.

In 2021, Boyer was appointed to the Channel Kindness Advisory Board for being an aspirational and engaged youth making meaningful impacts in the community. (Channel Kindness is a digital platform created by Lady Gaga, a safe space for the young to tell their stories of kindness, resilience and community.)

Danielle Boyer has her whole decade of twenties to look forward and I am sure that we will see her performing many more beautiful acts, doing great things then and throughout her life to help others and improve the world around us through STEAM.

BELLA LACK: CAMPAIGNER FOR ANIMAL RIGHTS, CONSERVATION AND ENVIRONMENT

Bella Lack is an amazing, articulate young English girl, a nature lover. She performs acts of beauty through her passion for nature and trying to preserve it; protecting animal rights and the environment, raising awareness of these issues and trying to effect positive change so that we all share a better world. And she is doing so without her parents' guidance. 'At times, they've tried to convince me to stop. I don't think I ever would, or ever could, stop.'

'From a young age, I've always loved animals. It started as a toddler... enchanted by the diligent ants and lethargic snails that resided in my garden. This has blossomed into an ever-growing wonderment and love of the diversity of creatures that our planet possesses.'

At the age of 11, she experienced an awakening after watching a video of how the palm oil industry had decimated orangutans, her favourite animal. 'I watched the baby orangutans orphaned and crying out pitifully for their mothers. I watched the verdant patchwork of forest being stripped and ravaged. How on earth could we be so willingly and mindlessly be causing so much destruction?' This awareness propelled her to take action to change the status quo.

In 2018, at 16, Lack's campaigning for animal protection impacted on the law. She initiated a petition to ban wild animal acts in circuses and collected 200,000 signatures. This young girl effected change when a bill in England was passed into law, prohibiting the use of wild animals in travelling circuses in 2019.

She is a young ambassador of the RSPCA (Royal Society for the Prevention of Cruelty to Animals that rescues, rehabilitates, rehomes and release animals in England and Wales) and a member of the Ivory Alliance campaign, a group of influencers and politicians working to combat the Illegal Wildlife Trade and stop the slaughter of elephants for their ivory tusks.

At 17, she was appointed Ambassador for The Born Free Foundation, an international wildlife charity that campaigns to keep wildlife in the wild, protects wild animals in their natural habitat, campaigns against the keeping of wild animals in captivity and rescues wild animals in need. 'Born Free epitomizes my ideals; I love their compassionate approach to conservation and I have always agreed with keeping "wildlife in the wild."'

As Ambassador for The Born Free Foundation, Lack has been working on a documentary entitled *Animal* with primatologist and conservationist, Dame Jane Goodall, meeting with scientists and activists around the world to figure out how humans can live alongside other species.

She is also raising money to make a documentary, *Losing Wild,* to highlight how disengaged young people are from nature and how different it was for previous generations. Lack is Ambassador for Save The Asian Elephants, an organisation that raises awareness to influence politicians and change commercial practices. She notes how these elephants are exploited as amusement for tourists for commercial profit – giving tourists rides and training to perform. These elephants are often beaten with iron rods, locked in cages, dehydrated and starved. They are chained and kept in small cages, needing a large area to roam. The documentary she is making will raise awareness of the cruelty encountered by this endangered species. We need to 'change from campaigning to action,' said Lack, who hopes to see Prime Minister Boris Johnson focus attention on wildlife, restoring and re-wilding it.

She has taken action to conserve the forest through her involvement as Youth Director for Reserva Land Trust, a platform for young people to use their voice and power. The trust 'empowers youth to make a measurable difference in the future of our planet through projects in conservation, education and storytelling,' she said.

The trust is currently working on the first fully youth-funded nature reserve in the Choco rainforest in Ecuador. Youth includes those under 26. 'Every three dollars a child donates protects a plot of rainforest the size of a classroom.' Lack advocates that we be proactive in creating a beautiful future through creative means like developing stories and narratives in books, films and music, sending messages of change to protect rather than exploit other forms of life.

The conservationist says that we need to change the economic narrative of endless growth and consumption to a humanist one where 'values of respect, compassion and wellbeing are at the heart of what we do. Viruses and disease are environmental issues. About 75% of emerging diseases are zoonotic. We are bound to the laws of the natural world, and will never be exempt from the havoc we wreak upon it.'

One wonders where this young girl finds the time to do everything. She is currently writing a book, *The Children of the Anthropocene*, that looks at how the climate crisis is hitting young people, to be published by Penguin in June 2022.

Lack wants to see a future where individuals assume responsibility for the natural world including a change in lifestyle and leaders taking action to protect our planet. She says that we can re-wild our gardens; keep informed and educate others to drive change forward; consider the impacts of our consumer product choices; decrease our consumption of animal products as 'carnivorous habits are ravaging our climate, biodiversity and oceans-and our health.'

I am sure that Bella Lack will play her part performing acts of beauty to do whatever she can to help effect further change to protect animals and the environment.

MARI COPENY (LITTLE MISS FLINT): SOCIAL JUSTICE ADVOCATE/ ACTIVIST AND PHILANTHROPIST

Mari Copeny's social conscience was stirred very early in life: she became an activist at the age of four or five, helping her grandmother give people food for free who could not afford to buy it. The beautiful act of giving to and doing for others is integral in this young girl's make up as she continues to advocate for others wronged and fundraises to support underprivileged children in her community and the United States.

Copeny was just seven when in 2014, officials in Michigan switched the Flint water supply from Lake Huron and the Detroit River to the Flint River without properly treating it, consequently resulting in dangerously high levels of bacteria and lead. 'The bacteria resulted in an outbreak of Legionnaires' disease that killed 12 people and sickened another 79 mid-June 2014–October 2015; bathing in the water reportedly caused rashes and hair loss. More than 8000 children, including Mari, face a risk of long-term developmental problems as a result of possible exposure to lead in the water.' Mari said, 'It smelled funny and it was brown. It wasn't something you'd want to drink.' But 'we drank the water for two years before scientists discovered it was toxic. My siblings and I had to learn to turn off the tap when we brushed our teeth or washed our hands.'

'We could not drink. We could not cook (with the water).' 'We can't take baths. The water still burns our eyes. We're using bottled water for everything we consume.'

At the age of eight, Copeny made a bold move and in 2016, she wrote to the incumbent President of the United States, Barack Obama, about the water crisis in Flint, Michigan where she lives with her family. 'I am one of the children that is effected by this water, and I've been doing my best to march in protest and to speak out for the kids who live here in Flint... I know that this is probably an odd request but I would love for a chance to meet you or your wife.'

Obama responded by letter to Copeny: 'I am so proud of you for using your voice to speak out on behalf of the children of Flint... I'm coming to Flint...I'll use my voice to call for change and help uplift your community. Letters from kids like you are what make me so optimistic for the future.'

Not only did the President come to Flint and meet Copeny, he also declared a federal state of emergency. He authorised $100 million on January 16, 2016, to help repair Flint's water system. This little girl effected great change improving the water crisis in her hometown of Flint. She also distributed over 1 million bottled waters for the Flint children. Partnering with Hydroviv, a water filter company, Copeny produced and distributed water filters to places experiencing a water problem like Flint has.

This amazing young girl raised over $500,000 for projects to help and support Flint kids. She wants them to have access to the tools in life that will make them successful. She fights for issues like clean water, books, bikes and packs for kids and articulated so in a speech delivered to the 2018 Social Good Summit (a United Nations affiliated event connecting individuals, corporations, non-profits, government and grassroots organisations to inspire and discuss solutions for greatest challenges of our times.) 'I want to make sure that no child will ever find they're helpless and hopeless. I want to make sure that kids in Flint have the same shots at life as kids in the middle-class areas from our country. I want to teach kids that using the Internet can help them use their voice. I want to help build a generation of kids that know that they don't have to wait for a change in the world – that the world is ours now and it's up to us to save it.'

Copeny together with non-profit Pack Your Back raised funds to buy 16,000 backpacks filled with pencils, pens, markers, crayons notebooks, highlighters and books. She finds books by authors of colour for the Flint children as she sees representation as an important issue so that black children see themselves depicted in their culture. To that account, Copeny raised funds for underprivileged Flint children to see the screening of Black Panther about what it means to be Black in America, Africa and the world. Thinking of others, she also raised $18,000 for Christmas 2017 and had thousands of toys to give to children.

Mari Copeny is a member of the Flint Youth Justice League (a youth advisory board for Michigan State University-Hurley Children's Hospital) Members are chosen who are making a difference in their homes, community and the world in which we live. These members serve as a youth advisory council for the public health paediatric initiative to provide a perspective and guidance in public health. Their voices as youth leaders directly influence these activities and are greatly valued and viewed as role models.

Mari Copeny has her eye on the White House as President in 2044.

I will not be surprised if she wins that office. 'I love helping people, especially kids.'

And that's what makes her beautiful – this feeling she has that is translated into action to help others.

SYNTHIA OTIENO, AWOUR MACRINE ATIENO, STACY OWINA, PURITY ACHIENG, IVY AKINYI: RESTORERS – INVENTORS AND CO-FOUNDERS OF I-CUT APP FOR FEMALE GENITAL MUTILATION

Five girls aged (15–17) in Kenya came up with an idea to develop a cell phone application to fight Female Genital Mutilation (FGM). In doing so, they perform an act of beauty to help and protect young girls and women in their community, who are at risk from experiencing this barbaric cultural practice, considered a rite of passage and prerequisite for marriage that incurs a dowry for impoverished families. Although it is illegal in Kenya, a quarter of women have experienced FGM there.

In Kenya, a girl aged (10–14) becomes a woman in her tribe by undergoing FGM, the partial or total removal or cutting of her external genitals: labia minora and majora (inner and outer lips), including the clitoris. 'Traditionally, no anesthesia is used and the procedure is performed with a razor blade.'

And even though FGM is a violation of human rights, more than 200 million girls and women today have suffered FGM, not only in Africa but also in the Middle East, some countries in Asia and Latin America.

Apart from the emotional and psychological damage FGM causes, the act also presents serious health risks like infection, long-term urinary issues, increased risk of complications in childbirth and even the possibility of death. Girls inflicted by

FGM are less likely to complete school and marry in adolescence.

Synthia Otieno and her friends talked about the prevalence of FGM and noticed how the act changed their friend, a smart, bubbly girl with a bright future, who never returned to school after going through that. Otieno together with the other four girls talked about trying to do something to fight FGM. 'FGM is a big problem affecting girls worldwide and it is a problem we want to solve,' shared Synthia.

That's when Synthia, Stacy, Purity, Awour and Ivy created i-Cut, an app for a mobile/cell phone, providing young girls with medical and legal advice and assistance about FGM. Girls forced to undergo the FGM procedure can use the app to 'alert authorities, report violations and find local shelters and help centres. The interface has five simple options: help, rescue, report, inform, donate/give feedback.' The group named themselves the Restorers as they wish to 'restore the hopeless and helpless girls in society.'

Owino joined the group when she realised there was no current platform to connect FGM victims to rescue centres or authorities and wanted to provide that platform. While a large percentage of Kenyans own smartphones, in remote areas, feature phones (the Restorers target) are heavily used so the group developed a technical shortcut that can be used with them and works like the app.

Synthia shares that 'We started by making prototypes where we sketched out ideas of different screens. The paper prototypes acted as a guide on how the app would look like and function on the phone. We then learnt different variables.'

She is grateful for her sponsored education and the opportunity it gave her at the Compassion Center (a Christian humanitarian aid organisation) where she fell in love with technology and is developing code. Synthia aspires to become a computer scientist and role model for other girls.

In 2017, the Restorers applied for the Technovation Challenge, a global competition that encourages girls to solve their community problems via technology. The group came runner-up, awarded $10,000 USD to use the funds at working out how to make the app available. 'We were very excited. We were not only representing Kenya, but the entire continent,' Syhthia shared.

The following year, the Daily Trust newspaper in Africa selected the Restorers as winners of the African of the Year (2018) for developing the i-Cut application. In 2019, the Restorers were shortlisted for the European Parliament's Sakharov Prize for Freedom of Thought, an honorary award for individuals or groups who have dedicated their lives to defending human rights and freedom of thought. 'Their nomination marks an important step in the fight against FGM, empowering young people to play a role in their own communities.'

The Restorers were interviewed after these accolades and commented: 'The app has been successful so far and we are particularly happy at the progress we are making with girls across the country by educating them on how to uses the app and the kind of positive feedback we are receiving from them. We made this app for them.'

The group has registered i-Cut as a foundation and wish to reach as many young girls as possible in Kenya. They are described as 'young girls who have embraced technology for the social good.'

I am sure the girls will innovate some more technologically to find solutions to local problems, performing beauty in helping others. They are stars with hearts.

JULIETA MARTINEZ: CHILEAN SOCIAL ACTIVIST

Julieta Martinez is a bright, caring young girl who performs beauty by thinking of others and has clear ideas about the kind of future she sees for girls and women. She contracted type 2 diabetes at the age of three and felt privileged to have access to a costly insulin pump that those less fortunate could afford. This disparity became her social consciousness calling and she wanted to help close this gap.

Her activism stemmed from this social consciousness that began when, at ten years of age, Martinez marched with her family to demand that the universal health care plan in Chile include diabetic pumps. This social consciousness grew stronger inside Martinez who assumed a leadership role and launched a social media platform, *Tremendas*, to connect young girls and women, their talents and causes across Chile. 'Julieta wanted to establish a space where those searching for activism could collaborate with others, improve lives and instigate social change.

Martinez reached out to family and friends and sought alliances with various companies and organisations and she became known after appearing on television programs and through growing support via her Instagram platform.

Since inception *Tremendas* has grown into a foundation of young people from up to 22 countries with a presence in 17 Latin American countries.

Tremendas has launched some initiatives during the COVID-19 pandemic. It created a program, *Juntas en cuarantena* (*Quarantine Together*), connecting girls and teenagers who are confined in conversations with women of the United Nations. It also created a webinar seminar program, *prendid@s* (*excited*), that provides tools to young people who are committed to social entrepreneurship.

*Tremendas Dirigenta sal*so disperses social aid to the most vulnerable. Its recent innovation is the *Acadamia Climaticas* (*Climate Academy*) for girls, teenagers and young women from Latin America and the Caribbean as agents of change, providing a platform where young activists can use their skills to transition towards sustainable development.

A priority of Martinez and *Tremendas* is caring for the environment. Early on in her life after attending a social innovation with her parents hearing people speak, she realised the information relayed to the public on environmental issues was inadequate. She asked, 'How is it that in my country there are more than a million people without access to clean drinking water?'

Martinez says Chile has poor environmental education in communities and the school system. She sees education in climate change as imperative and for her, the solution. 'It's not just an environmental crisis but a human rights crisis too.'

Tremendas commits to working on girls' education as the driver of change to a climate solution and recommends that STEM (Science, Technology, Engineering and Mathematics) be brought innovatively into girls' lives and at an earlier stage than currently. 'We will build a strong academy that will periodically train young women and girls and adolescents in biological sciences, astronomical sciences and robotics. We are committed to enabling spaces that position girls, young women and adolescents as protagonists of the present. We will connect young women leaders with decision-makers, so that their perspectives are considered.'

Apart from taking action in attempt to effect change, Martinez is a powerful speaker. She says the young need to be integral to decision-making that effect social issues. 'We are part of the solution to problems. We need an intergenerational dialogue. We, the youth, are not only the future. We are also the present.'

'Solutions should not be simply for the girls; they should be created with girls. We want to be protagonists of change, not spectators.'

'We're bringers of social transformation.'

Gender equality is an important issue to Martinez. Her interest in feminism began during her pre-adolescence when she noticed the invisibility and absence of female characters in historical feats or perhaps it was how history was represented to her. 'That motivated me to empower girls as agents of change, so that no girl would ever again feel that she was a "second-class" individual, or that she was alone,' the activist said.

It's pretty impressive that in 2021, Martinez participated in an international Generation Equality Forum backed by the United Nations where she shared dialogue with former US Secretary of State, Hilary Clinton. They discussed their views on the progress made and barriers to gender equality. Martinez 'emphasized the importance of girls' empowerment and inclusion in decision-making processes as a transformative force to achieve a sustainable and equal future.'

Recently, Martinez was selected to participate and graduated in environmentalist Al Gore's Climate Reality Program. It equipped her with training and tools to educate others about climate change and drive change. Martinez is a member of the United Nations Youth Task Force that represents youth globally and Teen Council for My Voice Counts Program, a non-profit community organisation that performs community outreach and offers mentoring.

I believe Julieta Martinez will perform beauty through action to make our world and environment a better, fairer place.

It is wonderful to see these young girls making a difference in our world by helping and empowering others, trying to improve education, and protecting our environment and planet. They are fabulous young female role models who care about these important issues in life and perform beauty in achieving their ends. I hope anyone reading this book can cite their examples to other young girls and women to show what we can *do* and how we can *perform* beauty.

CHAPTER SIX: WOMEN PERFORMING BEAUTY

In chapter five, we learned about amazing young girls performing beauty by doing fantastic things to help others in various ways and care for our environment. Chapter six looks at the lives of women who are also performing beauty by doing wonderful things to aid others and making or trying to make our world a better place in some way.

Like the selection of ten girls, I have also chosen ten women who have touched me through their character and/or the work they do. I believe they are making a difference through their work: paid and unpaid. They are a diverse group from different parts of the globe and are written about here in no particular order. The women selected are also change-makers or trying to bring about some kind of change that will benefit society. Some are better known than others. They are wonderful role models in performing beauty and opened my eyes in the multitude and various ways this can be accomplished.

SEGENET KELEMU: SCIENTIST AND MOLECULAR PLANT PATHOLOGIST

Through her work as a scientist and plant pathologist, Segenet Kelemu performs beauty by trying to reduce poverty, increase food security and help to care for the environment and people's health. Her focus is to solve scientifically based problems in Africa that also apply globally. 'I wanted to live a purposeful life contributing to society.'

'I want to make a difference for people who are not able to solve a problem for themselves (like farmers). As a scientist, I'm fortunate that I'm given this priceless knowledge and education. So I have to use it,' she says.

As an Ethiopian girl, she broke the mould and carved out a big career as a scientist who has worked around the world. The scientist shares that she defied the cultural norms placed on and expected of women raised in her remote conservative Ethiopian village. 'I had done all of the back-breaking work that was somehow reserved by the society for women and children: the weeding, the picking of coffee berries, the collection of firewood, the fetching of water, the washing clothes, the grinding and pounding of grains, the carrying of farm produce to long-distance markets. The work was endless... Amidst all those chores I had to do, I focused on and excelled in school, perhaps because I understood early on that good education was my only ticket for getting out of poverty.'

In Ethiopia, school was free except for notebooks, pens and pencils that her parents paid for. Kelemu is one of seven children and once they had their own income, her older brothers invested in her (higher) education.

Kelemu graduated at the top of her class with a Bachelor degree in Ethiopia, then went to America and earned a Master of Science degree in plant pathology and genetics, followed by a doctorate (PhD) in molecular biology and plant pathology. She went on to work as a senior scientist in Columbia, South America and in research of plant pathology. But Kelemu felt she had to return to her homeland, Africa, where she is needed to solve the country's scientific problems like helping farmers grow more food and preserve their ecosystems. This scientist has a lot to offer, the recipient of numerous awards (too many to list) and is described by philanthropist Bill Gates as a 'hero'.

Kelemu now works as Director General of the International Centre of Insect Physiology and Ecology (ICIPE), a research facility in Nairobi that solves problems created by insects to public health. So just how is Kelemu helping the farmers and agricultural community that comprises 60–70 percent of Africa's population?

For her, edible insects are a solution to the undernourishment problem in Africa. They reproduce quickly, require little or no water and are a valuable source of protein, vitamins and minerals like zinc, omega 3 and antioxidants, the scientist says. 'Insects have a significant role to play in improving food and nutritional security... form part of the traditional diet of at least 2 billion people in Africa, Asia and Latin America; traditional chicken and wildlife consume insects.'

'Insects clean the environment in being the workhorse of farms.' They pollinate many of Africa's crops and decompose waste. The soldier fly, for example, is an insect that is very good at processing a lot of waste, converting it to fertiliser, she says.

Kelemu has created a program, Insects for Food, Feed and Other Uses, to deal with these issues. She sees current food supplies as being inadequate for a growing global population, diminishing land supply and water resources, climate change and persistent poverty land as a threat to current food and economic systems.

Kelemu informs that as other feed production is becoming unavailable and unsustainable, insects can provide a good substitute with its high protein and amino acid. They lead to lower greenhouse emissions. 'Insect farming thus benefits the environment and can mitigate climate change.' She shares that America has approved insects as a protein source for chicken feed.

Locusts are a double-edged sword. Africans eat them as a food source that can significantly lower cholesterol and minimise heart problems. However, they can also destroy crops overnight. Together with other researchers, Kelemu discovered a locust outbreak in East Africa, Kenya, Sudan and Uganda, threatening livelihoods, food security, the environment and economic development of the region. They suggested that ground surveillance be strengthened to manage the pests cost-effectively in an environmentally friendly way.

Fruit flies have damaged horticultural farming, especially fruit cultivation in Kenya. ICIPE launched a commercial protein bait factory to produce a bait 'fruit fly mania' to control fruit flies. It is intended to stop damages by insect pests that adversely affect yields and cause great financial losses. 'Kelemu said Africa loses 2 billion US dollars every year as a result of fruit flies... Studies done by ICIPE shows that the use of protein food baits against fruit fly can reduce insecticides by 46 percent and increase the income of farmers by 40 percent.'

The scientist has identified a problem with Striga, a parasitic weed in Africa that attacks staple food like cereal crops, rice, maize, sorghum and millet. It attaches itself to the roots of its host and takes out the nutrients, resulting in a ruination of crops. ICIPE has technologies that can eradicate the Striga's produced seeds that shed into the soil. The Tsetse fly has been another problem in Africa, infesting much fertile land there, causing people to leave. ICIPE has a product to deal with this fly that comes from wildlife.

Kelemu and ICIPE discovered that not all mosquitoes transmit malaria; there are those that harbour bacteria in the body and don't transmit the malaria parasite. She says that it is possible to significantly reduce malaria transmission if we know what that microbe does to the insect to make it resistant and incapable of transmitting the malaria parasite. ICIPE recently has been awarded a grant for over $2 million to investigate this issue for effective and sustainable malaria control.

Kelemu says that bees are very important in Africa because 70% of the crops need them for pollination and they are resilient. She identifies the need to study bees, their genome, character traits, breeding systems and establish a sperm bank for them. 'Bees are number one to protect.'

The scientist sees science as capable of making a real positive difference in our lives, like the discoveries of antibiotics has, for example.

Her work would not be considered glamorous, a word that has been traditionally associated with external beauty. Instead, it focuses on improving lives and livelihoods and that's a deeper, more meaningful beauty.

GRACE TAME: SEXUAL ASSAULT SURVIVOR AND AUSTRALIAN OF THE YEAR 2021

Grace Tame performs beauty by giving sexual assault survivors a voice. She is a courageous woman who was molested at the age of six when an older child forced her into a cupboard with her clothes off. And at 15, she was repeatedly sexually abused by her Mathematics teacher. But Tame did not let these experiences define her. She rose up and fought against the injustice inflicted upon her by trying and succeeding to change laws that ban survivors from being allowed to speak about their experiences publicly. And Tame was named Australian of the Year for 2021, an annual award honouring exceptional Australians, for her advocacy for survivors of sexual assault.

So who is Grace Tame? She is a Tasmanian who loved to be outdoors playing sport as a child. 'As a kid, I was full of love, life and energy. I was a tomboy climbing trees.'

Her parents divorced when Tame was just two years old and each remarried. She says she knew she was loved but did not have a strong concept of stability and consistency, shuffling between the two homes. Tame was vulnerable and her teacher preyed on that. 'Abusers are looking for people who are vulnerable who don't have stable circumstances; lonely isolated people. He got me at a weak point but he underestimated my resilience.' Tame had been hospitalised for anorexia and her mother was due to have a baby when he targeted her.

A school scholarship winner who achieved top grades, Tame was taken advantage of and her sexual innocence stolen by that teacher, Nicolaas Bester. Over six months, the 58-year-old raped her 20–30 times, usually in his office, when she was legally underage for any sexual encounter. This man told her he had been a former soldier in South Africa who had the experience of killing others. While he had won her trust as her teacher, she also feared him knowing of his past.

He knew her timetable and lurked in the doorway, staring. And he'd sit in his car at night outside her home. She saw him when looking out of her window. 'He was everywhere.'

Tame had confided in Bester about the molestation and he re-enacted it by ordering her to undress and enter a cupboard as she did at the age of six. 'I was in a state of disbelief and sheer terror.'

When Tame re-emerged out of the cupboard in her underwear, naked Bester was facing her. 'He had his arms outstretched and walked towards me and pulled me into his naked body,' she said.

Tame shares that 'sexual abuse is characterised not just by physical abuse or violence, but by incredibly meticulous, calculated psychological manipulation.' 'Predators weaponise our fear. That's the foundation of their psychological manipulation which is a huge element of prolonged sexual abuse.'

She explains the grooming process that leads up to the abuse.

Step one involves targeting a victim, one who is vulnerable or isolated. Step two entails winning the trust of that person, establishing a rapport and then conning them into thinking they are validated and supported. Step three engages the predator to identify a need, a gap in the victim, then filling it. In step four, the predator drives a wedge between the victim and their support networks. Step five is the sexualisation – introducing the idea of sex into the conversation, exposing the victim to sexual content through media. Step six is maintaining control. Bester threatened Tame that he'd lose his job if she spoke out.

Eventually, Tame mustered up the courage to end the abuse. She knew that Bester had abused other girls before as he had told her and that she could end any further abuse by protecting future victims. Tame confided in another teacher about what had happened. They met with the school principal and the police and her parents were called in. 'My dad vomited after I told him. My mum was shattered. Everyone was shattered.'

Bester was convicted and sentenced to two years and six months in jail for maintaining a sexual relationship with someone under 17. Tame argued that the word 'relationship' was misleading and needed to be renamed 'abuse' as in other jurisdictions. 'We need to change some poorly worded (legal) charges. We need to change the glaring inconsistencies in our legislation that pertain to sexual assault in general. (In Australia) we have eight jurisdictions, eight different definitions of consent, eight different definitions of sexual intercourse, eight different definitions of what sexual intercourse is, and until we establish a uniform, standardised consistent approach (in legislation) we cannot possibly educate around these issues.'

After her ordeal with Bester, Tame left Tasmania to start afresh so went to California where she studied theatre and liberal arts, becoming a yoga instructor and illustrator. Even though the sexual abuse stopped, the effects didn't. 'I went on to abuse drugs, prescription and illegal. I drank. I cut myself. I covered myself in piercings.'

After learning that Bester bragged about his sexual encounters with Tame on social media (2015) and hearing how he played the victim (2017) in an interview, saying how he had lost everything: his marriage, children, home, job and status in the community, she took action. Tame contacted anti-sexual assault advocate and journalist Nina Funnell and together they found the archaic law in Tasmania that prevented victims from speaking out in the media. Funnell with Tame's input and fronting the campaign created #LetHerSpeak to overturn this law and others. And they succeeded impacting the law in three jurisdictions: Tasmania, Northern Territory and Victoria. Tame was free to legally speak out. In Victoria, parliament passed a law in 2021 that allows families to publicly speak the names of their deceased loved ones who had been sexual assault victims.

Tame's Australian of the Year platform has helped sexual assault survivors have a voice and elevate them. She felt a huge acknowledgement and respect in her nomination as representative of those survivors. 'When I first reported my abuse, there was shame and stigma. Today we have people carrying signs (in support).'

Tame reportedly has offered invaluable insights into the workings of child grooming to the Los Angeles Human Trafficking Squad.

Grace Tame sees the way forward with education on grooming as a primary preventative means in schools, workplaces, other institutions, followed by legislative change. I am sure that Tame will continue to fight for this, performing beauty as a force for change and reform for survivors of sexual abuse.

SIVAN YA'ARI: SOCIAL ENTREPRENEUR

Sivan Ya'ari is a special woman as she performs beauty by changing people's lives, giving them what we in the west would expect to have without thinking about it. She used her studies in finance and international energy management and work experience to provide water and electricity to villages in Africa using Israeli technologies.

Born in Israel and educated in the United States, Ya'ari lives in the former with her husband and three children. In 2008, she founded 'Innovation Africa', a non-profit organisation that has provided more than 300 water, solar and agricultural installations in remote villages in Africa, giving 1.8 million people clean water and electricity across ten countries.

Ya'ari first travelled to Madagascar at the young age of 20 when she worked for a multinational financial corporation. Seeing first-hand how people lived in their homes, schools and hospitals with no water or electricity had a profound impact on her. Ya'ari discovered that more than 600 million Africans had never been exposed to electricity. Less than 10% of Africans had proper access to it. 'I arrived in Madagascar and witnessed people waiting in hospitals without receiving proper care. People were in the dark. I also noticed that there weren't many children attending schools.' She had learned that mothers gave birth to babies with torches and kerosene lamps, resulting in low survival rates. Ya'ari tried to understand why this was happening and realised it was because of the lack of electricity.

She saw that due to no electricity, clinics had no refrigerators, medicines or vaccinations. Ya'ari witnessed adults and children physically digging for water with their bare hands because the water was underground. It had to be pumped out and needed electricity to do so.

These problems that she witnessed touched her deeply and led her to think how could they be resolved and how could she help. Ya'ari figured out that the root cause of the Africans' low quality of life, while still tied to the lack of technology, was actually the access to water. She had solar panels installed in rural villages to provide light to homes and schools and founded 'Innovation Africa' to bring the technologies of Israel into the African villages and change the lives of people there so positively. For her, the power of human connection was a formidable push to help these people. She brings 'water where there is drought; light where there is darkness; hope and dignity to where there is despair.'

Her beginning was marked by two solar panels installed as a clinic roof in Tanzania. This innovation changed the African residents' lives by giving them electricity in schools, enabling both children and adults to study. For the first time, nurses could care for their patients without using candles in the evening for light. The vaccines and drugs were refrigerated and did not spoil.

Her Israeli technology solved the water problem too. A solar pump was brought in to draw water drilled from deep in the ground. And through the solar collector water is then drawn into an enormous tank. 30,000 litres of water flows into the faucets that 'Innovation Africa' assembles in the villages. Clean water has been pumped to more than 1.7 million people across ten African countries. 'Innovation Africa' has completed over 275 projects, proving light, clean water, food and proper medical care to those people.

Having water means that villages can grow food all the time, not just when the rain comes. The residents sell the fruits and vegetables they grow and flourishing businesses are born. Ya'ari modestly says, 'We used the sun water that was theirs, and brought a few solar collectors to release the water underground.'

'Innovation Africa' operates in eight African countries:

Tanzania, Malawi, Uganda, Senegal, Ethiopia, Cameroon, The Democratic Republic of Congo and South Africa. The group builds much-needed medical clinics, installs computers in classrooms and powers solar refrigerators. To date, they've installed solar power in 133 villages that has enabled villagers to recharge cellular phones without having to travel outside them.

Ya'ari shares that she feels, happier when she's in the villages. 'Seeing the joy in the faces of the children and the hope in the eyes of the mothers, it's so rewarding.'

To identify potential issues before they affect communities, 'Innovation Africa' has developed a remote monitoring system that broadcasts real-time updates on the functioning of the solar pumps and villages' water consumption. The technology also enables villages to acquire information to see the amount of water being pumped as well as electricity consumption by the clinics. Ya'ari informs that the United States' donations fund many of the projects to bring water and electricity to the villages.

'My goals is to continue to help village after village, until the situation improves and people will finally have the minimum they need to lead a normal life.'

During the coronavirus pandemic, Ya'ari has had teams working across New York, Israel and Africa to ensure their work on the ground is completed efficiently and fast. 'People's lives are at risk,' she says. At this time, 'Innovation Africa' committed to doubling their effort, working remotely but with strong, local teams on the ground, local contractors and engineers, largely Israeli-trained.

'I'm constantly inspired by the women I meet in Africa. Their emotional and mental strength push me to continue... I want my children to be as independent as possible from the beginning. I keep showing them what I do at Innovation Africa and I took my eight-year-old daughter with me to live in a village and experience Africa for the first time...One of the core values I want to impart on my children is not to be bystanders. We need to help others. We should do it because what is happening right now in parts of the world is unjust.'

And that's Ya'ari's social conscience shining through. She performs beauty by changing lives in Africa, giving its people the basic human needs they have been of deprived for so long. She is a star who will undoubtedly continue to help others in need. And that's her real beauty.

ELIF SHAFAK: INTERNATIONALLY ACCLAIMED NOVELIST, STORYTELLER AND SOCIAL COMMENTATOR

Writers perform acts of beauty through the words they employ, emotions they express and ideas they convey. In both non-fiction and fiction, messages about life and the world we live in are inscribed via the characters, through action and dialogue. Award-winning British-Turkish writer Elif Shafak writes in both genres, performing beauty in the messages she transmits about the world and people in it via both mediums. A recurring theme in her writing is the creation of a fairer more just world. I see that as beautiful.

Shafak was exposed to the harsh realities of life early on in her childhood, growing up in a 'very conservative, patriarchal middle-class Muslim neighbourhood.' Her parents had divorced when Shafak was very young and her maternal grandmother raised her until she was ten so that her daughter, Shafak's mother, could go to university and attain a degree and she did. Shafak's mother became a diplomat.

Her formative years shaped Shafak under the care of her grandmother who she describes as 'extraordinary, colorful and compassionate'. Living there in Ankara, Istanbul, Shafak observed life in the inside and outside of her grandma's home. Inside, she watched her grandmother heal others with ailments like skin conditions, mood disorders, chronic fatigue and depression, happily passing on that knowledge without payment.

Shafak was soothed by this woman's voice inside their home while painfully aware of the turmoil outside: 'It was in the late 1970s. Outside the house there were strikes, gunshots, suicide bombings, demonstrations. People died. People disappeared. Far-right were fighting far-left, nationalists were fighting Turkish nationalists, even supporters of the same ideology fighting among themselves.' She weaves these experiences into her books later.

From the age of ten, Shafak travelled with her mother because of the diplomatic work that necessitated it. She credits her grandmother and mother with being strong albeit different, yet sharing a bond and inculcating her with no patriarchal expectations. From watching them, Shafak learned about solidarity and sisterhood – a strong theme that was woven into her books *The Bastard of Istanbul* (2006) and *Three Daughters of Eve* (2016).

The author's writing began at the age of eight when she wrote stories. Books to read were her companion as she felt lonely, an only child with no friends to play with growing up. 'Books helped me to dig tunnels of escape, tunnels to freedom.'

Shafak writes about humanity and those who have been dehumanised, a theme in her book *The Gaze,* the story of a fat woman and dwarf who become lovers and how they deal with being stared at by others. It explores the ideas of external beauty and ugliness, body image and desirability and the damage done by our desire to look like others. 'I believe that as human beings we learn from people who are different than us.' The fat woman and dwarf as characters serve as a vehicle for our acceptance and empathy, a worthy part of our humanity.

In her book *Honour* (2011), Shafak explores the duality of hope and despair: connections and clashes; the individual and society; family love and bonds; immigration and displacement; fitting into a new society. She questions honour killings as part of a society, culture and traditions, seeing them as an extreme way of oppressing women.

In *Forty Rules of Love* (2009), she blends ideas from the East and West, drawing parallels between the 13th and 21st centuries in terms of cultures, civilizations, religions and class. She explores the theme of love and the characters of Rumi from the 13th century and Ella from the 21st century symbolising our needs and longing in the modern world.

Shafak views identity and belonging in an interesting way. She sees identity not as a 'badge of who you are or stamps in your passport, but a fluid set of relationships.' It 'is not a once-and-for-all condition (but) a constant self-examination and dynamic revision of where we are, who we are and where we want to be.'

In terms of the global picture, Shafak values social, economic and political diversity saddened that Turkey has lost it. And she favours international security, peace and co-existence for a multiplicity of voices and views and is also concerned about seeing digital technology spreading hatred and violence.

Now living in London, Shafak wants to see the world as a better place. One example is through bridging the gaps dividing society into 'boxes of class, race and identity politics. The Britain I want to see flourish is one where there is a substantial decrease in the number of hate crimes; where gay couples are not beaten on the bus; a Jewish father out with his son is not harassed on the Tube; Muslims are not stigmatised; black young men are not singled out and searched on the streets; families living on the periphery of big cities are not left out. A country where women do not have to fight any more for equal pay. How do we get there?'

About her writing … 'I believe in the power of literature to help us transcend the boundaries of the Self and to build bridges across cultures, religion and nations.' 'Words, for me, connect us, make us more aware, more human, more compassionate.'

And that is what Shafak aims to do and succeeds in her writing, performing beauty, communicating with words and messages transmitted through them.

WENDY CAISHPAL: LEGAL ADVOCATE FOR THE RIGHTS OF DISABLED PEOPLE

Wendy Caishpal is an amazing woman whose purpose and work is to help the disabled and in doing so, performs beauty. She is paralysed from the waist down after being gunned down when 16 in El Salvador where she lives. Her story is both heart-wrenching and heart-warming.

A respected lawyer today, in 2004, Caishpal accompanied her cousin to sell bread. He was shot dead and she had been hit by five bullets: in the leg, back and arm. 'I collapsed,' she said. Wendy had lost a lot of blood and two policemen took her to the hospital. 'While we were going to the hospital, he shook me and asked me not to die. I felt like I was disappearing, but he did not allow me to, so I survived.'

Caishpal was taken into surgery immediately; however, she ended up in a coma for 14 days after. She was permanently paralysed with too much damage done to her spinal cord. She had been an active sporty girl until the shooting.

'My legs were my life. At first I refused to realize that I was paralyzed and thought that one day I could walk again. This made it extremely difficult for me to sit in a wheelchair. I hated it in the beginning. Above all, I was ashamed and did not want anyone to see me. I covered my legs and pulled away from my friends. Now I understand that it was because I could not escape who I had become.'

In El Salvador, gang members get tattoos to show their gang affiliation. Caishpal's cousin had a tattoo but it was unrelated to any gang. Before the shooting, the assailants tried to force him to show them his tattoo. He refused and was killed.

Caishpal recognised the shooters who came to the hospital and threatened to kill her and her family if she did not withdraw charges against them. Her aunt said she would not reveal their identity for the sake of the family. Then, the men stopped threatening her.

Apart from going through the trauma of the shooting, Caishpal had to accept her new identity and live as a disabled person. She needed to have rehabilitation and experienced personal development through an organisation, known as Red de Sobrevivientes, that promotes the inclusion of disabled people in El Salvador and focuses on their health, human rights and economic opportunities. She was also assisted by the privately run Humanium Metal initiative that removes illegal firearms seized by authorities and recycles that metal. Caishpal sees the latter as a vehicle to change the culture of violence in El Salvador and build peace in her country. She is the 'face of Humanium Metal against gun violence worldwide.'

This woman is more than a survivor; she rises to challenges, studying to become a lawyer and is a human rights defender with two children to bring up.

After her first child was born, Caishpal saw first-hand the potential harm that can occur if someone disabled is not aware of their rights. 'When my first child was born, the doctor came up to me with a form and said, "You have to sign here so we can sterilize you."' She believes the doctor's view was that persons with disabilities should not have children. She refused and told the doctor that she would hold him personally responsible for anything that happened to her.

Caishpal has founded an organisation called Ahuachapan Sin Barreras – Ahuachapan Without /Barriers (Ahuachapan is a city and municipality in western El Salvadore). She is the Director there and gives free legal guidance to the disabled, educating them about and defending their legal rights, including those that protect their health and has assisted more than 400 clients. 'The idea of Ahuachapan Sin Barrera sprang from the lack of infrastructure for her mobility at her local university. She was actually stuck in an area with no access to get out. And there was nobody there to help her. The young woman remembered that as a child, the vision was always to help other people.' She is certainly doing that now. 'I see it as my task to pave the way so that it will be easier for those who come after me. I am doing everything I can to remove obstacles for others.'

Through Ahuachapan Sin Barrera, Caishpal has improved park facilities so that those in wheelchairs or people with other disabilities can use them. She helped to update two existing parks in her town ensuring that the new parks are 100% accessible. The organisation has organised pool parties in the parks for disabled children with wheelchair access to shallow pools with wide steps. 'That's where I have seen the smiles of children who have gotten into a pool for the first time in their lives,' Caishpal shared.

Championing disability rights and representing El Salvador, Caishpal attended the Women's Institute on Leadership and Disability (WILD) in Oregon, America, wanting the tools and training to further this role that she performs. She has co-authored a book, *The Region that Comes: Looks on Central America,* championing social inclusion of the disabled in Latin America, stressing the importance of rehabilitation and education as 'fundamental pillars for the inclusion of people with disabilities.'

She cites poverty as a challenge that is limiting access of youth to education and then leading to little opportunity in life. Her message to youth: 'It is allowed to fail, but what is not allowed is not to get up. We must learn from mistakes, they must be part of our growth. We must give thanks even for the bad things that happen to us and see how they helped us.'

Other issues of concern to Caishpal are the present barriers facing the disabled community such as in architecture, the environment and attitudes. She would like to see them all removed. 'For nearly two decades, there has been a law designed to give people with disabilities equal access to jobs and transportation. (The law) talks about adaptability inclusion. The problem is that there is no follow-up.'

Wendy Caishpal was named as one of BBC's 100 inspiring and influential Women of the Year globally in 2020. I look forward to seeing how she continues to perform beauty in the future by helping the disabled in her community and thinking of others as she has done in the past.

WHITNEY WOLFE HERD: SOCIAL AND BUSINESS ENTREPRENEUR

Smart, savvy tech head Whitney Wolfe Herd performs beauty through connecting people and bringing them together via her Bumble app that she launched in 2014. She created Bumble, 'the first app of its kind to bring dating-friend-finding and career building into a single social networking platform.' Users can access Bumble in different modes: to date (Bumble Date), find friends through BFF or grow a professional network and build careers through Bumble Bizz. In 2020, Bumble reached 100 million users, becoming Tinder's primary competitor for those under 35.

Apart from creating Bumble Date, BFF and Bumble Bizz,

Herd has added Chappy, an app for gay men; Bumble Fund, an investment fund and a venture capital arm investing in business led by women; Bumble beauty and a skincare healing line.

'Nearly six years and countless Bumble weddings and babies later, we're a community over six continents. We've celebrated 1.5 billion moves. And we're just getting started... Bumble is a platform rooted in kindness and respect,' says Herd.

'Bumble's other core values include accountability, equality and growth.'

Herd's mum and grandma have connected with others using Bumble as have her parents' friends who met their new partners that way. Her own friends divorced and remarried through finding partners on Bumble.

Herd was tech-savvy before developing Bumble; she co-founded Tinder, the dating app, with ex-boyfriend Justin Mateen. Creating Bumble was primarily born out of Herd's painful life experience. Herd says that she was violently abused on the Internet by random people. 'I was broken.' 'It devastated me and made me so depressed. I started to realize there was something wrong with the Internet – a lack of accountability on these social networks ... At 24 I had a successful career, great friends and family and could barely get out of bed, barely sit straight; it depleted every ounce of confidence that I've ever had. It scared me for what it meant for a 13, 14 or 15 year old in junior high going through this and so I started to understand the danger of the Internet. After exposure to different areas of high tech industry, I was going to start a female only social network where you could only be kind to one another.'

That was the underlying motivating force that started Bumble, to empower women, make them feel confident and in control, giving them a platform where they made the first move. Women are the initiators on Bumble. 'We want to encourage women to be equals and to be seen as equal,' says Herd.

The other motivator in her creation of Bumble was her witnessing the fantastic women in her life waiting for men to make the first move: ask them out, get their phone numbers or strike up a conversation on a dating app. That made her wonder why couldn't a woman be the first mover of the dating game, seeing the 'gender dynamics of dating and romance largely outdated' (where the man is expected to make the first move).

Herd's mission to empower women starts at the top. The majority of her management team and board of directors are women as is 82% of her staff. 'Our values permeate our workplace,' Herd shares.

A female-fostered culture is evident at Bumble in its offering of a private lactation suite that can be reserved and is stocked with lactation-boosting drinks and snacks. Bumble also gives staff a flexible work-from-home policy even before COVID-19 hit.

Bumble wants to redress the male dominance in the filmmaking industry and so has introduced an initiative to support that goal: Bumble Female Film Force that awards grants to aspiring female filmmakers (writers, directors and producers) to make a short film 'with its rooted theme in Bumble's values of kindness, respect. And equality.'

Bumble has produced a biannual magazine run by volunteers that focuses on UK wildlife. Its core is struggling species and the magazine advises readers on how to assist. It also features international artists who drew their inspiration from nature. The magazine is subtly educative so that readers can learn about the ecological world around them. And Bumble has added a lifestyle magazine as well, another offline component that presents celebrity interviews, features, advice and guides to products. It provides a way of connecting with existing and new clients. 'The company wants to be more broadly known as a woman-centric lifestyle brand where users can network online and off in all aspects of their lives.'

If you are a Bumble user who is travelling to another location, with Bumble's new travel feature, you can access Bumble worldwide. Current Bumble users are located in the US, Europe, Canada, Europe, Canada, Australia, Mexico and Latin America and it has recently launched in India where Herd feels it could be helpful in a country that has a high rate of sexual violence and where dating is relatively new.

Herd shared, 'We need to go where we're needed the most. Actress Priyanka Chopra, A Bumble investor advised the company on its roll out in India in 2018.' She wants to empower women of India and provide a safety space for them in dating. Herd has added photo verification as a global feature to the app. Bumble has added a private detector safety feature so it can detect any nude or lewd images sent from someone. 'We need to hold people accountable. The less anonymity given to the other side of the table is actually a great way to reduce friction, harassment and abuse,' she said.

Herd had planned for Bumble Brew to open in Soho, New York during 2021, a daytime café that converts into a nightly wine bar, hosting events and programs and providing an 'empowering space for (its) community to bring their Bumble dates.' At the time of writing this book, it has not yet opened.

Apart from being tech-savvy and business-minded, Herd comes across as a people's person. Relationships are important to her and that's what I find beautiful. She likes to treat her co-workers like friends, checking in to see how they and their families are, not just what they offer her. Her employees (mainly women) are treated to manicures and movies with food and cocktails. 60 recently went with Herd to see the documentary *RBG* on the late Justice Ruth Bader Ginsburg.

Employees are also treated to blow-waves twice a week and hair trims plus a $100 monthly stipend and 16 weeks' paid parental leave. Herd is said to have voiced her intention to offer stipends to parents that can be used towards childcare, tutoring or whatever would improve a work-life balance. 'I've always wanted parents to prioritize the children's well-being alongside their job. So I never wanted them to feel like they have to choose one or the other. I don't think that's a fair position to be in.'

She encourages her staff to bring the problems to her but with an exit strategy with the best solutions and reasons for them.

In her early days of Bumble, Herd invited her staff to her home 'so that they felt like family in a non-boundary crossing way...eg Saturday, I'd have them over to my house making sure they had a great day, explaining my pains points that I've lived through in my life and why this company is going to make a difference. And share how we can have a real impact on the world, and not just a paycheck or the potential to be a big valuation one day. You can change the world by affecting one person... I'm so proud (of my staff) because they're all new leaders in their own right. I want them to feel like mini-CEOs in their own way...they're just as impactful as I am to the company. And that's how I wanted it to be.'

During the COVID-19 pandemic, 'Bumble became a beacon of light for connection.' Herd commented that 'it's uniting people and we're seeing that from our data. We have never seen such an active audience...humans need emotional and intellectual connection.' Herd provides that beautiful connection not only through Bumble but also her emphasis on relationships. Advising her staff: 'Make time to call your grandparents, or call an old friend, or take an afternoon off to spend with your parents.'

Apart from creating Bumble as a connector of humans and fostering good working relationships, perhaps her greatest act of beauty is this: 'I cannot sleep at night unless I text my mom good night and say I love you.' I do find this especially beautiful.

MANURI GUNAWARDENA: MEDICAL APP ENTREPRENEUR

Sri Lankan-born Manuri Gunawardena lives in New South Wales, Australia. She had spent five years studying medicine but her invested care in patients pulled her away from completing the degree. Gunawardena performs beauty through her attempts to help cancer patients survive and her innovative work to achieve that goal. She is the founder and CEO of HealthMatch, which started in 2017 – an online clinical trial-matching platform that matches patients to available trials, not only for cancer treatments but for other health issues too and free of charge.

But what had led her to where she is today?

'I was a nerdy kid, a major tomboy who loved Science and investigating things,' she shared. Gunawardena also had a solid mathematics and science education at Brisbane Girls' Grammar School where she was also lucky to have inspiring teachers and developed an interest in problem-solving through her extra-curricular activities there. Having a mother who was a science teacher may have also influenced her interests and the direction of her working life.

During her tertiary study, Gunawardena had spent three years as a neuro-oncology research scientist working on personalised medicine for brain cancer patients. Her mentor, Associate Professor Kerrie McDonald, Head of Cure Brain Cancer Neuro-Oncology Group, Lowy Cancer Research Centre, taught Gunawardena 'to think outside the box,' evident in her innovative idea: HealthMatch. The pair had worked together to try and achieve new and more targeted treatments to improve survival rates of their patients.

Gunawardena's cancer patients had reached out to her asking for a clinical trial. And she tried, spending hours, if not days, to find those trials that suited the patient. She informs that usually patients learn about clinical trials through their doctor, existing medical trials or from the clinic or hospital they attend and the criteria to qualify is specific. She says it is also difficult for doctors to keep up with every new clinical trial and overwhelming for patients to navigate through clinical trial options.

With this in mind, her interests in problem solving and experience in working with Associate Professor McDonald, Gunawardena faced a turning point in her career. She witnessed two patients – one whose family had the resources to get a cancer-stricken daughter into clinical trials. That patient survived and returned to work as a solicitor. The other patient didn't have those resources and passed away. Seeing this sparked the awareness in Gunawardena that 'all patients should have access to all treatment options.'

It all led to Gunawardena thinking 'outside the box' about how she could help patients equally access treatments. She 'thought to build a platform that could inform and match patients with ongoing research into their condition, making it easier for researchers to fill their trials.' And she wanted to impact as many lives as possible connecting patients to clinical trials effectively and efficiently.

Wanting to help cancer patients access clinical trials motivated her to leave her medical studies and pursue this goal full-time. But she knew she needed someone who had technical know-how to help her. Through LinkedIn, she found a medical doctor and software engineer, Aaron Schlosberg, who had the skills in clinical medicine, statistics and computer science that could marry the medicine side with the technology needed. 'Can we build a platform?' Gunawardena reached out and asked him.

He agreed to head up the technical division, responsible for building the algorithms and managing the strategic growth and development of the platform.

He built the first prototype of HealthMatch with Gunawardena in 2017. She pitched the idea to the inaugural Tech Crunch's Startup Battlefield Australia. 15 startups competed. After a pitch and live demonstration in front of investors, entrepreneurs, technologists, live stream viewers and difficult Q and A sessions from the judges, Gunawardena won it. 'HealthMatch launched in 2019, free for patients and makes its money by charging the sponsors of the research trials, whether that be a pharmaceutical company, university researcher or biotech firm.'

Gunawardena secured a group of investors in HealthMatch that has 'grown into a team of 35 software engineers, doctors and business minds.' Recently, she secured $18 million led by Square Peg Capital: Paul Bassat, co-founder of Seek Ltd, the online job search website. Bassat was one of the first investors to back HealthMatch leading a $6 million series when she started. Former Prime Minister of Australia Malcolm Turnbull and his wife Lucy have joined the latest investment round. Mrs Turnbull is 'inspired and excited about the potential for HealthMatch to democratise access for everyone to clinical trials and accelerate the rate of recruitment for subjects in clinical trials.' Since inception, HealthMatch has raised more than $25 million.

'The funding allows us to grow and scale the business. Having helped 120,000 patients create profiles on HealthMatch has allowed some 11,000 people to be placed in clinical trials in just two years.'

Gunawardena's interest in science and technology has also led her to another passion: to propel STEM (Science, Technology, Engineering and Mathematics) education forward for girls by mentoring female students at the New York Academy of Sciences Global STEM Alliance, a global initiative aiming to ensure a future generation of female STEM innovators. She wants female students of STEM to know about the 'varied possibilities that STEM supplies. There are undertones that if you remain in STEM, you are being in a laboratory running assays all the time which is just not real. We require to not be one-dimensional in just how we discuss STEM. The reality is lots of task possibilities remain in STEM-related self controls. We require to be giving that expertise so girls can recognise there are lots of wonderful possibilities.'

She is a living example of what a woman can achieve through the study of science and technology. In 2019, the entrepreneur was recognised in the Forbes '30 Under 30 Asia' list that includes the brightest innovators, entrepreneurs and drivers of change. In 2021, she was the named winner of the Bold Future Award to honour exceptional leaders by French champagne producers Veuve Clicquot.

Investor Paul Bassat commended Gunawardena's 'metric of success', seeing a positive impact on patients' lives rather than being motivated by financial gain. And that's what is beautiful about Gunawardena: her authentic caring about and interest in patients' health and wellbeing and wanting to genuinely help them achieve that.

BARBARA KRUGER: CONCEPTUAL ARTIST

Barbara Kruger is an American contemporary artist who uses words and visual images to convey her ideas. Her art smacked me in my face – Google her to see what I am talking about.

'I try to make my work about how we are to one another,' Kruger says. And that picture is not always pretty. But encoded in her art is the underlying message that we can do better in the way we treat and regard one another. Now, that is an act of beauty.

'Visually, Kruger's graphic style hits you through her cryptic statements scripted in a bold white font (Future Bold Italic), usually encased in red bands, printed on vinyl black and white photographs. They are the three colors she uses that have a striking effect, prompting the viewer takes notice. It's like seeing advertising, and it's everywhere: in the street; on billboards; posters; postcards; T-shirts; matchbooks; umbrellas; tote bags; mugs; galleries; museums; in magazines and books.' On buildings, buses and bus stops, in train stations, stairs, exterior storefronts and parks. She wants her art to be accessible for all to see. And Kruger is global.

Her artistic method is informed by her study at Parsons School of Design in New York City and her experiences as a designer and editor at Conde Nast publications. She is a successful artist as her art has flourished for over five decades.

I became enchanted with Kruger's bold, inventive work because it really makes me think about what message she is trying to convey and how she is trying to tell us something about the world, ourselves, the viewers and society. She wants us to critically engage with this. This is evident in her creation of a mural in a train station in Strasbourg, France in 1994 where many people would have passed through and seen this work. It reads 'Empathy can change the world.' She wants to see the world as a kinder, more understanding place. That certainly is beauty.

Her creative form critiques issues surrounding gender, race, sex, religion, power and greed. Kruger is also critical of consumer culture, imploring her viewers to question the mass media's role in advertising. Kruger raises the point about our contemporary society being obsessed with the consumption of material goods, rather than engaging in critical thought.

This is evident in her work 'I shop therefore I am' (1987). It is a photographic silkscreen with white bold Futura text, 'I shop therefore I am' in a red rectangle, layered over a black and white image of a hand. The red rectangle could be seen to represent credit cards, symbols for shopping and consumerism. The hand stretching out represents a 'strong yearning to obtain material possessions' and Kruger is saying the public is defined by what they own, rather than what they think.

Kruger's point is that being a shopper shouldn't define who you are – your identity needs to be something deeper than that. She is advocating that the viewer should question their identity and reflect upon the purpose/s of their shopping. Identity is a recurrent theme in her art and Kruger is also asking the public to look inward at their personal attributes, ideas and accomplishments rather than focusing on shallow material possessions, their public appearance and image.

Kruger's art is also critical of America's treatment of women exemplified in her work, 'Your body is a battleground' (1989). This example of the white text inside the red encasing is written onto a black-and-white photograph of a woman's face. The image is very powerful. It is of a young woman's face, split into two sides with a dividing line separating them. The left side is a regular black and white photograph image while the right side appears as a negative of that. The text overlaid on the visual image reads: 'Your body is a battleground'.

This piece of art was made for the Women's March on Washington protesting against a new wave of anti-abortion laws chipping away at Roe V Wade (1973), the landmark case legalising abortion for women in the United States.

I think the divided face symbolises opposing views on abortion. On the left side of the photograph, Kruger is advocating for women, their freedom and right to choose for their bodies and lives in this piece. It is a statement of feminist struggle.

The negative image of the photograph on the right side of the face symbolises Kruger's negative view of the landmark legislation ever being overturned. The artwork is still relevant today such as in Texas, for example, where the state has recently legislated against abortion in 2021.

Kruger's art also examines gender stereotypes, expected roles and fe/male identities. 'We don't need another hero' (1985) is an example. This work of art depicts a young boy, tight-lipped, his jaw clenched, flexing his bicep to show his muscular strength, stereotypically associated with men in Western culture. Next to him, is an older girl, perhaps his sister, touching his bicep either in awe or perplexed. A red border frames the picture with white text written inside a red band 'We don't need another hero' across the middle of the image above the boy's flexed arm.

The boy looks angry yet determined and I think Kruger is asking the viewer to question and challenge stereotypical masculinity associated with physical strength and its value. Perhaps she is anti-war: the image and text refer to male physical strength possibly used in combat. Perhaps she is asking the viewer to think about another kind of masculine hero that is not defined by strength but by other qualities. And the girl is more passive, looking on assuming a stereotyped position here. Kruger said, 'The most important question is the extent to which we comply or resist the stereotype of our own destruction.'

Kruger's work 'You are not yourself' (1982) is an image of a woman's face, her eyes closed, visibly distressed in a shattered mirror encased by a red border. On the left side is an image of one closed eye and eyebrow and on the right, her full face is divided, fragmented into three separate parts. The woman's distressed face shows how unhappy she is. The text reads 'You are not yourself' but 'not' is minuscule compared to the size of the other words. In this piece, I think Kruger is telling women to be themselves, who they really want to be and not be what society expects them to be. She alludes that the expectations placed on women are not realistic, too demanding, not working for them and they should abandon it. 'The parts do not fit together as a whole.'

The '(Untitled) Skate' installation (2017) shown at Coleman Skatepark, Manhattan (for the Performa 17 Biennial) is a thought-provoking work of varied sized white-on-red Futura bold typeface in capital letters displayed on panels: 'WHO IS FREE TO CHOOSE? WHO OWNS WHAT? WHOSE HOPES AND FEARS? WHOSE VALUES? WHOSE JUSTICE? WHO DOES THE CRIME? WHO DOES THE TIME? WHO IS HEALED? WHO IS HOUSED? PLENTY SHOULD BE ENOUGH.' 'These are ideas in the air and questions that we ask sometimes – and questions that we don't ask but should ask,' Barbara Kruger said.

The beauty lies in Kruger wanting the viewer to think about these questions and comments and the other issues touched upon by her and see how we can make our world a fairer, more just place. Essentially, she is asking us to think about who holds the power and who is valued in society. And question it. Is it just? Is it fair? Are we too greedy?

Celebrity Kim Kardashian graced the cover of W Magazine in 2010. Looking coiffed, fully made up, oozing sensuality and confidence, she was nude, cloaked in Barbara Kruger's white words, encased in a red rectangle, splashed across her body so that her private parts were hidden. In this piece by Kruger that is in colour, 'Untitled' (2010), the text reads: across her bust, 'It's all about me'; across her navel, 'I mean you' and across her genitals, 'I mean me'. So what is Kruger saying here?

'It's all about me' banded across her breasts could imply she is a reality superstar with a perfect body. 'I mean you' decorating her mid-rift may imply the viewer wants to look like Kardashian and other perfect-looking women in magazines; 'I mean me' draping her genitals affirms this was never about you but all about Kardashian basking in her reality television glory.

I think Kruger is asking the viewer to question the construct of beauty, perhaps how it came to be and whose values does it reflect. And are they worthy? The air-brushed image begs the question: how many women look like Kardashian or can even achieve and sustain that look? Kruger is critical of reality television as 'voyeurism and narcissism'. Kruger reminds us that 'Those reality shows tell us important things about value, materialism and consumerism.' Is Kruger saying that this cover of Kardashian beauty is actually lacking in values? I think so. And perhaps she is also critiquing the media's role in cultivating such values represented in their images. Kruger asks 'Can we exist without having a camera pointed at us?' She questions people seeing the world through lenses and screens like Facebook and reality television. She is asking: can't they form their own independent opinions without these?

The artist says she is interested in 'what makes us who we are in the world and how culture constructs and contains us.' 'We need to question images we are exposed to everyday in this commercial world,' she says. Her art is also very much about this.

Associate Professor of Art History, Dr Tom Folland, notes that 'Today, Barbara Kruger is regarded as one of the most influential artists of our time and working across disciplines, and using the power of words to challenge the basis of all social, political and cultural constructs.' And the beauty lies in her art, prompting the viewer to think about these elements to improve our lives and world.

ILWAD ELMAN: HUMANITARIAN, PEACE AND SOCIAL ACTIVIST

Ilwad Elman performs beauty by aiding those in need and deriving satisfaction from that. She is an amazing Somalian woman who devotes her life to securing human rights, building peace where there is conflict and helping sexually abused women. Elman's inspiring parents were her role models, setting an example in their work.

Her deceased father, Elman Ali Ahmed, was a social and peace activist, and her mother, Fartuun Adan, a social activist. As a much-loved peace activist, Elman tried to talk to local leaders to end the civil war in Somalia. He had rehabilitated child soldiers, setting up small businesses to employ them and others.

Educated as an engineer overseas, Elman returned to Somalia, wanting to give back that education to vulnerable youth like orphans and street kids living there. He owned vehicle repair garages and electronic shops in many districts and 'wanted to present youth skills and livelihood so they wouldn't contribute to violence.'

'My father injected the notion of social responsibility – of doing something for your community – in a time when there was absolute chaos. He was a social innovator – he promoted human rights, education and was incredibly unique at the time. He inspires me every day,' shared Ilwad.

Sadly, her father was shot dead for his efforts in disarming children in 1996. Shortly after his death, Ilwad, her mother and her two sisters relocated to Canada. But in 2006, Adan felt compelled to return to her homeland to help her people in need. She and her husband had run the Elman Peace and Human Rights Center to promote peace in Mogadishu during the 1990s. 'It was a haven for child soldiers.' After his death, the centre was closed. Upon her return to Somalia, she re-opened the centre to include rehabilitation for victims of sexual violence.

Ilwad was a young teenager when she left a comfortable life in Canada to return to Somalia in 2010 to visit her mother. 'I fell in love with the work that she was doing – just going into the office for one day could actually change somebody's life. My mother is someone that I very much look up to.'

Ilwad chose to remain in Somalia and work with her mother who she considers a mentor. Mother and daughter are changing lives; through the rape crisis centre, they established 'Sister Somalia' in Mogadishu. They have saved women and girls who had been raped, supporting them emotionally, helping them regain their health and providing counselling and free housing.

As Director of the centre, Ilwad helps the victims of rape and gender-based violence through innovative programs that she runs in the centre. She helps these women reconnect with their bodies, gain control of their lives perhaps for the first time and also provides education and alternative livelihood opportunities. She has become a spokesperson for women's justice.

'As we started we found there was an outpouring of women and girls who needed this service. And we started in dialogue and advocacy with the government and advocacy internationally to raise awareness of the human suffering in Somalia especially as it pertains to women.'

Ilwad reports that Sister Somali has expanded to nine different regions with former victims in charge of the new centres, becoming ambassadors for justice. She can see other changes too. Before the opening of Sister Somalia, gender-based violence like rape was not talked about. But since the vocal support of the centres, 'rape is on the social and political agenda.'

Women in Somalia are raised not to talk about rape and gender-based violence. But another change Ilwad has seen is victims of these crimes speaking out to create awareness. 'It's very much about overcoming a culture of silence... times are changing.' 'The center is not only working on response, but also on prevention and challenging social norms that continue to perpetuate conflict and subjugation of women. We work with young men and boys to have these conversations.'

Ilwad's work also includes peacebuilding and helping those affected by violence, continuing to take in child soldiers. She has taught traumatised former fighters to surf after discovering the healing power of the waves.

And this incredible woman also designs interventions in the area of security reform creating an inclusive space for women in building peace and develops programs to disarm, rehabilitate, empower and reintegrate child soldiers and adults leaving armed groups. 'We are working with children handed over to us by the Ministry of Internal Security and young people who have gone through our programs have become ambassadors to their peers. We know it works. And now we're actually scaling outside of Somalia and bringing our solutions to other countries like Mali, Cameroon, Nigeria and other epicenters of violent extremism.'

Former Ghanian diplomat and former Secretary General of the United Nations Kofi Annan (now deceased) mentored Ilwad influencing her thinking about global diplomacy and governance. Ilwad is now considered a global authority on ending conflict and preventing violent extremism. She is the youngest member on a committee that advises the United Nations Secretary General on global conflict.

Iwad Elman and Fartuun Adan have been honoured to receive numerous humanitarian awards for their work. And may I say, well deserved. Ilwad has also been nominated three times for the Nobel Peace Prize. I won't be surprised if she wins it one year soon.

Ilwad leaves us a significant thought: 'To achieve success in creating more peaceful, just societies, we must create a world, an environment where any girl can choose her future.' She Is dedicating her life to work for gender justice, human rights, protection of peace and security. And this is beautiful.

PASHTANA DURRANI: ACTIVIST FOR GIRLS' EDUCATION AND WOMEN'S RIGHTS

Pashtana Durrani is a courageous, resolute woman who performs beauty by providing and fighting for Afghan girls to attain an education in Afghanistan, a country where, during 1996–2001, the governing Taliban banned girls from accessing it and work. The fear is that the Taliban may do so again now since it has resumed rule in 2021 after years where women had secured these rights amongst others when they were not in power.

Why is education so important, you may ask? According to The Economist, 'educating girls liberates them. When girls learn how to read, write and do sums, they lead longer, healthier lives. They are much less likely to become child brides or teenage mums, and are also less likely to suffer domestic violence. If all women completed primary school, the number who die in pregnancy and childbirth would fall about two-thirds. If all women finished secondary school the number of child deaths would fall by half and 12 million fewer children would suffer from stunting caused by malnutrition.'

This is why Durrani is standing up to fight for her girls. While half of Durrani's friends have fled Afghanistan, she is there for the long haul. The fearless teacher says, 'there are different kinds of freedom, and the one that is most important to me right now is the education of Afghan girls. I can't turn my back on them... My focus is on protecting our basic rights such as education – because we have earned it.'

Durrani reminds us that since the Taliban took control of Afghanistan in 2021, there are two spun narratives, two stories. One is what they are trying to show and the other is what is really happening. They're saying that women and girls can go to educational institutions and work but that's not their practice. Girls in Herat and Kandahar, large cities in Afghanistan, are at home, not going to university or their bank to work. Durrani says the Taliban seeks legitimacy but doesn't work for it. Durrani would like to see some mechanism in place whereby world leaders can check on what the Taliban is doing – what the literacy rate is, the workforce rate and how women are involved and pressure the Taliban to accept women's rights.

As I write this, she is currently hiding, working remotely having moved seven times since the Taliban took over. As an outspoken advocate for girls' education, her life could be in danger from the Taliban. 'Everything around me is packed in boxes. I am not safe because I have been vocal and visible. I am an Afghan educator and run a nonprofit that seeks to empower women. I'm in hiding because that is the only way my voice remains free.'

Durrani says the Taliban have re-opened schools for male students from the seventh to the 12th grade. Since she wrote (above) the latest news released from Kabul is that in several provinces of northern Afghanistan, the Taliban has allowed middle and high school girls to go back to school. Not all female students have returned to class where they are allowed, as many families have fled the city of Kunduz; there are parents who fear that the Taliban fighters may harass their daughters on the way to school and others just don't trust the Taliban's word.

This is reflective of how in patriarchal Afghanistan, girls have been assigned an inferior role, Durrani informs. The male child is celebrated at birth, fed and educated first at a private school whereas the girl goes to an under-resourced public one and is not celebrated at birth. There are no functioning toilets or running water in the schools for the girls and many can't afford sanitary napkins so they don't attend.

So what has Durrani been doing to help girls? She founded and is Director of Learn Afghanistan, a non-profit, innovative education organisation. The impetus for this organisation came from seeing her cousins learn from television due to their families not affording to send them to school. Education via technology was the way forward in Durrani's thinking. Learn has an offline app where students can access courses as well as materials accessible via tablet. Teachers can also see what the students accessing the app are interested in learning and can prepare classes accordingly.

The organisation works with girls who live where there are no schools or infrastructure. Learn offers a general education; STEM education focusing on biophysics, chemistry and technology.

Learn also 'uses community schools as a pathway to reach thousands of children and youth in Afghanistan to educate and empower them by providing quality educational resources, mentorship, training, innovative technology tools and means.'

Durrani would like to build community centres in rural areas and urban slums where children can learn coding. Learn has developed four projects, including: Project Zarghona, maternal health care that has trained women to become midwives – 30 are currently trained; Project Soraya, educating future leaders through digital literacy, reaching 900 students in Kandahar; Project Malalai Maiwand, menstrual hygiene management (teaching how to use sanitary pads and keep clean), working with rural communities to support girls with this – 150 girls have been trained; and Project Ayesha Durrani, teacher training, equipping teachers with new methods of teaching and learning. 80 teachers have been trained in digital literacy.

'I have an international platform right now and I can be a voice for at least 7000 girls who don't have the opportunity (to study)', Durrani says. 'They don't have Internet. They don't have electricity. They don't have access to international media. I have all that, so why not talk about it? It's my responsibility. It's my country. Education is the one thing I'm willing to put up a fight for … I'm going to make sure that girls can access their rights one way or another. If they cannot do it legally, we are going to find a way… All these centuries men have been in charge and they haven't made very good decisions. I think it's time we claim our space. We need to come together and make sure the next generation doesn't have to worry. We all have to choose our battles. This is mine. I'll raise an army, just like they did – except mine will be of educated, determined Afghan women.'

Durrani concludes that 'When I think about the future of my country, I think of a girl like me. I want her to have more influence, more opportunities, a better life. I don't want her to live in fear of the Taliban. So I have to keep going – if not for me, then for her.'

For promoting educational access for girls and women in Afghanistan, Durrani received the Malala Fund Education Champion Award in 2020.

So one can see how beautiful Durrani is: she wants Afghan girls and women to have a better life through access to education. She is risking her own life to fight for them to secure this goal. I think that's beautiful.

The women in these pages inspire me as they perform beauty in such different ways, whether by working to reduce poverty and increase food security; giving a voice to trying to help sexual assault victims; providing technology to enable villagers in a developing region of the world access water and electricity; using the power of the written word in literature or social commentary to improve the world we live in; championing disability rights and trying to change the culture of violence; connecting people globally in their personal and business relationships through technology improving medical access to clinical trials through technology; relaying messages about our society and the world we live in through art wanting to improve both; promoting peace and fighting for human rights and working to improve girls' education and women's rights. As we turn the page, we learn about some other fabulous women who are performing beauty in other ways too.

CHAPTER SEVEN: CELEBRITIES PERFORMING BEAUTY

In chapter six, we learned about amazing women performing beauty by doing wonderful things to help others improve their lives. I thought it would be interesting to see how some celebrities have also performed beauty through their actions and tried to make a positive difference in the world.

In this chapter, I have chosen five very different women in this category. They are a privileged group because of their fame and financial status. There are fewer women in this category because I felt it was important to showcase more of the women and young girls who have changed lives and/or our world for the better, who were not famous to start with. But the women in this chapter who became famous early on in their lives are equally as special for their performance of beauty and should also be equally acknowledged.

KATE MIDDLETON, PRINCESS OF WALES: SOCIAL CHANGE-MAKER

Kate Middleton, Princess of Wales; wife of Prince William, Prince of Wales and mother of Prince George, Princess Charlotte and Prince Louis is a world-famous figure because of this position that she occupies. But importantly, we also see Her Royal Highness in another way – performing beauty through her warmth, empathy and authenticity, embracing charitable causes that are meaningful to her in an attempt to make a positive difference in others' lives. In this limited space, I focus on a few examples as there is much written about her.

Middleton wants to help improve early childhood for children. Why, should we ask? For the last nine years, she has spent time exploring how early childhood experiences are at the core of social challenges like family breakdown, poor mental health, suicide, addiction and homelessness. Experiences from conception to the age of five shape a developing brain and crucial to that is one's positive physical, emotional and cognitive development. Her Royal Highness has consulted with academics, practitioners, service providers and charities working to strengthen families and communities and has recently met with parents to ascertain their views about the development of young children. 'The early years are not simply about how we raise our children. They are about how we raise the next generation of adults. They are about the society we will become,' she shares.

Recently, through the Royal Foundation, which supports any charitable initiatives that the Prince and Princess of Wales initiate, Middleton launched a landmark public survey in the United Kingdom to spark a national conversation about young children with the view to better their lives. It was the first time the UK public was consulted in an open survey for its view on early childhood.

The Duchess travelled on a nationwide tour to Cardiff, Birmingham, Woking, London, Belfast and Aberdeen to speak to parents about their thoughts and experiences on child development.

The 2020 survey 'Five big questions on the under fives' asked participants' opinions on what influences children's development (newborn-five) and which period of a child's life is most significant for their happiness. Participants were given a list of possible answers and had to rank them according to what they thought the most to least important.

> Question 1 asks: '**What do you believe is most important for children growing up in the UK today to live a happy adult life?** Good physical and mental health; good friendship and relationships; access to opportunities; access to good education.
>
> **2. Which of these statements is closest to your opinion?** It is primarily the responsibility of others in society to give children aged 0-5 the best chance of health and happiness; it is the shared responsibility of parents and others in society to give children aged 0-5 the best chance of health and happiness; don't know.
>
> **3. How much do you agree or disagree with this statement?** The mental health and wellbeing of parents and carers has a great impact on the development of their child(ren).
>
> **4. Which of the following is closest to your opinion of what influences how children develop from the start of pregnancy to age five?** Mostly the traits a child is born with (i.e. nature); mostly the experiences of a child in the early years (i.e. nurture); both nature and nurture equally; don't know.
>
> **5. Which period of a child and young person's life do you think is important for health and happiness in adulthood?** Start of pregnancy to five years; 5-11 years (primary school) 11-16 (secondary school) 16-18 (further education) 18-24 (young adulthood); don't know; all equally important.'

Some findings of the survey have been disclosed. 98% of participants believe that nurture is essential to lifelong outcomes and a child's future is not pre-determined. However, disturbingly, 'only one in four recognized the importance of the first five years of a child's life.' 90% of people saw parental mental health and wellbeing as critical to a child's development but only 10% of parents mentioned they took time to care for theirs when preparing for a baby.

Three themes emerged out of the survey: the need for parental education on the primacy of the early years, the provision of support networks for parents to enhance their mental health and well-being and society to be more supportive of parents, carers and families during those early childhood years.

Since the survey, the Duchess has taken action and launched the Royal Foundation Centre for Early Childhood to help children and parents. The centre is staffed by professionals working with the private and voluntary sectors to raise awareness of the first five years of life as important for future outcomes and to work out how to create a happier, mentally healthier, more nurturing society and inspire change.

'My ambition is to provide lasting change for generations to come.' Middleton is interested in seeing a support system in place during the early years of life. 'We are at the heart of raising the next generation. The science proves the importance of the early years but the next step is knowing how best to support parents and families to do the best job they can.'

During the COVID-19 pandemic, the Duchess enthusiastically engaged in video calls with frontline heroes and she wrote personal letters to charitable organisations like Evelina Children's Hospital and Action on Addiction, a UK charity working to treat alcohol and drug addicts, and working on prevention, research, aftercare, professional education and providing family support. Middleton is patron of the latter. The following letter she wrote illustrates her beauty as she shows the staff compassion, care and support in these trying times:

To all staff at Action on Addiction,

I'm writing to tell you how much I am thinking of you all at Action on Addiction at this hugely difficult time.

I know you are doing all you can to ensure you are still there for those suffering from addiction and their families-despite challenges you are now under. Whilst you are having to adapt your services, it is wonderful to hear how you are very much continuing with your vital work.

Like you, I am deeply worried about the impact of the pandemic on vulnerable families and children, and the negative effect that the stress and anxiety could have on those who suffer with addiction. But I am heartened to hear that you are ready to support people, right now and well into the future.

I have no doubt that you will be helping each other through the pressures of juggling your professional and personal lives and I hope you are taking time to look after yourselves.

Now more than ever, it will be crucial to pull people together to ensure we're in the strongest position for what lies ahead.

Thank you for all you are doing in these incredibly challenging circumstances, and please take care

Catherine.

The Duchess performs beauty in her sheer connection, actively engaging with people, young, old and in-between. Carolyn Asante, head of a day care centre in Cardiff, South Wales, observed the Duchess interacting with the centre's preschoolers; she is 'a natural with children. She was so brilliant I even offered her a job.'

Middleton also performs beauty by leaning in, rolling up her sleeves and getting out to help 'hands on' when it is needed. Recently, wearing their apron with the logo on it, she helped to unpack donations given to Baby Basics, a baby bank run by volunteers that supports financially struggling families with baby essentials and equipment in Sheffield in the UK. There are around 100 baby banks in the UK that provide nappies and maternity pads, good quality second-hand baby clothes, blankets, towels, toiletries, toys, prams and other equipment donated by others. Her Royal Highness shared how after visiting a baby bank and talking to families there, she 'went home and burst into tears, their stories were so moving.'

Her compassionate heart did not close there. As the Duchess became aware of the substantial increase in the need for more donations due to baby banks because of COVID-19, she took action. Middleton convinced 19 baby brands and retailers to donate items. They provided more than 10,000 items.

Her big heart continues to perform beauty through her support of the mental health issue, one that she has championed. Place2Be is a children's mental health charity that helps children in school with mental health issues that she supports. 'I know I was lucky. My parents and teachers provided me with a wonderful and secure childhood where I always knew I was loved, valued and listened to. But of course, many children are not so lucky. Imagine if everyone was able to help just one child who needs to be listened to, needs to be respected and needs to be loved – we could make such a huge difference to an entire generation,' Middleton said.

The Prince and Princess of Wales and Prince Harry have led a mental health initiative Heads Together, a campaign that changes the conversation about mental health and the stigma that has been attached to it, along with fundraising for new mental health initiatives. Their royal foundation is rolling out mental health programs in schools and work. Prince William credited the Duchess with the idea. He said 'It was Catherine who realized that all three of us (Prince William, Prince Harry and her) were working on mental health in our individual areas of focus. She had seen that at the core of adult issues like addiction and family breakdown, unresolved mental health issues were often part of the problem.'

And the Duchess is bringing her mental health campaign, Heads Together, into schools by introducing a program delivering online resources for teachers and school staff to help students with their struggles. She informs that she has seen 'firsthand that the simple act of having a conversation about mental health – the initial breaking of silence – can make a real difference.'

'My own commitment is to the youngest and most vulnerable in their early years –babies, toddlers and primary school-age pupils – and to support all those who care for them, including teachers. The ultimate goal is that no primary school teacher, anywhere in the country, (UK) should in future have to wonder where to turn when it comes to the well-being of children in their care.'

Her beauty shines through trying to improve the lives of others in the other numerous causes she supports, like the homeless youth 16-25; helping families who have lost a child grieve and rebuild their lives; underprivileged children and the mental well-being of children suffering with HIV in third-world countries; vulnerable youth who are unemployed or excluded; couples who cannot afford to marry; young athletes who cannot afford to compete at elite levels; teenagers with cancer in hospital; and UNICEF (a global organisation that defends children's rights, saves their lives and helps them fulfil their potential in childhood and adolescence). And there are more.

Gary Smith, Kate Middleton's uncle (her mother's brother), describes the Princess as 'nicer on the inside than on the outside: she is a very beautiful soul.' Middleton just happens to be beautiful on the outside. But she performs beauty by trying to help those in need in numerous ways, wanting to improve outcomes for society and the world. Katie Nicoll, journalist and *Vanity Fair*'s Royal Correspondent described the Princess as 'paving the way as a new way of being royal – being real, able to connect and being relatable.' This is also an act of beauty.

OPRAH WINFREY: MEDIA PERSONALITY, PHILANTHROPIST AND CULTURAL FORCE

Oprah Winfrey performs beauty by helping others through her kindness, empathy, generous philanthropy and sharing stories that have positively impacted on people's lives. She has achieved this notwithstanding her fraught childhood and teen years. Let's first take a look at the early period and get a glimpse of some of the wonderful acts of beauty she has performed.

Winfrey was born into rural poverty, raised by her grandmother until she was six while her unwed mother worked as a maid. Grandma Hattie Mae taught her to read before she was three. Believing children should be seen not heard, she whipped her so badly for the 'slightest reasons, (like) spilled water, a broken glass, the inability to keep quiet or still.' Winfrey says she had bleeding welts on her back from the beatings.

After age six, she was shuttled between her two unmarried parents, Vernita Lee and Vernon Winfrey, and life was very challenging for her. 'I first learned about sex the year I was nine when a 19-year-old cousin raped me. As I trembled and cried, he took me for ice cream and convinced me not to tell – and for 12 years, I didn't. When you are sexually violated, it's not the physical act that destroys you. It's the weight of the secret you feel you have to keep, the person you have to become so no one will discover what you're hiding. It's losing a sense of appropriate boundaries and unconsciously confusing mistreatment with love. It's holding onto the belief I had all the way into my thirties that I had done something to cause the abuse. That I was a bad girl. The single greatest feeling I carried with me through childhood was of being alone.'

Until the age of 14, Oprah various men trusted by her family had repeatedly sexually abused her. She had become pregnant to one of her abusers and had the baby at 14 but he died two weeks later. 'I hit rock bottom. I hid the pregnancy. I'd intended to kill myself actually.'

Winfrey went to stay with her father during her pregnancy after her mother wanted to throw her out and place her in a detention centre. He helped her to turn her life around, move forward and put the painful past behind her. And guided her in her learning. Her life was starting to change for the better.

Winfrey's intelligence was evident after she skipped kindergarten to jump to prep and again after graduating from high school when she won a scholarship to the University of Tennessee. She majored in Speech Communications and Performing Arts and landed an anchor job on the six o'clock news, afterwards appearing as co-host and host of television morning talk shows. Winfrey used her performing arts skills to star in the movie *The Color Purple*, directed by Steven Spielberg, and other movies.

When I was home feeling unwell, I loved to watch the Oprah Winfrey morning talkback show where she performed beauty in that role. She reached out to viewers, openly sharing her problems publicly on air, connecting with her live audience and those, like me, watching at home. Oprah has observed 'a commonality in human experience...If it's happened to one person, it has happened to thousands of others. Our shows are hour-long lessons.' 'Her celebrations of the singular experience as a way to connect to everyone became a defining experience of the show.'

On that show, she performed beauty by empathising with her guests who had suffered in life and was so generous in helping others. The television host 'has touched the lives of millions.' Her show also launched careers of various guests.

Cheryl Hallett from Wellington, Florida is an example of Oprah's affirmation. A guest on Winfrey's show, Hallett shared that she had a drinking problem. After appearing on *The Oprah Show*, Hallett entered a recovery program, crediting Oprah as the catalyst for her change. Hallett commented that appearing on *The Oprah Show* gave her a feeling of being valued and worthy.

Another guest, Kiley Russell, who appeared on Oprah's show was a recipient of Oprah's generosity and received a brand new car from her: a Pontiac G6. Russell sold the car as seed money to turn her idea of making scrubs and soaps into a business. She put $20,000 into her fledgling business, Big Girl Cosmetics. Her business had expanded beyond online sales and is currently sold in Macy's department stores in the US. Russell 'created Angel's Halo lip gloss in Oprah's honor. The case is shaped in a circle, an "O" for Oprah. "I really feel like she's my angel in disguise."'

Winfrey performs beauty by changing lives for the better. Oprah's Angel Network, supporting her other charitable projects, has raised more than $80 million with 100% of the donations funding them and grants across the globe. Her private foundation committed $13 million to Covid relief efforts in 'home cities' in the United States.

Winfrey's performance of beauty is bountiful in her commitment to helping others access education. She has financed and founded the Leadership Academy for Girls in South Africa, a 'gleaming campus with 21 state of the art classrooms, six labs, a 10,000 volume library, manicured grounds, a 600-seat theatre and modern dorms equipped with features hand picked by Winfrey herself. 528 girls have graduated from OWLAG. 90% of the school's graduates attend college. Graduates have attended top universities including Spelman, Oxford and Stanford Medical School. In South Africa, only 20% of students attend college.'

'I wanted to build a school for girls like me. I wanted to create an environment that I would want to be part of. This school is my greatest legacy,' shares Winfrey.

Winfrey has a 'fierce love' for her girls at the Academy. 'They're the daughters I never had. They are my greatest, deepest joy,' said Oprah.

And they feel the same about her. Winfrey 'is like a mother to these girls – they call her "Mama O".' (Evident in the following letter written to her by a former graduate of the school.)

'At 12 you saw a future worth investing in and from there we took off – internships, jobs, titles, tears, joy, mistakes, accolades, but through it all nothing but consistency and unconditional love from you. Words, actions, accomplishments can never express how grateful I am towards you, but even more so for believing in me even when my own didn't. I love you and when I walk across that stage this is for us. We did it.'

The Head of the School said of Oprah, 'She's not just giving her time she's giving of her talent. She's visible, she's present she is amongst the students. That is a very unique feature for any founder of a school to be so personally invested.'

Education is very important to Winfrey and she donates generously to a charity, 'Free the Children's Organization', that is dedicated to building schools for children in developing countries. The organisation focuses on the issues of education; water; health; and food and economic opportunity in Asia, Africa and Latin America. Building schools is currently a current focal point. Her charitable foundation in collaboration with the Herrendorf Family Foundation offers an Oprah Winfrey Scholarship to academically gifted students from diverse backgrounds for four years to attend college or university in the United States.

African American History and Culture is important to Winfrey who has donated $21 million to the Smithsonian National Museum of African American History and Culture. She is the museum's largest individual donor. In 2018, the museum honoured her by putting on an exhibition highlighting her accomplishments, and contributions to American culture and her work as an activist for African American rights. The exhibition began by introducing Winfrey the person, progressing to her show and representing her as a 'force for change' and her global influence known as the 'Oprah Effect'. The curators of the exhibition note how Oprah connects with people 'in a way that really gets to the heart of what it means to be human, what it means to be a woman and what it means to be African-American.'

The media personality has and continues to use her voice to effect change and make a positive difference in people's lives. In the 1990s, wanting to protect children, she led a campaign to establish a national database of convicted child abusers, an act of beauty, looking out for the vulnerable young. In 1993, then-President Bill Clinton signed what was dubbed the 'Oprah bill' into law. It is called the National Child Protection Act where each state is required to report or index child abuse information.

Winfrey says she feels that she accomplished a mission where *The Oprah Show* served as a 'mirror for people to see themselves, in other people, in others' stories; and by watching those stories of other people, be lifted, be inspired, be encouraged in a way that makes you think you can do better in your own life.'

Winfrey performed another act of beauty by showing her mother empathy when she was dying. 'It must have been hard for you as a 17 year old pregnant, scared girl in Mississippi. Many people no doubt told you to get rid of that baby. To have an abortion or give me away. But you didn't. And for that I thank you. I know you did the best you could with what you had. And for that I thank you. And look how it's all turned out.'

Oprah Winfrey suffered a lot in her early life and perhaps those difficult experiences helped to shape her into the compassionate, empathetic and generous person she is. And in this limited space, we glean how she performs beauty by improving others' lives in various ways.

CERRIE BURNELL: ACTOR, AUTHOR, TELEVISION PRESENTER, CHILDREN'S ADVOCATE AND CHAMPION OF DIFFERENCE

Media personality Cerrie Burnell has worked in theatre, in small parts on television and as a BBC preschool presenter for children. She has also written best-selling children's books. Burnell, however, performs beauty by championing the issue of inclusion in the books that she writes, embracing and normalising difference like race and disability and publicising the issue in a recent documentary. Burnell also performs beauty as a children's advocate in the various charities she supports and participates in.

Born without a right forearm and hand, it didn't occur to her parents that Burnell's disability would stop her from doing anything. She recalls having a 'lovely childhood' with her parents and younger brother. 'I was riding at two, did ballet from three, and swimming a little later; I also did trampolining, gymnastics and tap dancing. (My parents) imbued me with a can-do attitude.'

And Burnell always found a way to manage things; she even worked in pubs and bars internationally. She has only known the body she occupies and says the disability isn't the problem but other people's perception of it. For her, it is normal.

'Having a disability is not a negative label. It doesn't make you vulnerable, it doesn't mean that you're lesser in any way it doesn't mean that your life isn't enriched. It just means that you are a minority... Being disabled is only a small part of your life and is not the most interesting thing about you,' she so wisely informs.

When she started as presenter of the BBC children's channel *CBeebies*, featuring in the shows *Discover and Do* and *The Bedtime Hour*, Burnell faced prejudice by parents who complained that her disability was scaring their children but the BBC and disability organisations defended her right to be there.

Her 'talent, warm friendly disposition as a presenter, however, soon became evident; she defended her own right to be a presenter on various television shows, gaining widespread public support.' And through that, she publicly exposed the issue of prejudice against the disabled, bringing the issue to the fore and sparking conversations. 'She hoped these complaints encouraged parents to discuss disability with their children and eliminate the prejudice the disabled face.'

As a disability advocate, she has recently explored the negative attitudes towards disability in a BBC Two documentary, *Silenced: The Hidden Story of Disabled Britain.* In this documentary she asks why the prejudice that is historic continues today. 'Contemporary attitudes, she learns, were shaped by the segregation of disabled people, first in workhouses and then in 20th century institutions that admitted children with physical and learning disabilities and where they remained shut away for decades.'

In the documentary, she meets 'trailblazers' and 'crusaders' who had campaigned for disability rights, inclusive education and independent living. Despite these positive strides, Burnell is concerned about welfare payment and social care cuts making it more difficult for disabled people to live independently. She is also worried about the high death toll among the disabled during the coronavirus. 'Figures from the Office for National Statistics show that in England and Wales, disabled people account for almost six in ten (59%) of all deaths involving Covid-19.'

In our post-pandemic world, Burnell wants to see improved

access to spaces – from workplaces to cafés and other venues and better awareness of disability issues. 'She especially wants disability to no longer be viewed as a barrier to employment, learning and living a full life.'

Burnell champions the issue of disability in the children's books that she writes. They serve as a platform to dispel this kind of prejudice against the disabled for being different. Disabled characters are normalised in the storylines; for example, in *The Magical Playroom*, *Mermaid* and *Fairy Magic*. In her books, she creates diverse characters to represent not only disability but also race, ethnicity and faith. Her book *Snowflakes* is about a girl of mixed race like her daughter Amelie, who she is raising as a solo parent.

Her new book, *I Am Not a Label: 34 disabled thinkers, athletes and activists from past and present*, is an illustrated anthology of biographies about disabled people. And it celebrates the different ways people experience disability. 'We need more disability storylines that are based on truth, and more disabled icons,' Burnell says.

Representation matters in books, films, theatre and art. 'Representation matters so greatly. It's not acceptable for children to grow up with a singular narrative … every child deserves to have their life represented by the beauty and power of story.'

Her work as a writer, experience and advocacy of disability has led her to be invited to be an ambassador for book charities. Burnell became an ambassador for BookTrust, the UK's largest reading charity that delivers books to over three million children annually, reaching babies during their first year of life, involving educators and the publishing world. Its recent target groups are economically disadvantaged and vulnerable families. As Ambassador, she publicly works with the organisation to encourage children to read.

Burnell was selected as an Inclusion Champion for 'Inclusive Minds', a group of people working towards changing the face of children's books so that children can see inclusion, diversity and equality in children's literature. Her role is to champion Inclusive Minds' growing network of Inclusion Ambassadors.

She is also an active supporter of the Get London Reading campaign that aims to get all children reading well in England by the age of 11. Burnell publicly shared in the press how she struggled with dyslexia and couldn't read until the age of ten with the view to inspire others to read.

Children hold a special place in Burnell's heart. Burnell's concern and care for others, especially children, is an example of her beauty extending to the charities she supports, like the Thai Children's Trust, a registered organisation that provides a loving home, food, shelter, medical care and access to education to needy children, those with AIDS who are HIV positive, street children, orphans, abandoned children and disabled children.

Burnell has supported the charity Happy Child by helping to fundraise and organise publicity for the organisation that provides food, health care and accommodation for street children in Brazil. 'I have spent time there and experienced its charms and challenges. Seeing street children living on the streets struggling to feed and protect themselves is very difficult.' She performed beauty in her youth when she helped in a children's home in a leprosy centre where she experienced changing nappies.

Her beautiful commitment to helping children continues with Burnell's appointment as an ambassador for CORAM, a group of specialist organisations that help to find adoptive families for children and help struggling parents to provide stability for their children. And yet again with her nomination as a Fellow for the Foundling Museum which archives the Foundling Hospital that continues today as the children's charity CORAM. 'The museum is about childhood and also documents different attitudes to children across different historical periods and societies,' shares writer Grayson Perry, another Fellow of the museum.

As part of her Fellowship, Burnell had to investigate the relationship between single mothers and their children since the 18th century. And she created a drama workshop for disabled children in her role as Fellow.

Burnell also uses her creative talent to work with the charity organisation Body Gossip, contributing to their films and live shows. Body Gossip is a charity that empowers every*body* to be the best version of themselves through the arts and education. The charity, for example, has run a drama workshop combining live theatre and creative writing with years 7–9 students to explore bodies, encouraging young people to re-evaluate their concept of perfection, learn to accept and celebrate their unique appearance in a culture that has tended not to deem every*body* worthy of attention. Sounds like we all should be supporting this charity, deconstructing and abandoning the cultural concept of perfection.

Cerrie Burnell is an upstander for the causes she believes in. She performs beauty by championing inclusion, whether it is disability or race or any other form of representation via her children's books or documentary, and through her varied charity work as a children's advocate, wanting to improve their plight. I am sure she is just warming up. Watch this space.

STELLA MCCARTNEY: FASHION DESIGNER

The name Stella McCartney is synonymous with fame and fortune. Celebrity too.

But Stella McCartney, the daughter of former Beatle Sir Paul McCartney, stands firmly on her own laurels. She is a talented fashion designer with her own fashion house and label and a global leader in sustainable fashion. McCartney performs beauty from her inner consciousness, wanting to create a cleaner world environment through her sustainable and eco-consciousness fashion brand and business model, protecting animal rights and preventing animal cruelty.

McCartney attributes her love of animals and nature to the McCartney parents for teaching her to be environmentally conscious, spending a lot of time growing up on an organic farm. Her parents were vegetarians. Stella's mother Linda McCartney (deceased), an animal rights activist and a pioneer in vegetarian cooking before it became trendy, had a huge impact on Stella in terms of these ideas and lifestyle. Stella is also vegetarian. Recently, she, her sister Mary and their father Sir Paul McCartney have reinvented 90 of Linda's plant-based recipes found in the current publication *Linda McCartney's Family Kitchen*.

McCartney trained in design at London's Central St Martins College of Art and Design. At her graduation in 1995, she asked supermodels Naomi Campbell and Kate Moss to model her collection. And those designs worn by the supermodels launched her career into the fashion world, boutiques and department stores. Two years later, McCartney secured the job as head designer for *Chloe*, an upmarket fashion house in Paris. She launched her own fashion house in 2001 in partnership with the haute couture Gucci Group (now Kering). McCartney's collections include women's and men's wear, accessories, lingerie, eyewear, fragrance and children's clothing.

Further success has followed with 51 freestanding stores across the globe. Adidas sportswear label appointed her Creative Director in 2012 to design the Olympic and Paralympic apparel. And again, in 2016, she designed the athletes' clothing for the Olympics.

McCartney was one of the first fashion designers to create and make luxurious beautiful products that are also sustainable, caring for our environment. No leather, fur or feathers are used out of care and respect for animals. While she adopts cutting-edge technology to create the *Stella* look, she protects animals and endangered forests to achieve it. That's performing beauty. She creates fake fur from corn fibres and produces vegan micro silk and mycelium-based leather.

Her cashmere yarn made of factory scraps is re-engineered and viscose sourced to protect ancient forests. She uses organic cotton, products that enrich the environment, recycled nylon and polyester. Wool is sourced from top quality hand-selected animal welfare farms. Italy supplies 65% of raw materials and finished goods production, her largest and most important sourcing country. She says, 'I have to find the balance between this conversation of fashion and the conversation of consciousness – and they have to compliment each other.'

Other key sourcing countries include Hungary, Spain, Portugal, China and India.

All Stella McCartney stores, offices and studios in the UK are powered by wind energy and abroad, they use renewable energy to power their stores and offices. 45% of their operations are run on 100% renewable, green energy. Her collections use as much organic cotton as possible and she continues to research new materials and new ecological processes... 'all Stella McCartney locations have recycling systems.'

McCartney has created a sustainable eyewear collection made from more than 50% natural and renewable resources using raw materials from natural origins such as castor-oil seeds and citric acid; the biodegradable soles made from a bioplastic called APINAT™, which degrades when placed in mature compost and her lingerie line uses recycled metal for hardware and organic cotton for gussets.

'I design clothes that are meant to last. I believe in creating pieces that are not going to get burnt, that are not going to fill landmines and that are not going to damage the environment. It's really the job of fashion designers now to try and ask questions about how you make that dress, where you make that dress, what materials are you using,' says the designer.

McCartney's social consciousness about the environment and her performance of beauty also extends to her charity. In 2018, she established the Stella McCartney Cares Foundation, a non-profitable charity platform with a dual focus: breast cancer and an awareness of sustainability in fashion. Her mother had died of breast cancer in her mid-fifties so this cause is very personal to her. The Stella McCartney Pink platform is dedicated to the prevention, early detection and treatment of breast cancer through education, awareness and support.

Since 2014, McCartney has heightened awareness about breast cancer through informative global campaigns and donating product proceeds to leading support centres and charities globally. From 2018, she has donated her Louise Listening post-operative mastectomy compression bras to women. 'I found that the mastectomy bras available at the time were just another moment where (breast cancer patients lost their femininity and they lost a sense of who they were as a woman. I wanted to create a product that really is still beautiful and still feminine and still celebrates the power of being a woman.'

The Stella McCartney Cares Green charitable platform wants to bridge the gap between the fashion industry and an informed understanding of sustainability.

The foundation works towards securing a future that will see the next generation of animal-free sustainable materials. In 2019, as part of her Green platform, she launched a social media campaign with her celebrity friends – actresses Gwyneth Paltrow and Drew Barrymore, and singer Pink – to raise funds to save Indonesia's Leuser Ecosystem (ancient tropical rainforest covering more than 6.5 million acres. The rainforest water provides clean air, water and livelihoods for millions of people).

In terms of sustainability, McCartney says, 'We're in the farming industry in fashion. We look at the biodiversity and the soil.' McCartney is so committed to ensuring sustainability in fashion that her business measures their greenhouse emissions, water use, water pollution, land use, air pollution and waste across her global supply chain. She is motivated to do better from this information from sourcing her materials to the way her clothes are made. 'We believe the way to be a modern business is to truly understand the impact we have on the environment,' the designer says.

Even though Stella McCartney is the daughter of famous former Beatle Sir Paul McCartney, she has become a successful fashion designer in her own right, a world leader in performing beauty by trying to create fabulous fashion in a healthy environmental way to protect our planet and animals. No doubt, she will continue her mission and influence others to follow.

PRIYANKA CHOPRA: ACTRESS, HUMANITARIAN AND PHILANTHROPIST

Priyanka Chopra is a successful Indian actress who lives in the United States. She performs beauty by working for social causes that resonate with her, contributing to humanitarianism and philanthropy. Her beauty shines through in her mantra: 'To be a philanthropist you just have to look around you and ask, "What little bit can I do? Whose life can I touch?"' And she is touching many lives through her support, advocacy and donating money. Chopra particularly targets girls, women and children, staunchly advocating for their education and medical care.

Philanthropy was an important part of Chopra's family life. From the age of nine, she would accompany her parents, both

Indian Army doctors, to villages where they gave their medical care for free to those who could not afford or access it. It was on those trips that she noticed how daughters were not being treated for their health but the sons were. 'I couldn't understand but from that moment, I vowed to help those sick girls as much as I could. That experience and the time I spent working with my parents are what drove me to use my name and voice to support the education and empowerment of girls.'

The daughters were probably not treated because of Indian custom. In India, there has been a strong tradition for boys to be more highly valued because they continue a family's lineage while girls leave their families upon marriage with a dowry and live with their in-laws.

Chopra uses her name and voice to advocate for the girl child and champions a change in attitude about the value of girls in India and developing countries. She is trying to improve the lives of girls. That's beauty. She speaks out for them, working as a Goodwill Ambassador for UNICEF and GIRL UP (a campaign of the United Nations Foundation dedicated to securing social and economic opportunities for underprivileged girls in developing countries: education, medical care and a life free of violence.)

Working with UNICEF, Chopra said she 'had to show people perspective that the girl child is just as important as the boy... educate your child, she'll be able to stand on her own feet, and take care of her family *that* much better: Because she'll know what hygiene is, or what medications to give her kids when they're sick... It's the lack of education and formal knowledge that limits your mindset. That has to change.'

Through her work as a UNICEF ambassador, she has supported the Deepshikha campaign that has endeavoured to empower girls socially, economically and politically. 70,000 girls and women in the Indian state of Maharashtra who participated in the program have learned entrepreneurial skills and developed confidence through financial education and leadership education.

Chopra visited a Deepshikha training centre and wanted to hear what the girls had learned through the program. One girl shared that there were three child marriages in her house and Deepshikha gave her the courage to say no to child marriage because it was 'her right,' she explained. Another participant said Deepshikha taught her how to make decisions for herself.

Her work with UNICEF includes supporting and advocating for the digital AAAZ Do campaign that empowered citizens to demand that children have a right to education. More than eight million 6–14-year-olds were out of school in 2009. That year, India's Parliament passed the Right of Children to Free and Compulsory Education Act guaranteeing children's right to elementary education. The digital campaign was intended to get children into school, particularly disadvantaged groups like child labourers, migrants and special needs kids.

Chopra supports other organisations like Nanhi Kali and Save Girl Child. The former helps to educate girls from low-income families to complete ten years of formal schooling. The organisation has impacted over 450,000 girls who are given academic support and access to adaptive learning software via digital tablets, a sports curriculum and a school kit comprising a school bag, stationery, pullover/raincoat and a supply of sanitary napkins for 12 months. Save Girl Child is a campaign against female foeticide, committed to bringing changes in attitudes about the girl child and educating people about her importance.

The actress/philanthropist also performs beauty through her work at The Priyanka Chopra Foundation for Health and Education, providing support to underprivileged children in India. She pays for the medical care and education of 70 students, 50 of them girls, potentially changing their lives for the better. And she knows them all personally.

Chopra performs beauty by publicising worthy causes and creating awareness about the plight of girls in developing countries and how education could change their lives for the better. An example is her being the voice-over in Hindi and English in the documentary *Girls Rising*, which follows nine girls from Haiti, Sierra Leone, Nepal, Ethiopia, India, Egypt, Peru, Cambodia and Afghanistan, exposing the difficulties they face such as child marriage and child slavery as they attempt to have an education. In the documentary, Chopra endeavours to show the girls in developing countries struggling to get an education and illustrate the changes that education could make in those poor places.

She helped to publicise the Dare to Care campaign, a movement aimed at demanding the lives of marginalised young women be improved and has supported the End Violence Against Children campaign, which talks about the physical, emotional and sexual violence against women in India and child marriages there.

Chopra performs beauty in supporting environmental causes. She personally removed rubbish from the banks of the Yamuna River in Agra to increase awareness of the need to care for the environment. Another example is her being the brand ambassador for *New Delhi Television Limited* (NDTV) Greenathon, which raises money to light up villages with no access to electricity through clean, sustainable solar lighting while protecting the environment. NDTV partners with Toyota in the Greenathon and runs a twenty-four-hour telethon effort to raise this money. 'Almost a billion and a half of people on earth have no access to electricity and almost four hundred million of them live in India.'

Chopra visited villages to see the situation for herself. 'No light, no electricity, water shortages. I saw firsthand how a lantern had improved their lives in so many ways, from studying to delivering a baby, they could now do these with more ease and not have to deal with the fumes and heat generated by the kerosene lamps that they used before.'

People could work into the night and charge their cell phones. The Greenathon educates how to go green.

Chopra has worked for the welfare of some villages and has raised awareness about the need to care for the environment. 'I don't think that any awareness in these villages about the environment exists... One of the most distressing sights for me was the sight of plastic and other garbage strewn around the village.'

She says that individuals as well as governments and businesses need to be mindful in our daily life in how to care for our environment. 'Simple things like switching off lights and fans when not in use, car-pooling, saving paper, recycling of all the materials we use has the power to make such a difference.'

Chopra demonstrated her beauty when she donated five million dollars to a suburban hospital in Mumbai to facilitate the establishment of a cancer ward in her late father's name, Dr Ashok Chopra, in 2013. Sadly, he had lost the battle to cancer, aged 62. Her donation is to honour his name and help cancer patients fight the disease.

These are just *some* examples of Priyanka Chopra performing beauty by trying to make a positive difference in and for the lives of children, girls and women in Indian society, and the environment. Undoubtedly, she will continue to support these causes while they need help and because they are very meaningful to her.

All the women in these pages are performing, doing beauty by trying to help others in different ways and proving examples of what *beauty* really can be. They demonstrate this through their charity and philanthropy work: trying to help improve mental health and childhood for children (including championing their right to an education and trying to help secure that for those who don't have it and the disadvantaged); advocating for inclusion and diversity of characters such as the disabled and those from different races and ethnic groups to be represented in children's literature; providing a plurality of narratives and caring for our environment by creating and providing sustainable products.

Now, it's time for us to review.

CHAPTER EIGHT: CONNECTING THE DOTS

RECAPPING

When girls 7–10 think they are valued more for their looks than their character and achievements, we have a problem. When 10–11-year-old girls are using filters to make them look good, we have a problem. When teenage girls want to access cosmetic procedures so that they can look like their filters, we have a problem. When adolescent and teenage girls are unhappy with their bodies, we have a problem. If girls see beauty as a source of happiness, we have a problem that can be damaging and lifelong.

And the problem is coming from society's message that you are beautiful according to how you look on the outside.

We need to change this for the health of our girls. We need to change this measure of their self-worth. We need to abandon the idea that external beauty is the goal. We need to overthrow the value attributed to outward appearance by society in spite of the big business of the beauty industry constantly advertising external beauty, trying to jam it down our throats.

We need to reframe the idea of beauty as kind, loving, fair, caring, considerate, courageous, charitable, capable, smart, resilient and funny. And any similar characteristics you wish to throw into the mix. We need to teach our young that beauty can be in the work they do positively impacting on society and the environment.

We need girls and boys, our future women, men and those who identify as other, to be educated from a young age as a toddler all the way throughout school about the shallowness of external beauty as a measure of one's worth.

I don't want this next generation to feel like I did when my cancer was surgically removed from my face. It is now eighteen months since that surgery. I can still see slight redness and the scar. And it still bothers me to see my flawed skin. I shouldn't feel that. And I get angry with myself for feeling that way. I shouldn't care about how it looks but I do. And that is because of years of socio-cultural messaging and inculcating the value of external beauty, including flawless skin. At the same time, I am really grateful that the cancer could be incised and be removed from my body keeping me healthy. I know this is far more important.

I see beauty as a concept and have discussed some influential ideas about beauty in this book. *The Beauty Myth* by Naomi Wolf argued that men created the 'beauty myth' idealising women's physical beauty as young, thin and white, largely through advertising this image bombarding women with it as valuable and necessary so that it is their focus rather than concentrating on advancing in the public arena. I don't see any male conspiracy here but rather commercial opportunism and big bucks to be made out of the hard sell of beautification and products needed to achieve it. It's all about money.

In *Face Value*, Autumn Whitefield-Madrano found through interviewing women that their relationship with beauty is not clear-cut. She found that many of the women felt positive about the way they looked after seeing images of women in the media. She discovered an important finding that the women who had good self-esteem and a positive sense of their own body image were less likely to respond negatively to the media images of women. It was those women who did not have a good self-esteem to start with who were adversely affected by the media images of women. We need this finding to be publicised more and help women who suffer from low self-esteem to work on improving it so that it is not based on their external looks.

Beauty rituals and routines can be fun and harmless. There is nothing wrong in experiencing pleasure with them. It is when they dominate one's life and unhealthy eating patterns assume control, when exercising becomes excessive and compulsive, when too much cosmetic surgery and filter use etc. take over that we have a problem.

In *Perfect Me,* Heather Widdows argues that beauty is a moral ideal but does not really explain what she means or how this ideal manifests in contemporary beauty practices. She generalises a lot without quantifying how many women actually buy into it as a moral ideal. I don't agree with her when she says women judge themselves as a total failure if they don't achieve the feminine beauty ideal. We are much more than a body. We are multiples selves with more than one form of identity. She also ignores that women have other values in their lives: work, relationships, love of animals and nature and/or the arts and sport, for example.

The evolutionary perspective explains women's physical beauty differently to the other views. According to this understanding, women's value serves as a mate, providing genetic success based on their physical beauty. But men don't always partner with what is generally thought to be an attractive woman. There are men who choose a mate for other reasons like their lovely character or nature, compatibility, great sex, common interests, etc.

Could we value external beauty merely because we derive great pleasure looking at it, like a pretty face? Is it as simple as that?

I like the idea of 'doing beauty' in Susie Orbach's *Bodies.* She says in terms of physical beauty, it requires a production and action. We do our hair: wash and blow-wave it. We do our makeup – apply and remove it – we do diets, exercise and remove unwanted hair. We dress ourselves and it all becomes a performance.

As the historians have demonstrated early in this book, we do beauty to lure a partner and/or gain political power. This has occurred for centuries, not just the 17th or 18th centuries but also in ancient times. Models are a great example of doing beauty as they strut the catwalk and deliver a performance. And they do diets and exercise to keep in good physical shape.

Sadly and unfairly, there are perks: social and economic rewards for looking beautiful, fitting the feminine ideal of beauty of the day.

But beauty standards are not static. As I have shown, they change according to the zeitgeist from the ancient Greeks to modern day. They are often a response to an initiation of ideas in the particular historical, political, socio-cultural contexts and are a part of that. We saw that the Kardashian body shape was heavily influential and perpetuated in social media. (2000–2010)

Then emerged the body positivity and body neutrality movements in an attempt for women to embrace the bodies they were living in rather than trying to be the skinny ideal that was so dominant for a long time. The latter encouraged a shift in focus to the emotional and mental aspects of identity like compassion and good humour.

Soon after, Instagram celebrated a new feminine ideal – the body with a flat stomach, boobs and an hourglass figure. However, the Millennials brought a healthy new perspective, wanting an acceptance of diverse bodies and creating their own sense of style and swagger. Those of them working in the fashion and beauty industry were driving diversity, wanting to see everyone represented in fashion. There have been other forces supporting diversity like Ivan Bart President of IMG Models, leading an international agency and representing diverse models, using his voice publicly to influence this change in the industry.

And there are many others, as discussed in this book.

We are now seeing diverse models like those who are Trans and who have dark skin represented as beauty in woman's magazines and on the catwalk, although the thin white model still tends to dominate. The disabled are not very visible yet as representatives of beauty in magazines and on the catwalk. However, there are disabled advocates like Xian Horn and Sinead Burke who are actively working in the fashion world to ensure disabled representation and accessibility for disabled employees. They are recommending that a disabled person be part of the fashion design team and part of the decision-making process, not only centre stage on the catwalk, on billboards or in magazines in the public eye. Disabled model Jill Mercado has worked as a disability advocate hoping to see a future where brands produce work reflecting the world we see.

There are some fashion labels like Tommy Hilfiger, Salvatore Ferragamo, Izzy Camilleri, Zappos and Target who are designing for the disabled. Some brands are developing products for the disabled like more accessible makeup brushes. Some skincare companies are providing braille in their external packaging.

Change has begun with singer Rihanna introducing many more shades of makeup for dark-skinned women to access who could not before because it was unavailable. Makeup and fashion labels are introducing products like more accessible makeup brushes for the disabled.

Australian entrepreneurial young women, Carly Warson and Stephanie Korn from Form and Fold swimwear address the issue of size, particularly a fuller bust, filling a void in the market. Their website showcases diverse women in different shapes and sizes modelling their swimwear. This issue of size is still a problem on the catwalk and design of luxury clothing. In the May and November Fashion Weeks in Australia, larger sizes were not so well represented while Indigenous designs and models took the limelight. In the autumn-winter Paris Fashion Week 2021, there was still a dominance of thin white models amongst a few Asian and black ones. Kerby Jean Raymond's label Pyer Moss made a statement with all his models being black. It was the reverse of an all-white model cast.

Diversity in beauty and fashion needs normalisation for it to fully work. Design schools should be accepting diverse students who can contribute and create designs that reflect their diversity. The diverse students' input should be included in the various stages of the design process.

The Barbie doll has traditionally represented American feminine beauty in its design: thin and beautiful, the stereotype that has dominated the catwalk, billboards and magazines for many years. The designer of Barbie, Ruth Handler, had said that through the doll, the little girl could be whoever she wanted to be. Barbie was a fictitious character with whom a player could imagine all sorts of things. Over time, the Barbie doll was available in all sorts of occupations, spanning two hundred different careers and not feminine stereotypes.

The original doll had been criticised for being too thin, contributing to unhealthy ideals although not all researchers agree with this. Recently Mattel has introduced a diverse range of dolls to reflect our world today, a fuller figure doll, black dolls, those with skin issues like vitiligo, and a wheelchair Barbie that sold well, for example. There is a Barbie with a prosthetic leg, one wearing a hijab. The fuller Barbie doll has not been as popular among girls as the original thin one and this could be because cultural messages about body shape have been so pervasive that the girls have internalised them.

If images of different body types would be the norm then perhaps girls would not gravitate towards the thin Barbie doll. They need to be taught that 'skinny is not the only way a human body should be viewed and loved.' And that 'feeling beautiful and being wonderful are emotions that should exist outside of what we see in the mirror.'

We need to teach young children that diversity is the norm of life, that people come in different shapes and sizes, skin colour, pigment, ethnicity, disability, gender and sexuality. We need to teach them that as a society, we must accept and embrace all people and not them by how they look on the outside. This should be taught formally in preschool and reinforced in primary and high school. Once the children are old enough and have the cognitive ability, schools should teach them how to critically evaluate media representations of beauty and any stereotypes it projects. They should be made aware that they have the choice not to follow external beauty ideals, not to be influenced or persuaded by all the advertising.

The children need to be taught of inner beauty in our internal character and identity: kindness, compassion, thoughtfulness, fairness, consideration, courage, resilience, a sense of humour and finding our capabilities. This should be the focus of beauty, like helping others as so many of my wonderful girls and women represented in this book have.

We have now learned about amazing young girls performing beauty through caring for and making other's lives better, correcting injustices and caring for our environment, doing community work and helping disadvantaged kids or those from poor socio-economic backgrounds to access education, protecting animal rights and engaging in philanthropy: Marley Dias, Khloe Thompson, Ruby Kate Chitsey, sisters Isabel and Melati Wijsen, Katie Stagliano, Danielle Boyer, Bella Lack, Mari Copeny, Synthia Otieno, Awour Macrine Atieno, Stacy Owina, Purity Achieng, Ivy Akinyi and Julieta Martinez.

And we have learned about fabulous women performing beauty by trying to reduce poverty; increasing food security; caring for the environment; giving sexual assault victims a voice;

providing water and electricity in villages that don't have it; trying to create a fairer world through the power of words and messages inscribed in books; protect girls from genital mutilation; helping the disabled; connecting others; helping the sick access medical trials and through art trying to persuade onlookers to think about our society and how we can treat one another better: Segenet Kelemu, Grace Tame, Sivan Ya'ari, Elif Shafak, Wendy Caishpal, Whitney Wolfe Herd, Manuri Gunawardena, Barbara Kruger, Ilwad Elman and Pashtana Durrani.

We also learned about some celebrities who perform beauty through trying to change other's lives for the better like helping children and families struggling to buy baby essentials and equipment; helping street children in third world countries; supporting addicts and trying to remove stigma associated with addiction; providing mental health programs in schools and at work; supporting the homeless, grieving families, underprivileged children, children suffering from HIV in third world countries, vulnerable unemployed youth and teenagers with cancer; helping young athletes who can't afford to compete at elite levels; supporting UNICEF; generously engaging in varies kinds of philanthropy; educating girls who could not afford it for free, connecting with and support them; advocating for girls' education; trying to protect children through law; promoting inclusion of minorities in books to ensure diverse representation that reflects our world; advocating for the disabled; protecting animal rights; caring for our environment by ensuring sustainability; supporting cancer charities and contributing financially to establish a cancer ward in a hospital: Kate Middleton, Princess of Wales; Oprah Winfrey; Cerrie Burnell; Stella McCartney and Priyanka Chopra.

I hope that you, reader, will feel inspired by these individuals. They inspired me.

Obviously we are all different, but these women individually and collectively demonstrate that we can all perform beauty in some way. They have taught me how we can do it through how they are living their working lives.

The girls and women in this book show us a variety of things we could do, but there is no pressure to do big things. It's often the little things in life that mean a lot, like showing kindness and compassion to someone in need or who is not in a good place in their life. That, too, is performing beauty.

Reframing Beauty gives you an idea of what beauty could be and perhaps the book may even change your view of beauty as external. You may even free yourself of any pressure that you may feel in trying to look outwardly beautiful and refocus on your inner beauty and how you can perform beauty. We all have this choice. And this is yours.

ACKNOWLEDGMENTS

I extend special thanks to the Shawline team for helping me bring this book to life.

To Bradley Shaw, Managing Partner, I am very grateful that you saw this topic of 'beauty' as significant, warranting publication of my thoughts and research in book form.

To Katrina Burge, my editor, thank you for pushing me that bit further to reflect a little harder along the way in my writing of the text, adding that deeper layer to the book.

To Kit Cronk, I love the edgy cover you designed that encapsulates the thrust of the book.

And to my family, it makes me feel warm inside that you are proud and supportive of me writing.

My dear friends deserve a special mention for kindly reading the first few pages of a draft and encouraging me to write more: thanks to Idit Benjamin; Bonnie Blashki and Sharon Marcus. To Sharon, I appreciate you generously referring me to some interesting research. And to Michelle Marks and Elana Warson, thank you for your interest and our engaging chats about this work.

BIBLIOGRAPHY

60 Minutes Australia (2021). The rise of Kate Middleton: why she is desperately needed by the Royal family | 60 Minutes Australia. YouTube. Available at: https://www.youtube.com/watch?v=6uP-PaXu2BY.

Action For Nature (2019). 2019 International Young Eco-Hero Award Winners. [online] Youtube. Available at: https://www.youtube.com/watch?v=u7FVSUjXYqU.

Adams, C. (2014). "Venus of the Capitol": Madame Tallien and the Politics of Beauty under the Directory. French Historical Studies, 37(4), p.619.

Adams, C. and Adams, T. (2015). Female beauty systems : beauty as social capital in Western Europe and the United States, Middle Ages to the present. Newcastle Upon Tyne, Uk: Cambridge Scholars Publishing, p.160.

Africanews. (2016). Meet Egypt's daring and ambitious wheelchair model. [online] Youtube. Available at: https://www.youtube.com/watch?v=l5bUtRSF_KQ.

Aging Well With Cybill Shepherd, Bo Derek and Beverly Johnson, (2019). Super Soul.

Allen, M. (2020). Brown-Girl Beauty Editors Share Their Thoughts on Diversity in the Industry. [online] Byrdie. Available at: https://www.byrdie.com/diversity-in-the-beauty-industry.

Alliance, C.P. (2020). Xian Horn makes her mark through the adaptive fashion revolution | Cerebral Palsy Alliance. [online] CerebralPalsy.org. Available at: https://cerebralpalsy.org.au/sstposts/StoryId1604016801705

Andaloro, A. (2021b). The Tragic Story Of Oprah's Childhood. [online] TheList.com. Available at: https://www.thelist.com/346339/the-tragic-story-of-oprahs-childhood/#:~:text=Oprah%20was%20living%20there%20at.

Anderson, A. (2021). The body neutrality movement as an alternative to body positivity? [online] The Daily of the University of Washington. Available at: https://www.dailyuw.com/arts_and_culture/the-body-neutrality-movement-as-an-alternative-to-body-positivity/article_bb6da560-abce-11eb-b4a4-47228e04f87e.html.

Anschutz, C. (2016). HuffPost - Breaking News, U.S. and World News. [online] HuffPost. Available at: https://huffingtonpost.com.au/entry/depressing/issues-n_57c71d23ecbo7858lf10be6a.

Anschutz, D.J. and Engels, R.C.M.E. (2010). The Effects of Playing with Thin Dolls on Body Image and Food Intake in Young Girls. Sex Roles, 63(9-10), pp.621–630.

Appell, F.(n.d) Victorian Ideals: The Influence of Society's Ideals on Victorian Relationships. [online] Available at: https://www.mckendree.edu/academics/scholars/issue18/appell.htm).

Arimus Media (2014). ALD Interview with Dr. Segenet Kelemu. www.youtube.com. Available at: https://www.youtube.com/watch?v=4dHh6_IXTFc.

Armstrong, K. (2017). Barbie Is An Incredible Role Model for My Kids. [online] Redbook. Available at: https://www.redbookmag.com/life/mom-kids/a48137/barbie-is-a-good-role-model/.

Ashley O'Brien, S. (2019). She sued Tinder, founded Bumble and now, at 30, is the CEO of a dating empire. [online] CNN. Available at: https://edition.cnn.com/2019/12/13/tech/whitney-wolfe-herd-bumble-risk-takers/index.html.

Ashoka.org. (2021). Julieta's Changemaker Journey | Ashoka | Everyone a Changemaker. [online] Available at: https://www.ashoka.org/en/story/julieta-changemaker-journey.

Associated Press (2017). FACT CHECK: Obama, Trump both had role in Flint water relief. [online] Michigan Radio. Available at: https://www.michiganradio.org/politics-government/2017-03-27/fact-check-obama-trump-both-had-role-in-flint-water-relief.

Azerta. (2021). Tremendous Leadership. [online] Available at: https://www.azerta.cl/en/tremendous-leadership/.

Baer, A.A., Drake (2014). 11 scientific reasons why attractive people are more successful in life. [online] Business Insider Australia. Available at: https://www.businessinsider.com.au/beautiful-people-make-more-money-2014-11?r=US&IR=T.

Bahadur, N. (2014). It's Amazing How Much The "Perfect Body" Has Changed In 100 Years. [online] HuffPost. Available at: https://www.huffpost.com/entry/perfect-body-change-beauty-ideals_n_4733378.

Barbera, A. (2015). 1950s Beauty. [online] A Pretty Addiction. Available at: https://allisonbarberamakeup.wordpress.com/2015/02/09/1950s-beauty/.

Barbera, A. (2016). 2000s Beauty. [online] A Pretty Addiction. Available at: https://allisonbarberamakeup.wordpress.com/2016/10/11/2000s-beauty/.

Barbiemedia. (n.d.). Barbie Fast Facts. [online] Available at: http://www.barbiemedia.com/about-barbie/fast-facts.html#:~:text=Barbie%20is%20the%20most%20diverse.

Bart, I. (2017). An Open Letter To The Fashion Industry From IMG Models' Ivan Bart. [online] Refinery29. Available at: https://www.refinery29.com/en-us/2017/03/145548/modeling-industry-diversity-letter-ivan-bart.

Bassat, P. (2019). Investment notes: HealthMatch AU$6m Series A. [online] Squarepegcap.com. Available at: https://www.squarepegcap.com/blog/investment-notes-healthmatch.

Bauck, W. (2020). How Sinéad Burke Went From Elementary School Teacher to Accessible Design Advocate. [online] Fashionista. Available at: https://fashionista.com/2020/01/sinead-burke-fashion-style-career-interview#:~:text=Jan%208%2C%202020-.

BBC My World (2021). Mari Copeny: FIGHTING for clean water in the US - BBC My World. Youtube. Available at: https://www.youtube.com/watch?v=6ZZwpV300t8.

BBC News. (2020). BBC 100 Women 2020: Who is on the list this year? [online] Available at: https://www.bbc.com/news/world-55042935.

BBC News. (2021). Bella Lack: Teenage environmentalist hopeful for post-Covid world. [online] Available at: https://www.bbc.com/news/uk-england-sussex-56497289.

Beal, D. (2018). EXCLUSIVE: Bumble Is Launching a Beauty Line. [online] Marie Claire Magazine. Available at: https://www.marieclaire.com/career-advice/a23335721/whitney-wolfe-herd-bumble-beauty-line/.

Beard, M. (2020). How to Stay Sane in an Age of Division by Elif Shafak review – a poignant look back at another age. [online] The Guardian. Available at: https://www.theguardian.com/books/2020/aug/21/how-to-stay-sane-in-an-age-of-division-by-elif-shafak-review.

Beautiful with Brains (2011). Beauty History: Women And Cosmetics During World War II. [online] Beautiful With Brains. Available at: https://www.beautifulwithbrains.com/beauty-history-women-and-cosmetics-during-world-war-ii/.

Berg, M. (2018). Bumble's Whitney Wolfe Herd Swiped Right To A $230 Million Fortune. [online] Forbes. Available at: https://www.forbes.com/sites/maddieberg/2018/07/11/whitney-wolfe-heard-bumble-net-worth/.

Bergstein, R. (2016). The beauty routine of a Victorian woman was anything but glamorous. [online] New York Post. Available at: https://nypost.com/2016/10/23/the-beauty-routine-of-a-victorian-woman-was-anything-but-glamorous/.

Betterplace.org. (n.d.). Thai Children's Trust. [online] Available at: https://www.betterplace.org/en/organisations/11095-thai-children-s-trust.

Bggs.qld.edu.au. (2019). Manuri Gunawardena to share her passion for pairing patients to life-saving clinical trials - Brisbane Girls Grammar School. [online] Available at: https://www.bggs.qld.edu.au/news/alumnae-news/manuri-gunawardena/.

Bird, I. (2021). A year of Grace: Life as the Australian of the Year. [online] The Canberra Times. Available at: https://www.canberratimes.com.au/story/7326011/a-year-of-grace-life-as-the-australian-of-the-year/.

Bitmead, C. (2020). Beauty And Disability Inclusivity - Are We Really Doing Enough? [online] ELLE. Available at: https://www.elle.com/uk/beauty/a34234323/beauty-disability-inclusivity/.

Boardman, M. (2017). James Scully On the Increasing Diversity of Fashion Week. [online] Paper Mag. Available at: https://www.papermag.com/casting-director-james-scully-on-diversity-during-fashion-week-2489860042.html.

Booktrust.org.uk. (2020). Cerrie Burnell: I Am Not A Label. [online] Available at: https://www.booktrust.org.uk/news-and-features/features/2020/july/cerrie-burnell-i-am-not-a-label/.

Boor, A.S. (2021). Danielle Boyer | Ojibwe | The STEAM Connection | Winds of Change. [online] Woc.Aises.org. Available at: https://woc.aises.org/content/danielle-boyer-ojibwe-steam-connection.

Born Free Foundation (2019). Born Free Podcast #3 | Bella Lack. Youtube. Available at: https://www.youtube.com/watch?v=fVnlFZ4uUCQ.

Born This Way Foundation. (2021). Born This Way Foundation. [online] Available at: https://bornthisway.foundation/advisory-board-2021/.

Bornfree.org.uk. (2021). Bella Lack. [online] Available at: https://www.bornfree.org.uk/bella-lack.

Bourbon, N. (n.d.). New Perspectives. [online] Alumni.pace.edu. Available at: https://www.alumni.pace.edu/humanconnection.

Bovet, J. (2018). The Evolution of Feminine Beauty. Exploring Transdisciplinarity in Art and Sciences, pp.327–357.

Boyer, D. (2020). Larissa Aniceto - Changemaker Feature. [online] Human Projects. Available at: https://bagpipe-caper-8n74. squarespace.com/blog/danielle-boyer-changemaker-feature

Brewer, T. (2018). 60's Fashion for Women (How to Get the 1960s Style). The Trend Spotter. [online] 6 Nov. Available at: https://www. thetrendspotter.net/60s-fashion-for-women/.

Brewer, T. (2020). 90's Fashion (How to Get The 1990's Style). [online] The Trend Spotter. Available at: https://www.thetrendspotter. net/how-to-rock-the-90s-fashion-trend-in-2016/#:~:text=90s%20 Fashion%20Trend.

Brown, K. (2020). "Disabled People Love Clothes Too." The New York Times. [online] 26 Jul. Available at: https://www.nytimes. com/2020/07/26/style/functional-fashion.html.

Brown, M. (2020b). From Student to STEAM Educator to Entrepreneur. [online] Engineers Rule. Available at: https://www.engineersrule. com/from-student-to-steam-educator-to-entrepreneur/.

Bulo, K. (2017). The Gibson Girl: The turn of the century's "ideal" woman, independent and feminine. [online] The Vintage News. Available at: https://www.thevintagenews.com/2017/06/14/the-gibson-girl-the-turn-of-the-centurys-ideal-woman-independent-and-feminine-2/.

Bumble Buzz. (2021). Bumble - Switch on Bumble's Travel feature in your app's settings, and make connections anywhere in the world! [online] Available at: https://bumble.com/en/the-buzz/travel#:~:text=With%20Bumble

Bumble HQ (2019). Here's How To Apply For Bumble's Female Film Force 2019. [online] The BeeHive. Available at: https://thebeehive.bumble.com/uk-blog/heres-how-to-apply-for-bumbles-female-film-force-2019#:~:text=We%20want%20to%20do%20our.

Bumble. (2021a). BFF & Bizz. [online] Available at: https://bumble.com/en/help/what-is-bumble-bff-bizz#:~:text=Bumble%20BFF%20is%20a%20simple.

Bumble. (2021b). Bumble. [online] Available at: https://www.bumblemagazine.co.uk/.

Burke, S. (1498). Why design should include everyone. [online] Ted.com. Available at: https://www.ted.com/talks/sinead_burke_why_design_should_include_everyone?language=en.

Burnell, C. (2010). My family values: Cerrie Burnell. [online] the Guardian. 27 Mar. Available at: https://www.theguardian.com/lifeandstyle/2010/mar/27/cerrie-burnell-cbeebies-family-values.

Businesswire. (2020). Barbie® Unveils 2020 Campaign Team Set to Encourage All Girls to Raise Their Voice. [online] Available at: https://www.businesswire.com/news/home/20200728005341/en/Barbie%C2%AE-Unveils-2020-Campaign-Team-Set-to-Encourage-All-Girls-to-Raise-Their-Voice.

Caban, A. (2020). Katie's Krops providing free meals to those in need at Summerville YMCA. [online] WCIV. Available at: https://abcnews4.com/news/local/katies-krops-providing-free-meals-to-those-in-need-at-summerville-ymca.

Cairo Scene. (2016). 16 of 2016: The Egyptian Men and Women Changing the Country. [online] Available at: https://cairoscene.com/LifeStyle/16-of-2016-Egypt-s-Real-Influencers.

Cancer.org.(n.d). What is Cancer? Cancer Council. [online] Available at: Cancer.org.au/cancer-information/what-is-cancer.

Castro, E. (2021). appreciate the privilege of having a voice to share my ideas in this book. [online] ElPaisque. Available at: https:// elpaisqueviene.org/2021/07/wendy-caishpal/?lang=fr.

Cavallo, A. (2021). Defining an Era of Beauty: Twiggy's '60s Mod Makeup Looks - Twiggy Model 1960s Eye Makeup. [online] Lofficielusa. Available at: https://www.lofficielusa.com/beauty/ twiggy-model-mod-eye-makeup-60s.

Channel Kindness. (2020). Channel Kindness Radio: An Interview with Khloe of Khloe Kares. [online] Available at: https://www. channelkindness.org/channel-kindness-radio-an-interview-with-khloe-of-khloe-kares/.

Chopra, P. (2014). Opinion | What Jane Austen Knew. The New York Times. [online] 4 Dec. Available at: https://www.nytimes. com/2014/12/04/opinion/priyanka-chopra-on-educating-girls.html.

Chung, M. (2017). Revlon Names Sabrina Carpenter, Gigi Gorgeous and More as Newest Ambassadors. [online] FASHION Magazine. Available at: https://fashionmagazine.com/beauty-grooming/revlon-gigi-gorgeous-sabrina-carpenter/.

Clark, M. (2020). "Seeds of Change" inspires new crop of young gardeners during coronavirus pandemic. [online] The Tennessean. Available at: https://www.tennessean.com/story/news/american-south/2020/09/11/during-coronavirus-seeds-change-inspires-new-crop-young-gardeners/5746734002/.

Cloer, L. (n.d.). Society and Culture: Barbie Turns 50 | Vision. [online] Vision.org. Available at: https://www.vision.org/society-and-culture-barbie-turns-50-672.

Cocoa Swatches. (n.d.). About - Cocoa Swatches. [online] Available at: https://www.cocoaswatches.com/about-cocoa-swatches-1-1.

Collins, M. (2017). 1960s Fashion in Australia. [online] Prezi. Available at: https://prezi.com/innv52mmm1r2/1960s-fashion-in-australia/.

Coram.org.uk. (n.d.). Coram | Better chances for children since 1739. [online] Available at: https://www.coram.org.uk/.

Cosmato, D. (2012). 1950s Fashion for Women. [online] LoveToKnow. Available at: https://womens-fashion.lovetoknow.com/1950_Fashion_for_Women.

Cramer, M. (2020). After All These Years, Barbie Is Still Reinventing Herself. The New York Times. [online] 29 Jan. Available at: https://www.nytimes.com/2020/01/29/business/mattel-barbie-dolls-vitiligo.html.

Create & Cultivate. (2020). Bumble Founder Whitney Wolfe Herd's Career Advice for Aspiring Entrepreneurs Is Good, Really Good. [online] Available at: https://www.createcultivate.com/blog/entrepreneur-whitney-wolfe-herd-create-cultivate-100/.

Crunchbase. (2021). Crunchbase. [online] Available at: https://www.crunchbase.com/organization/innovation-africa.

Curkovic, F. (2021). 2min Art Analysis: Barbara Kruger. [online] www.youtube.com. Available at: https://www.youtube.com/watch?v=N8SZb72Sm18.

Curry, D. (2020). Bumble Revenue and Usage Statistics (2020). [online] Business of Apps. Available at: https://www.businessofapps.com/data/bumble-statistics/.

Daijiworld.com. (2013). Priyanka Chopra donates 5 million to fight cancer. [online] Available at: https://daijiworld.com/index.php/news/newsDisplay?newsID=196613.

Deloza, L. (2018). Marley Dias on Inspiring Activism, Diversifying Children's Literature, and Her Latest Reads. [online] Literacyworldwide.org. Available at: https://www.literacyworldwide.org/blog%2Fliteracy-now%2F2018%2F05%2F31%2Fmarley-dias-on-inspiring-activism-diversifying-children%27s-literature-and-her-latest-reads.

Dezign Ark (2016). Barbara Kruger – Consumerism, Power and the Everyday | Fresh Perspectives | Tate Collective. [online] Dezign Ark. Available at: https://dezignark.com/blog/barbara-kruger-consumerism-power-and-the-everyday-fresh-perspectives-tate-collective/.

Dias, M. (2020). "Let Us Help You Lead": Marley Dias on Why Young People Must Be Included in the Fight for Racial Justice. [online] ELLE. Available at: https://www.elle.com/culture/career-politics/a33336406/marley-dias-black-lives-matter-essay/.

Diep, F. (2017). The Science of Barbie's Effect on Self-Esteem. [online] Pacific Standard. Available at: https://psmag.com/social-justice/i-am-a-barbie-girl-in-what-is-not-a-barbie-world.

Dill-Shackleford, K. (2016). Barbie and the negative body image effect. [online] OUPblog. Available at: https://blog.oup.com/2016/02/barbie-body-image-social-psychology/.

Dinsdale, E. (2020). The power of Barbara Kruger's art, in her own words. [online] Dazed. Available at: https://www.dazeddigital.com/art-photography/article/48055/1/the-power-of-barbara-krugers-art-in-her-own-words.

Dittmar, H., Halliwell, E. and Ive, S. (2006). Does Barbie make girls want to be thin? The effect of experimental exposure to images of dolls on the body image of 5- to 8-year-old girls. Developmental psychology, [online] 42(2), pp.283–92. Available at: https://www.ncbi.nlm.nih.gov/pubmed/16569167.

DoGoodJamaica. (n.d.). "Raising Marley: Nurturing A Literacy Rockstar" – Do Good Jamaica. [online] Available at: https://dogoodjamaica.org/raising-marley-nurturing-a-literacy-rockstar/.

Donham, M. (2019). With #GivingTuesdayKids, 12-Year-Old Changemaker Encourages Kids to Unlock Their Power to Improve to World. [online] Points of Light. Available at: https://www.pointsoflight.org/awards/with-givingtuesdaykids-12-year-old-changemaker-encourages-kids-to-unlock-their-power-to-improve-to-world/.

Drae, C. and Caichpal, W. (2020). It's no secret that the disabled population is a vulnerable and forgotten sector. https://historico. elsalvador.com/historico/781491/salvadorenos-destacados-wendy-beatriz-caishpal-jaco-bbc-mundo.html

Dreamstress, T. (2017). The Ideal WWI era figure: Part I. [online] The Dreamstress. Available at: https://thedreamstress.com/2017/08/the-ideal-wwi-era-figure-part-i/.

Dunne, S. (2009). Chancing her arm on TV. [online] The Irish Times. Available at: https://www.irishtimes.com/news/health/chancing-her-arm-on-tv-1.714049.

Durand, C. and Kindelan, K. (2018). Princess Kate launches mental health program for schools: "My own commitment is to the youngest and most vulnerable." [online] ABC News. Available at: https:// abcnews.go.com/Entertainment/princess-kate-launches-mental -health-program-schools-commitment/story?id=52544635#:~:text= %22My%20own%20commitment%20is%20to.

Durrani, P. (2021). In Kandahar, It's a Dangerous Time for Women. [online] New Lines Magazine. Available at: https://newlinesmag.com/ first-person/in-kandahar-its-a-dangerous-time-for-women/.

Elmanpeace (2017). Ilwad Elman. [online] Elman Peace. Available at: http://elmanpeace.org/ilwad-elman/.

Encyclopedia of World Biography (2013). Oprah Winfrey Biography - life, family, childhood, parents, name, story, history, school, mother, young. [online] Notablebiographies.com. Available at: https://www. notablebiographies.com/We-Z/Winfrey-Oprah.html.

Engeln, R. (2013). An epidemic of beauty sickness,. [online] Available at: youtube.com/watch?v=j9vE4i017q4.

Engeln, R. (2017). Beauty Sick. New York: Harper Collins, pp.10, 11.

Entwistle, J. and Mears, A. (2012). Gender on Display: Peformativity in Fashion Modelling. Cultural Sociology, 7(3), pp.9, 10.

Essex News Daily. (2019). Marley Dias named to Time magazine's list of "25 Most Influential Teens of 2018." [online] Available at: https://essexnewsdaily.com/headlne-news/marley-dias-named-to-time-magazines-list-of-25-most-influential-teens-of-2018

Europarl.europa.eu. (2020). Female genital mutilation: where, why and consequences | News | European Parliament. [online] Available at: https://www.europarl.europa.eu/news/en/headlines/society/20200206STO72031/female-genital-mutilation-where-why-and-consequences.

Eveleeth, R. (2018). "Accessible" Fashion Lines Have a Disability Problem. [online] Vice. Available at: https://www.vice.com/en/article/8xkyxb/design-bias-disability-fashion-zappos-j-crew.

Fashion Journal. (n.d.). Fashion Journal. [online] Available at: https://fashionjournal.com.au.

Female Founders Fund (2019). An Interview with Bumble's Whitney Wolfe Herd. [online] Medium. Available at: https://blog.femalefoundersfund.com/an-interview-with-bumbles-whitney-wolfe-herd-d9ab69e21497.

Fenty Beauty (2017). Fenty Beauty Trailer. Available at: https://www.youtube.com/watch?v=Yp9qmTutr4k.

Ferriss, T. (2018). The Tim Ferriss Show Transcripts: Whitney Wolfe Herd (#316). [online] The Blog of Author Tim Ferriss. Available at: https://tim.blog/2018/06/26/the-tim-ferriss-show-transcripts-whitney-wolfe-herd/.

Fessenden, M. (2016). Madame de Pompadour's Legacy as a Patron of Arts Is Often Overlooked. [online] Smithsonian Magazine. Available at: https://www.smithsonianmag.com/smart-news/madame-de-pompadours-legacy-patron-arts-often-overlooked-180959062/.

Fetto, F. (2020). How Fenty Beauty Changed The State Of Play In The Industry. [online] British Vogue. Available at: https://www.vogue.co.uk/beauty/article/rihanna-fenty-beauty-diversity.

Fiell, C. and Emmanuelle Dirix (2016). 1930S Fashion. London: Goodman-Fiell, p.10.

Figueroa, S. (2019). Diversity is Beauty and Beauty is Everywhere. [online] Linkedin. Available at: https://www.linkedin.com/pulse/diversity-beauty-everywhere-shannon-figueroa.

Fisher, L. (2011). How Oprah Winfrey Changed My Life. [online] ABC News. Available at: https://abcnews.go.com/Entertainment/oprah-winfrey-changed-lives/story?id=13666585.

Folland, Dr.T. (n.d.). Barbara Kruger, Untitled (Your gaze hits the side of my face) (article). [online] Khan Academy. Available at: https://www.khanacademy.org/humanities/global-culture/concepts-in-art-1980-to-now/x247213a3:pictures-generation-and-post-modern-photography/a/barbara-kruger-untitled-your-gaze-hits-the-side-of-my-face.

Forbes. (2020). Manuri Gunawardena. [online] Available at: https://www.forbes.com/profile/manuri-gunawardena/.

Foster, E. (2020). Marley Dias starts a new chapter with Netflix. [online] Kidscreen. Available at: https://kidscreen.com/2020/08/31/marley-dias-starts-a-new-chapter-with-netflix/.

Foxley, D. (2018). Artist Barbara Kruger and Her Iconic Skatepark Installation Are Celebrated in a New Film. [online] Architectural Digest. Available at: https://www.architecturaldigest.com/story/barbara-kruger-performa-17#:~:text=The%20Report-.

Franklin, H. (2019). 1890-1899 | Fashion History Timeline. [online] Fitnyc.edu. Available at: https://fashionhistory.fitnyc.edu/1890-1899/.

Fuller, K. (2021). How To Practice Body Neutrality. [online] Verywell Mind. Available at: https://www.verywellmind.com/how-to-practice-body-neutrality-5120914.

Gannon, K. (2018). Herstory: A South Asian Superwoman | Her Campus. [online] Hercampus.com. Available at: https://www.hercampus.com/school/usf/herstory-south-asian-superwoman/.

Gates, B. (2018). No masks or capes, but these heroes are saving the world. [online] Gatesnotes. Available at: https://www.gatesnotes.com/About-Bill-Gates/These-Heroes-Are-Saving-the-World.

General Mills (2018). Katie Stagliano, Katie's Krops. [online] Youtube. Available at: https://www.youtube.com/watch?v=B6aA7TAzdAs.

Gersch, D. (2021). Building your child body image and self esteem. [online] Available at: https://familydoctor.org/building-your-childs-body-image-and-self-esteem/

Gillezeau, N. (2020). HealthMatch raises $18m as patients go online for clinical trials. [online] Australian Financial Review. Available at: https://www.afr.com/technology/healthmatch-raises-18m-as-patients-go-online-for-clinical-trials-20201202-p56k0n.

Girlguiding. (2016). Girls as young as seven feel pressure to look perfect. [online] Available at: https://www.huffingtonpost.co.uk/entry/girlguiding-2016-body-image-report_uk_57f258b3e4b00e5804f1f832

Givhan, R. (2017a). Perspective | Fashion is finally figuring out diversity — in ways that actually matter. Washington Post. [online] 6 Sep. Available at: https://www.washingtonpost.com/lifestyle/style/fashion-is-finally-figuring-out-diversity--in-ways-that-actually-matter/2017/09/06/a16333a6-88f0-11e7-a94f-3139abce39f5_story.html.

Givhan, R. (2017b). To Fight the Status Quo, the activists of 1968 harnessed the power of fashion. The Washington Post. [online] 5 Winter. Available at: https://www.washingtonpost.com/lifestyle/style/to-fight-the-status-quo-the-activists-of-1968-harnessed-the-power-of-fashion/2018/05/23/1d2f2ad2-44dd-11e8-bba2-0976a82b05a2_story.html#:~:text=Style-,To%20fight%20the%20status%20quo%2C%20the%20activists%20of,harnessed%20the%20power%20of%20fashion&text=In%201968%2C%20the%20American%20Dream,dark%20suits%20and%20slim%20ties..

Givhan, R. (2020). The idea of beauty is always shifting. Today it's more inclusive than ever. National Geographic.

Glamour Daze. (2013). The History of 1930s Makeup - 1930 to 1939 | Glamour Daze. [online] Available at: https://glamourdaze.com/history-of-makeup/1930s.

Glamour Daze.(n.d). 1970's in Fashion | Style Trends and History. [online] Available at: https://glamourdaze.com/1970s-fashion.

GoFundMe (2019). Meet Ruby Kate. [online] GoFundMe Stories. Available at: https://medium.com/gofundme-stories/meet-ruby-kate-3f34992e887d.

Gofundme. (2020). Khloe's community fridge, organized by Alisha Denise. [online] Available at: https://www.gofundme.com/f/khloes-community-fridge.

Gorman, A. (2021). "We are changing the narrative": meet the new faces of Australian fashion week. [online] The Guardian. Available at: https://www.theguardian.com/fashion/2021/may/24/we-are-changing-the-narrative-meet-the-new-faces-of-australian-fashion-week.

GrassROOTS Community Foundation. (n.d.). Home. [online] Available at: https://grassrootscommunityfoundation.org/.

Gray, C. (2019). Disability fashion: Stephanie Thomas shakes up fashion. [online] Uncomfortable Revolution. Available at: https://www.urevolution.com/en-au/blogs/magazine/disability-fashion-stephanie-thomas

Greenfield, B. (2017). When a stranger asked, "What's wrong with you?" this disability advocate had been the best response. [online] Yahoo. Available at: https://ca.news.yahoo.com/one-woman-considers-disability-blessing-life-181624067.html?guccounter=1&guce_referrer=aHR0cHM6Ly93d3cuZ2ludGVyZXN0LmNhLw&guce_referrer_sig=AQAAAK5oM00FSuFBful1CKWBTMhmsUkVViIO5D2A1KcclgPbzw7jigeTjBuF0KkORGq6DK-0fll4O-fx7aWRyMM7_i2_x0sEWp7C2oebCqPqfQNJXfjsdRx7lXVdB7Y2IBdV8x7lHKXwTw3ER50ZLCufik_igy6A8oFNr8rIaxTqtd8.

Griffin, A. (2019). At 60, Barbie has no discernible personality, and that is the best thing about her. [online] Quartz. Available at: https://qz.com/quartzy/1568829/is-barbie-a-good-or-bad-role-model-shes-neither/#:~:text=At%2060%2C%20Barbie%20has%20no.

Griffith, E. (2019). Whitney Wolfe Herd's Work Diary: Fighting Misogyny, One Bumble Brand at a Time. The New York Times. [online] 9 May. Available at: https://www.nytimes.com/2019/05/09/business/whitney-wolfe-herd-bumble-work-diary.html.

Gurman, S. (2021). Jillian Mercado Belongs Everywhere. [online] V Magazine. Available at: https://vmagazine.com/article/jillian-mercado-belongs-everywhere/.

Hamad, R. (2014). Human rights a family tradition for Sister Somalia founder Ilwad Elman. [online] Hiiraan.com. Available at: https://hiiraan.com/news4/2014/Mar/53744/human_rights_a_family_tradition_for_sister_somalia_founder_ilwad_elman.aspx.

Hamish Bowles (2019). Stella McCartney's Vogue Cover: How The Designer Became Fashion's Conscience. [online] Vogue. Available at: https://www.vogue.com/article/stella-mccartney-cover-january-2020.

Hansen, A. (2020). Kate Middleton's Charity Work Highlights Everything Fans Love About Her. [online] CCN.com. Available at: https://www.ccn.com/kate-middletons-charity-work-highlights-everything-fans-love-about-her/.

Harkin, S. (2021). Mari Copeny Biography for Kids. [online] Lottie.com. Available at: https://www.lottie.com/blogs/strong-women/mari-copeny-biography-for-kids.

Harriger, J.A., Calogero, R.M., Witherington, David.C. and Smith, J.E. (2010). Body Size Stereotyping and Internalization of the Thin Ideal in Preschool Girls. Sex Roles, 63(9-10), pp.609–620.

Harte, J. (2021). Texas abortion clinics struggle to survive under restrictive law. Reuters. [online] 1 Oct. Available at: https://www.reuters.com/world/us/texas-abortion-clinics-struggle-survive-under-restrictive-law-2021-09-30/.

Harveston, K. (2019). , Inside the "Body Neutrality" Movement. [online] Bust. Available at: https://bust.com.

Hayasaki, E. (2016). Priyanka Chopra's Secret Triumph: How the *Quantico* Star Is Helping Kids Go to School. [online] Glamour. Available at: https://www.glamour.com/story/quantico-star-priyanka-chopra-on-education.

Hayden, N. (2011). What Influenced Fashion in the 70s? [online] LEAFtv. Available at: https://www.leaf.tv/articles/what-influenced-fashion-in-the-70s/.

Herling, T. (2017). The entrepreneur that brought electricity and water to Africa. [online] Forbes Israel. Available at: https://forbes.co.il/e/and-then-there-was-light-the-female-entrepreneur-that-brought-electricity-and-water-to-villages-in-seven-african-countries/#:~:text=%E2%80%9CIt.

Hickman, J. (2019). Is the beauty industry really as diverse as it should be? Let's check in. [online] Well+Good. Available at: https://www.wellandgood.com/diversity-in-the-beauty-industry/.

Hidreley (2016). Barbie Celebrates Diversity By Creating Differently-Abled Dolls With Vitiligo And No Hair That Come In 35 Different Skin Tones. [online] Bored Panda. Available at: https://www.boredpanda.com/mattel-barbie-inclusive-dolls-diversity/.

Hitchings-Hales, J. (2020). UK Teen Climate Activist Says COVID-19 Is "Once-in-a-Lifetime" Chance to Save the Planet. [online] Global Citizen. Available at: https://www.globalcitizen.org/en/content/bella-lack-climate-activist-covid-19-uk/.

Hoffower, H. (2020). A very millennial decade: The trends, the looks, and the moments that defined each year of the 2000s for America's most controversial generation. Business Insider. [online] 20 Jan. Available at: https://www.businessinsider.in/slideshows/miscellaneous/a-very-millennial-decade-the-trends-the-looks-and-the-moments-that-defined-each-year-of-the-2000s-for-americas-most-controversial-generation/slidelist/73049112.cms.

Hogan, M. (2017). Mattel's stock swoons 17 percent after grim earnings, revenue letdown. [online] CNBC. Available at: https://www.cnbc.com/2017/01/25/mattel-plunges-10-percent-after-falling-short-on-revenue-earnings.html.

Horn, X. (2021). How inclusive beauty is expanding its definition | Avery Dennison | M_use. [online] my muse. Available at: https://www.my-muse.com/en/home/insights/tfl-inclusive-beauty.html.

Horton, C. (2021). Cerrie Burnell: "Disabled people have been shut away during the pandemic." [online] The Guardian. Available at: https://www.theguardian.com/society/2021/jan/19/cerrie-burnell-disabled-people-have-been-shut-away-during-the-pandemic.

Huffingtonpost.co.uk. (n.d.). Cerrie Burnell | HuffPost. [online] Available at: https://www.huffingtonpost.co.uk/author/cerrie-burnell.

Hyde, M. (2000). The "Makeup" of the Marquise: Boucher's Portrait of Pompadour at Her Toilette. The Art Bulletin, 82(3), p.462.

Icipe.org. (2020). Boost for icipe malaria reduction efforts | icipe - International Centre of Insect Physiology and Ecology. [online] Available at: http://www.icipe.org/news/boost-icipe-malaria-reduction-efforts.

Idealist Style. (2013). Beauty Ideals Over the Decadepart 3 : THE 2000's. [online] Available at: http://www.idealiststyle.com/blog/beauty-ideal-over-the-decades-part-3-the-2000s.

Idealist Style. (2014). Beuty Ideal Over the Decades part 9 : The 40's. [online] Available at: http://www.idealiststyle.com/blog/beauty-ideal-over-the-decades-part-9-the-40s.

Ilchi, L. (2020). 3 Ways Rihanna Electrified the Fashion and Beauty Industries. [online] WWD. Available at: https://wwd.com/fashion-news/fashion-scoops/how-rihanna-transformed-fashion-beauty-industries-fenty-1203494894/.

Ilse, J. (2020). The Duchess of Cambridge reveals 5 Big Questions results. [online] Royal Central. Available at: https://royalcentral. co.uk/uk/cambridge/the-duchess-of-cambridge-reveals-5-big-questions-results-152972/#:~:text=The%20insights%20are%20that%20 %E2%80%9Cpeople.

Innoafrica (2019). InspIring Israelis we met thIs decade. [online] Available at: https://www.innoafrica.org/assets/grapevine-article-sivan-yaari-2020.pdf.

Innovation: Africa (2020). Interview with Sivan Ya'ari. www. youtube.com. Available at: https://www.youtube.com/ watch?v=96ANT8XmTN0.

Interview with Autumn-Whitefield-Madrano, author of FACE VALUE. (2016). Available at: https://www.youtube.com/watch?v=2l8uKdsYYgU

Jackson, L. (2021). "It's a basic human right": the fight for adaptive fashion. [online] the Guardian. Available at: https://www. theguardian.com/fashion/2021/feb/26/its-a-basic-human-right-the-fight-for-adaptive-fashion.

Jacob, B. (2020). A strong survivor | Oprah recalls how she was raped as a child by her own cousin who bought her ice cream after the crime. [online] Explore.newsner.com. Available at: https://explore. newsner.com/oprah-windrey-childhood-abuse-trauma-life-family-pregnant-premature-baby.

Jahangir, R. (2015). How does black hair reflect black history? BBC News. [online] 31 May. Available at: https://www.bbc.com/news/uk-england-merseyside-31438273.

James, C. (1991). Critic's Notebook: Feminine Beauty as a Masculine Plot. The New York Times.

Jeffreys, T. (2010). Foundline, Father, Figurehead – an interview with Grayson Perry «Tom Jeffreys. [online] Tom-jeffreys.co.uk. Available at: http://www.tom-jeffreys.co.uk/foundline-father-figurehead-an-interview-with-grayson-perry/377.

Jellison, H. (2019). Top 10 Facts about Priyanka Chopra's Philanthropy. [online] BORGEN. Available at: https://www.borgenmagazine.com/top-10-facts-about-priyanka-chopras-philanthropy/.

Johnson, J. (2012). Oprah: I was raped when I was only 9. [online] Irish Examiner. Available at: https://www.irishexaminer.com/world/arid-20215310.html.

Johnson, M. (2018). During WWII, beauty was propaganda, but it might've helped win the war. [online] Upworthy. Available at: https://www.upworthy.com/during-wwii-beauty-was-propaganda-but-it-might-ve-helped-win-the-war.

Johnson, P. (2011). The Fashion That Was: The Sixties and How it influenced the Fashion World. [online] Buffalo Rising. Available at: https://www.buffalorising.com/2011/10/the-fashion-that-was-the-sixties-and-how-it-influenced-the-fashion-world/#:~:text=People%20were%20dressing%20in%20psychedelic.

Johnston, J. (2020). Q&A Interview with Melati and Isabel Wijsen, Founders of Bye Bye Plastic Bags | CoralVue. [online] Coralvue. Available at: https://www.coralvue.com/blog/bye-bye-plastic-bags-interview-melati-isabel-wijsen-september-1-2020.

Jones, G. (2012). Beauty imagined : a history of the global beauty industry. Oxford: Oxford University Press, p.53.

Karp, C. (2021). How an anorexic schoolgirl was preyed on by her maths teacher at 15. [online] Mail Online. Available at: https://www.dailymail.co.uk/news/article-9186001/How-anorexic-schoolgirl-preyed-maths-teacher-15.html.

Kat Stoeffel (2018). Barbara Kruger Forever. [online] The Cut. Available at: https://www.thecut.com/2018/02/profile-barbara-kruger-on-trump-supreme-and-harassment.html.

Katemiddletonreview (2020). Kate launches "5 Big Questions" survey – Kate Middleton Review. [online] Katemiddletonreview.com. Available at: http://katemiddletonreview.com/2020/01/kate-launches-5-big-questions-survey/.

KatiesKrops. (2021a). Katie's Krops Bringing Educational Programming to the Lowcountry with New Outdoor Classroom – Welcome to Katie's Krops ! [online] Available at: https://katieskrops.com/katies-krops-bringing-educational-programming-to-the-lowcountry-with-new-outdoor-classroom/.

KatiesKrops. (2021b). Media & Publications – Welcome to Katie's Krops ! [online] Available at: https://katieskrops.com/category/media-a-publications/.

KatiesKrops. (2021c). Storytime in the Garden – Welcome to Katie's Krops ! [online] Available at: https://katieskrops.com/events/storytime-in-the-garden/.

Kaufman, J. (2020). Mindset Matters: The Revolution Will Look Fabulous. [online] Forbes. Available at: https://www.forbes.com/sites/jonathankaufman/2020/08/12/mindset-matters-the-revolution-will-look-fabulous/.

Kelly, A. and Moss, P. (2021). Pyer Moss Will Make Haute Couture Debut in Paris for Fall/Winter 2021 - Kerby Jean-Raymond. [online] Lofficielusa. Available at: https://www.lofficielusa.com/fashion/pyer-moss-kerby-jean-raymond-first-black-american-designer-haute-couture-debut-fall-winter-2021.

Kelly, R. (2017). 7 of Duchess Kate's Most Prominent Charities. [online] Parade. Available at: https://parade.com/593885/roisinkelly/7-of-duchess-kates-most-prominent-charities/.

Kemp, N. (2018). Body positivity, diversity and strong women: the new rules of beauty advertising. [online] Campaignlive.co.uk. Available at: https://www.campaignlive.co.uk/article/body-positivity-diversity-strong-women-new-rules-beauty-advertising/1466761.

Kempter, V. (2018). Are the Kardashians inspiring or damaging to women? [online] The Perspective. Available at: https://www.theperspective.com/amp/debates/3395/kardashians-inspiring-damaging-women.html

Keyes, A. (2018). Oprah's Undeniable Influence on American History Recognized in New Smithsonian Exhibition. Smithsonian. [online] 7 Jun. Available at: https://www.smithsonianmag.com/smithsonian-institution/oprahs-undeniable-influence-american-history-recognized-new-smithsonian-exhibition-180969267/.

Kiefer, E. (2017). Your Role Model? No Thanks, Gigi Gorgeous Just Wants To Be Herself. [online] Refinery29. Available at: https://www.refinery29.com/en-us/2017/11/155789/who-is-gigi-gorgeous-youtube-transgender-advocate.

Kihlström, M. (2020). Humanium. [online] Humanium. Available at: https://humanium-metal.com.

Kimathi, E., Tonnang, H.E.Z., Subramanian, S., Cressman, K., Abdel-Rahman, E.M., Tesfayohannes, M., Niassy, S., Torto, B., Dubois, T., Tanga, C.M., Kassie, M., Ekesi, S., Mwangi, D. and Kelemu, S. (2020). Prediction of breeding regions for the desert locust Schistocerca gregaria in East Africa. Scientific Reports, 10(1).

King, E. (2019). How The Kardashians Became The Biggest Influencers Of The 2010s. [online] British Vogue. Available at: https://www.vogue.co.uk/arts-and-lifestyle/article/kardashian-jenner-familys-impact-on-the-world.

Kofiannanfoundation (2016). Ilwad Elman. [online] Kofi Annan Foundation. Available at: https://www.kofiannanfoundation.org/extremely-together/ilwad-elman/.

Koha, N.T. (2021). World of beauty in our nation's diversity. Herald Sun. 1 Oct.

Koigi, B. (2021). Fighting female cut: technology to the rescue. [online] FairPlanet. Available at: https://www.fairplanet.org/story/fighting-female-cut-technology-to-the-rescue/.

Komar, M. (2017). Makeup & War Are More Intricately Connected Than You Realized. [online] Bustle. Available at: https://www.bustle.com/p/makeup-war-are-more-intricately-connected-than-you-realized-51078.

Kong, J. (2020). 24 Minutes with disability fashion stylist, Stephanie Thomas. [online] BURO. Available at: https://www.buro247.my/fashion/insiders/disability-fashion-stylist-stephanie-thomas-interv.html.

Kościcka, K., Czepczor, K. and Brytek-Matera, A. (2016). Body size attitudes and body image perception among preschool children and their parents: a preliminary study. Archives of Psychiatry and Psychotherapy, 18(4), pp.28–34.

Kumar, A. (2011). The Hindu: Metro Plus Kochi/People/Green agenda. [online] Hindu.com. Available at: https://peoplepill.com/people/priyanka-chopra

Lane, K. (2019). How Women's Perfect Body Types Changed Throughout The Past Decade. [online] TheList. Available at: https://www.thelist.com/179261/how-womens-perfect-body-types-changed-throughout-the-past-decade/.

LaPorte, N. (2019). Inside Bumble CEO Whitney Wolfe Herd's mission to build the "female internet." [online] Fast Company. Available at: https://www.fastcompany.com/90396193/inside-bumble-ceo-whitney-wolfe-herds-mission-to-build-the-female-internet.

LearnAfghan (n.d.). Education | Learn | Afghanistan. [online] LEARN. Available at: https://www.learnafghan.org/.

Letusspeak.com.au. (2020). #LetHerSpeak | #LetUsSpeak. [online] Available at: https://www.letusspeak.com.au/.

Liechman, A. (2020). Israeli tech helps African villages protect against corona. [online] ISRAEL21c. Available at: https://www.israel21c.org/israeli-tech-helps-african-villages-protect-against-corona/.

Little, A.C., Jones, B.C. and DeBruine, L.M. (2011). Facial attractiveness: evolutionary based research. Philosophical Transactions of the Royal Society B: Biological Sciences, [online] 366(1571), pp.1638–1659. Available at: https://www.ncbi.nlm.nih.gov/pmc/articles/PMC3130383/.

LIVEKellyandRyan (2020). Good News: 13-Year-old Khloe Thompson is Providing Supplies For the Homeless. [online] Youtube. Available at: https://www.youtube.com/watch?v=UMSD0mvgjD4.

Livelifegetactive.(n.d). Body image, Self - Esteem and the Influence of Society. [online] Available at: https://livelifegetactive.com/blog/body-image-self-esteem/).

Lolli, A. (n.d.). Stella McCartney: Fashion And Sustainability. [online] Thefashionglobe. Available at: https://thefashionglobe.com/stella-mccartney.

London, L. (2020). Nikita Dragun On Trans Makeup, Entrepreneurship, And Pride. [online] Forbes. Available at: https://www.forbes.com/sites/lelalondon/2020/10/26/nikita-dragun-on-trans-makeup-entrepreneurship-and-pride/.

Lowry, M.P. (2018). This Is How One Sixth Grade Girl Helped Improve Flint's Water Crisis. [online] Oprah Daily. Available at: https://www.oprahdaily.com/life/a25383285/mari-copeny-barack-obama-flint-water-crisis/.

Lyons, S. (2021). Marley Dias' Heroes Are Black Women. [online] Teen Vogue. Available at: https://www.teenvogue.com/story/marley-dias-female-heroes.

MacBride, K. (2018). Getting to Work With Little Miss Flint. [online] Shondaland. Available at: https://www.shondaland.com/inspire/a19485789/getting-to-work-with-little-miss-flint/.

Madden, K. (2021). Grace Tame: "It's Terrifying To Do Something In The Face Of Evil." [online] Marie Claire. Available at: https://www.marieclaire.com.au/grace-tame-marie-claire-cover-full-interview#:~:text=Grace%20Tame%20Opens%20Up%20About%20Survival%2C%20Speaking%20Out%20%26%20Starting%20A%20Revolution&text=Grace%20Tame%20will%20not%20be.

Malcolm, B. (2021). Bridget Malcolm, former Victoria's Secret model: I was told to have sex as a minor and do cocaine to lose weight. [online] Marca. Available at: https://www.marca.com/en/lifestyle/2021/07/07/60e60647ca4741bc468b45a6.html#:~:text=Fashion-.

March, B. (2019). 16 beauty trends that sum up the 2010s. [online] Harper's BAZAAR. Available at: https://www.harpersbazaar.com/uk/beauty/beauty-shows-trends/a30180045/beauty-trends-2010s/.

Marley Dias. (n.d.). Marley Dias. [online] Available at: https://www.marleydias.com.

Mashable Experiential (2018). MARI COPENY continues to fight for clean water and inspires other folks to stand up and speak up. [online] Youtube. Available at: https://www.youtube.com/watch?v=M8BUiW77xUY.

Mason, H. (2017). Meet Smart Girl Mari Copeny aka "Little Miss Flint." [online] Medium. Available at: https://amysmartgirls.com/meet-smart-girl-mari-copeny-aka-little-miss-flint-4131419a31bd.

Mayo Clinic (2018). Eating disorders - Symptoms and causes. [online] Mayo Clinic. Available at: https://www.mayoclinic.org/diseases-conditions/eating-disorders/symptoms-causes/syc-20353603.

McCann, H. (2019). 'Look good, feel good. Overland literary journal, 237.

McDermott, R. (2019). The Beauty Premium: how society rewards pretty, and why it's a lose/lose game for women. [online] IMAGE.ie. Available at: https://www.image.ie/life/beauty-premium-society-rewards-pretty-loselose-game-woman-162996.

McGlinchey, S. (2013). The History of 1900's Makeup - 1900 to 1919 | Glamour Daze. [online] Glamour Daze. Available at: https://glamourdaze.com/history-of-makeup/1900-1919.

McGreevy, N. (2021). Major Barbara Kruger Exhibition Spills Out Into the Streets of Chicago. [online] Smithsonian Magazine. Available at: https://www.smithsonianmag.com/smart-news/barbara-kruger-survey-art-institute-chicago-180978802/.

McKay, L. (2012). Australians Outspend US on Cosmetic Procedures. [online] Costhetics. Available at: https://www.costhetics.com.au/news/australians-outspend-us-on-cosmetic-procedures/.

McKay, R. (2020). 90's Clothes for Women: How to Pull The Perfect Nineties Outfit. [online] New Idea. Available at: https://www.newidea.com.au/90s-clothes-women.

Melendez, M. (2019). Meet Ruby Kate Chitsey, the Young Girl Who's Raised Over $200,000 for the Elderly. [online] Scholastic. Available at: https://www.scholastic.com/parents/school-success/learning-toolkit-blog/three-wishes-for-rubys-residents.html.

Mendelson, B. (2014). In Your Face. Melbourne: Hardie Grant, pp.xi, 11.

Mental Health Foundation (2019). Body image in childhood. [online] Mental Health Foundation. Available at: https://www.mentalhealth.org.uk/publications/body-image-report/childhood.

Meyer, K. (2016). Asked and Answered: President Obama Responds to an Eight-Year-Old Girl from Flint. [online] Whitehouse.gov. Available at: https://obamawhitehouse.archives.gov/blog/2016/04/27/asked-and-answered-president-obama-responds-eight-year-old-girl-flint.

Michigan State University Division Of Pubic Health (2020). MSU's... - Michigan State University Division of Public Health. [online] ne-np.facebook.com. Available at: https://ne-np.facebook.com/MSUPublicHealth/videos/msus-pediatric-public-health-initiative-youth-advisory-group-the-flint-youth-jus/546928379531933/?__so__=permalink&__rv__=related_videos.

Million STEM. (2020). Danielle Boyer. [online] Available at: https://www.1mwis.com/profiles/Danielle-Boyer.

Minutaglio, R. (2021). Inside One Afghan Woman's Fight to Protect Educational Rights. [online] ELLE. Available at: https://www.elle.com/culture/a37340851/afghan-activist-womens-rights/.

Mollard, A. (2021a). (The (un)changing face of the future. Herald Sun.

Mollard, A. (2021b). How Did Airbrushed Perfection Become the New Normal? Herald Sun.

Monet, D. (2011). Women's Fashions of the 1920s - Flappers and the Jazz Age. [online] Bellatory. Available at: https://bellatory.com/fashion-industry/WomensFashionsofthe1920-FlappersandtheJazz-Age.

Monet, D. (2012). Fashion History—Women's Clothing of the 1950s. [online] Bellatory. Available at: https://bellatory.com/fashion-industry/Fashion-History-Womens-Clothing-of-the-1950s.

Montague, J. (2020). Sinéad Burke on her career, activism and forcing the fashion industry to shift its thinking about inclusivity. [online] Vogue Australia. Available at: https://www.vogue.com.au/celebrity/interviews/sinad-burke-on-her-career-activism-and-forcing-the-fashion-industry-to-shift-its-thinking-about-inclusivity/news-story/3143bbd1c63f2f9e9ff4bb940f4b543d.

Moore, C. (2017). How Sinead Burke is making the fashion world wake up to disability. [online] Irish Examiner. Available at: https://www.irishexaminer.com/lifestyle/fashionandbeauty/arid-20442022.html.

Moore, Z. (2019). YouTuber announces genderless makeup collection. [online] Good Morning America. Available at: https://www.goodmorningamerica.com/style/story/gigi-gorgeous-announces-genderless-makeup-collection-66211207.

Mros, S. (2020). History of the Mini Skirt: 60s Hedonism & Youth Rebellion. [online] Contrado Blog. Available at: https://au.contrado.com/blog/history-of-mini-skirt/#:~:text=A%20History%20of%20the%20Mini%20Skirt&text=It%20involves%20rebellion%2C%20sex%20and.

Mulkerrins, J. (2021). The question about men that made this woman a billionaire. [online] The Sydney Morning Herald. Available at: https://www.smh.com.au/lifestyle/life-and-relationships/the-question-about-men-that-made-this-woman-a-billionaire-20210507-p57q09.html.

Mutai, P. (2017). Kenya launches first fruit fly protein bait facility - Xinhua | English.news.cn. [online] Xinhuanet. Available at: http://news.xinhuanet.com/english/2017-03/29/c_136168711.htm#:~:text=MURANG.

Nanhikali. (n.d.). After School Education Support. [online] Available at: https://www.nanhikali.org/after-school-education-support/.

Napikoski, L. (2017). The Feminist Art and Found Images of Barbara Kruger. [online] ThoughtCo. Available at: https://www.thoughtco.com/barbara-kruger-bio-3529938#:~:text=Born%20on%20January%2026%2C%201945.

Nash, G.T. (2021). Subscribe to The Australian | Newspaper home delivery, website, iPad, iPhone & Android apps. [online] The Australian. Available at: https://www.theaustralian.com.au/life/style/a-new-report-by-the-australian-fashion-council-has-revealed-the-impact-of-the-local-fashion-industry/news-story/4b4eeebaa44242a7c41db817a521fb24

Nast, C. (2017). How to Update Jean Shrimpton's Sixties Bombshell Blowout. [online] Vogue. Available at: https://www.vogue.com/article/jean-shrimpton-bombshell-blowout-rollers-tips-how-to.

Nast, C. (2020). Jillian Mercado on Her Runway Debut and Fighting For the Disabled Community. [online] Teen Vogue. Available at: https://www.teenvogue.com/story/jillian-mercado-runway-debut.

Nast, C. (2020b). This Schoolgirl Conservationist Wants You To Be Positive About The Climate Crisis. [online] British Vogue. Available at: https://www.vogue.co.uk/news/article/bella-lack.

Nast, C. (2021a). Beauty weak spot: People with disabilities. [online] Vogue Business. Available at: https://www.voguebusiness.com/beauty/beauty-fails-people-with-disabilities-loreal-estee-lauder-unilever-wants-to-change-that.

Nast, C. (2021b). Dressed in Gucci, Director Jim LeBrecht Makes a Powerful Statement About Representation on the Red Carpet. [online] Vogue. Available at: https://www.vogue.com/article/sinead-burke-jim-lebrecht-gucci-oscars.

Nast, C. (2021c). Is the Beauty Industry Glossing Over Disability? [online] Allure. Available at: https://www.allure.com/story/disability-inclusion-beauty-industry-advertising.

Nast, C. (2021d). Tommy Hilfiger ramps up adaptive fashion. Who's next? [online] Vogue Business. Available at: https://www.voguebusiness.com/fashion/tommy-hilfiger-ramps-up-adaptive-fashion-whos-next.

Natsmith, E. (2020). yatu widders hunt is an advocate for indigenous fashion. [online] Frankie magazine. Available at: https://www.frankie.com.au/article/yatu-widders-hunt-is-an-advocate-for-indigenous-fashion-558415.

Navarro , H. (2019). Bumble Announces "Private Detector" So You Don't Have to Deal With Lewd Pics. [online] NBC Los Angeles. Available at: https://www.nbclosangeles.com/news/bumble-nude-pictures-offensive-filter-private-detector/163970/.

Ncurrie (2017). How Women Look: Standards of Beauty and Female Stereotypes in Product Advertising. [online] The Text Message. Available at: https://text-message.blogs.archives.gov/2017/03/23/how-women-look-standards-of-beauty-and-female-stereotypes-in-product-advertising/.

NDTV.com (2011). Video | NDTV launches Greenathon 3. Ndtv.com. Available at: https://www.ndtv.com/video/shows/ndtv-special-ndtv-24x7/ndtv-launches-greenathon-3-199067.

Neff, D. (2021). Pashtana Durrani. [online] The MY HERO Project. Available at: https://myhero.com/pashtana-durrani.

News.yahoo.com. (2010). "Awaaz Do" digital campaign urges Indians to speak for 8 million out-of-school kids. [online] Available at: https://news.yahoo.com/news/awaaz-digital-campaign-urges-indians-speak-8-million.html.

Newsoveraudio.com. (2021). Beauty Filters are changing the way young girls see themselves. [online] Available at: https://newsover audio.com/articles-beauty-thmselves-678382

NewsPsychology·March 14, F. and 2018 (2018). Are Barbie Dolls Really That Bad? [online] Neuroscience News. Available at: https://neurosciencenews.com/stem-barbie-8629/.

Newton, K. (2021). Flint's water crisis is far from over. Here's how 13-year-old Mari Copeny is taking matters into her own hands. [online] Yahoo. Available at: https://www.yahoo.com/lifestyle/flint-water-crisis-far-from-over-mari-copeny-13-doing-her-part-190625949.html.

Nicholl, K. (2020). Kate Middleton, "A Natural" With Children, Continues Her Whirlwind Tour. [online] Vanity Fair. Available at: https://www.vanityfair.com/style/2020/01/kate-middleton-early-years-survey.

Nichols, N. (2020). Former PM Turnbull backs $18m HealthMatch raise. [online] BusinessNewsAustralia. Available at: https://www.businessnewsaustralia.com/articles/former-pm-turnbull-backs--18m-healthmatch-raise.html.

Not So Secret, 60 Minutes, (2021). Channel 9. 12 Sep.

NYU CIC (2020). The peace activist fighting for women's rights in Somalia. [online] Pathfinders for Peaceful, Just and Inclusive Societies. Available at: https://medium.com/sdg16plus/the-peace-activist-fighting-for-womens-rights-in-somalia-3024426fa634.

Nz.news.yahoo.com. (2019). Stella McCartney praises dad Paul McCartney as a "change agent." [online] Available at: https://nz.news.yahoo.com/stella-mccartney-praises-dad-paul-151845360.html#:~:text=Stella%20McCartney%20praises%20dad%20Paul%20McCartney%20as%20a%20.

O'Grady, M. (2020). Barbara Kruger Offers a Dark Mirror for Our Meme-Driven Age. The New York Times. [online] 19 Oct. Available at: https://www.nytimes.com/interactive/2020/10/19/t-magazine/barbara-kruger.html.

Obama, M. (2018). Becoming. London: Viking, An Imprint Of Penguin Books, p.332.

Octipus, L. (2017). Fashion Influence in the 1960's. [online] theaquariumvintage. Available at: https://www.theaquarium vintage.com/post/2017/04/18/fashion-influence-in-the-1960s.

Olito, F. (2020). 12 transgender models who are changing the industry. [online] Insider. Available at: https://www.insider.com/transgender-models-changing-industry.

Omnicoreagency. (2021). Instagram by the Number: Statistics, Demographics and Fun Facts. [online] Available at: omnicoreagency.com/instagram-statistics.

Omny Studio (2019). Next Generation Innovators Podcast - Next Generation Innovators - Omny.fm. [online] omny.fm. Available at: https://omny.fm/shows/future-women-next-generation-innovators/playlists/podcast.

Oprah Winfrey Charitable Foundation. (n.d.). About Us. [online] Available at: https://www.oprahfoundation.org/about-charity.

Oprah Winfrey Charitable Foundation. [n.d.] Oprah Winfrey Leadership Academy For Girls - Oprah Winfrey Charitable Foundation. [online] Available at: https://www.oprahfoundation.org/portfolio-item/oprah-leadership-academy

Oprah.com. (2007). Building a Dream. [online] Available at: https://www.oprah.com/entertainment/building-a-dream.

Oprah.com. (n.d.). Oprah's Angel Network Fact Sheet. [online] Available at: https://www.oprah.com/pressroom/about-oprahs-angel-network.

Orbach, S. (2019). Bodies. London: Profile Books, pp.xiii, 16, 85.

Paddock, R.C. and Laula, N. (2020). After Fighting Plastic in "Paradise Lost," Sisters Take On Climate Change. The New York Times. [online] 3 Jul. Available at: https://www.nytimes.com/2020/07/03/world/asia/bali-sisters-plastic-climate-change.html#:~:text=The%20Saturday%20Profile-.

Pagana, A. (2020). Oprah Winfrey. [online] Biography. Available at: https://www.biography.com/media-figure/oprah-winfrey.

Paintpotsnurseries.co.uk. 2020. Could Kate Middleton's 5 Big Questions Impact Early Years' Development? – Paintpots Day Nurseries. [online] Available at: https://paintpotsnurseries.co.uk/could-kate-middletons-5-big-questions-impact-early-years-development/

PBS NewsHour (2021). As Afghan women see shrinking public spaces, one activist reveals how the world can help. [online] Youtube. Available at: https://www.youtube.com/watch?v=F03OtFZAAA0.

Perez, S. (2019). Bumble goes to print with its new lifestyle magazine, Bumble Mag. [online] TechCrunch. Available at: https://techcrunch.com/2019/04/04/bumble-goes-to-print-with-its-new-lifestyle-magazine-bumble-mag/.

Perry, S. (2021). How Kate Middleton Is Seizing a "Golden Opportunity" to Make a Difference in Kids' Lives. [online] Yahoo.com. Available at: https://www.yahoo.com/entertainment/kate-middleton-seizing-golden-opportunity-230100969.html

Petty, A. (2017). How women's "perfect" body types changed throughout history. [online] TheList.com. Available at: https://www.thelist.com/44261/womens-perfect-body-types-changed-throughout-history/.

Pidgeon, E. (2021). Manuri Gunawardena is changing the future of medicine with HealthMatch. [online] The CEO Magazine. Available at: https://www.theceomagazine.com/business/innovation-technology/manuri-gunawardena/.

Pileberg, S. (2015). Why we look at pretty faces. [online] Available at: https://www.sv.uio.no/psi/english/research/news-and-events/news/why-we-look-at-pretty-faces.html

Points Of Light (2019). Khloe Thompson Accepts The George H.W. Bush Points of Light Award. [online] Youtube. Available at: https://www.youtube.com/watch?v=d5pR5yLEuPQ.

Ponsonby, E. (2013). The First Rape Center in Somalia. [online] The Borgen Project. Available at: https://borgenproject.org/elman-center-helps-somali-victims-of-sexual-violence-2/.

Popsugar (2017). How 1 SoCal 10-Year-Old Helped a Village in Ghana Get Clean Water. [online] Youtube. Available at: https://www.youtube.com/watch?v=cr5oCj2mNZQ.

Positive Luxury. (2020). Diversity in Beauty: Why the Industry Must Champion Inclusivity. [online] Available at: http://www.positiveluxury.com/blog2020/07/diversity-in-beauty-why-the-industry-must-champion-inclusivity.

Pressreader.com. (2020). When Words Take Wing. [online] Available at: https://www.pressreader.com/uk/harpers-bazaar-uk/20200801/283485028407651.

Prnewswire. (2017). Girls on Beauty: New Dove Research Findings how Beauty Confidence Driving 8 in 10 Girls to Opt Out of Future Opportunities. [online] Available at: https://www.prnewswire.com/news-releases/girls-on-beauty-new-dove-research-finds-low-beauty-confidence-driving-8-in-10-girls-to-opt-out-of-future-opportunities-649549253.html

Pruitt, S. (2018b). How the Vietnam War Empowered the Hippie Movement. [online] History. Available at: https://www.history.com/news/vietnam-war-hippies-counter-culture.

Publicdelivery.org. (2021). Barbara Kruger's I shop therefore I am - What you should know. [online] Available at: https://publicdelivery.org/barbara-kruger-i-shop/#:~:text=The%20phrase%20means%20that%20provided.

Purcell, E. (2020). Interview with disabled actress Cerrie Burnell. [online] Disability Horizons. Available at: https://disabilityhorizons.com/2020/08/cerrie-burnell-disabled-actress-author-and-tv-presenter/#:~:text=Cerrie%20Burnell%20is%20a%20British.

Pynchon, V. (2012). Using Youth and Beauty to Get What You Want. [online] Forbes. Available at: https://www.forbes.com/sites/shenegotiates/2012/04/30/using-youth-and-beauty-to-get-what-you-want/

Queenscommonwealthtrust.org. (2020). Bella Lack: Youth Director for Reserva YLT. [online] Available at: https://www.queenscommonwealthtrust.org/inspiration/bella-lack-youth-director-reserva-ylt-environment/#:~:text=Bella%20Lack%20is%20a%20Youth.

Raines, L. (2017). International Supermodel Teddy Quinlivan Comes Out As Transgender | Lavender Magazine. [online] Lavender Magazine. Available at: https://lavendermagazine.com/big-gay-news/international-supermodel-teddy-quinlivan-comes-transgender/.

Ranosa, R. (2021). Bumble CEO gives all employees the week off to fight burnout. [online] Hcamag.com. Available at: https://www.hcamag.com/au/specialisation/mental-health/bumble-ceo-gives-all-employees-the-week-off-to-fight-burnout/258525.

Rasmussen, S.E. (2021). Afghanistan's Taliban Prohibit Girls From Attending Secondary School. Wall Street Journal. [online] 19 Sep. Available at: https://www.wsj.com/articles/afghanistans-taliban-prohibit-girls-from-attending-secondary-school-as-boys-return-to-classrooms-11631951310.

Reddy, K. (2018). 1920-1929 | Fashion History Timeline. [online] Fitnyc. edu. Available at: https://fashionhistory.fitnyc.edu/1920-1929/.

Reddy, K. (2019b). 1970-1979 | Fashion History Timeline. [online] Fitnyc.edu. Available at: https://fashionhistory.fitnyc.edu/1970-1979/.

Reilly, N. (2019). Young girls are rejecting curvy Barbie. But why? [online] The Sydney Morning Herald. Available at: https://www.smh.com.au/lifestyle/life-and-relationships/young-girls-are-rejecting-curvy-barbie-but-why-20191009-p52z7a.html.

Relph, D. (2020). Kate launches childhood survey to help under-fives. BBC News. [online] 22 Jan. Available at: https://www.bbc.com/news/uk-51192909#:~:text=The%20Duchess%20of%20Cambridge%20has.

Rendon, C. and Konstantinides, A. (2019). Oprah Winfrey reflects on struggle to say final goodbye to mother. [online] Daily Mail Online. Available at: https://www.dailymail.co.uk/tvshowbiz/article-6934145/Oprah-Winfrey-reflects-struggle-say-goodbye-mother-Vernita-Lee.html.

Rhode, D. (2017). Appearance as a Feminist Issue. SMU Law Review, [online] 69(4), pp.697, 705, 709. Available at: https://scholar.smu.edu/smulr/vol69/iss4/2/

Rieden, J. (2020). Deborah Hutton reveals the frightening truth about her scar. Australian Women's Weekly. [online] Available at: https://www.nowtolove.com.au/celebrity/celeb-news/deborah-hutton-skin-cancer-64586

Robin, M. (2019). Biggest Beauty Trends of the Decade (2009 to 2019). [online] Allure. Available at: https://www.allure.com/gallery/biggest-beauty-hair-makeup-trends-of-decade.

Rockett, D. (2020). Q&A with 15-year-old children's book guru Marley Dias, who spoke at the Democratic convention, on her latest project coming Sept. 1 to Netflix. [online] Chicagotribune. Available at: https://www.chicagotribune.com/lifestyles/ct-life-marley-dias-bookmarks-netflix-tt-0825-20200825-nkadw6zuhvgqnhhfekvwuynyua-story.html.

Rogers-Anderson, S. (2020). Celebrating moms: Sivan Ya'ari. [online] Thetot.com. Available at: https://www.thetot.com/mama/celebrating-moms-sivan-yaari/.

Romm, S. (1987). Beauty Through History. Washington Post. 27 Jan.

Rosenbaum, R. (2012). Barbara Kruger's Artwork Speaks Truth to Power. [online] Smithsonian. Available at: https://www.smithsonianmag.com/arts-culture/barbara-krugers-artwork-speaks-truth-to-power-137717540/.

Rothman, L. (2017). How the Fashions of the 1960s Reflected Social Change. [online] Time.com. Available at: https://time.com/4978502/mod-fashion-1960s/.

Royal.uk (2020a). The Duchess of Cambridge reveals the results of her 5 Big Questions survey. [online] The Royal Family. Available at: https://www.royal.uk/5BigInsights.

Royal.uk (2020b). The Duchess of Cambridge's work on the Early Years. [online] The Royal Family. Available at: https://www.royal.uk/duchess-cambridges-work-early-years.

Rspca.org.uk. (2021). details | rspca.org.uk. [online] Available at: https://web.archive.org/web/20211020110901/https://www.rspca.org.uk/-/ambassadors_bellalack

Rufolfo, K. (2020). How Face Filters on Instagram and Facetune Affect Mental Health. [online] women's health. Available at: https://www.womenshealthmag.com/beauty/a33264141/face-filters-mental-health-effect/.

Rus, M. (2019). A bold social commentary since the 1970s, Barbara Kruger's art is as incisive as ever. [online] Wallpaper*. Available at: https://www.wallpaper.com/art/barbara-kruger-profile#:~:text=incisive%20as%20ever-.

S, J. (2021). Oprah Winfrey's Top 5 Charities - Celeb Giver Extraordinaire | Jetsetty. [online] Jetsetty.com. Available at: https://www.jetsetty.com /celebrity-style/oprah-winfreys-top-5-charities-celeb-giver-extraordinaire/.

Saeed, S. (2019). Elif Shafak: "Istanbul is a city of dreams... but it also has scars and wounds." [online] The National. Available at: https:// www.thenationalnews.com/arts-culture/books/elif-shafak-istanbul-is-a-city-of-dreams-but-it-also-has-scars-and-wounds-1.927677.

Salemme, N. (2021). They told me: You're way too curvy,. Herald Sun, 11 Jul., p.6.

Saner, E. (2011). TV presenter Cerrie Burnell: "I don't care if you are offended." [online] The Guardian. Available at: https://www. theguardian.com/society/2011/feb/21/tv-presenter-cerrie-burnell.

Saputo, S. (2019). Fenty Beauty's inclusive advertising campaign. [online] Think with Google. Available at: https://www. thinkwithgoogle.com/future-of-marketing/management-and-culture/diversity-and-inclusion/-fenty-beauty-inclusive-advertising/.

Sargeant, C. (2017). Teenage girls in Kenya create app to stop female genital mutilation. Topics. [online] Available at: https://www.sbs.com. au/topics/voices/culture/article/2017/08/04/teenage-girls-kenya-create-app-stop-female-genital-mutilation#:~:text=The%20teens%20have%20created%20an.

Saval, M. (2017). Oprah Winfrey's Leadship Academy for Girls Marks 10 Years. [online] Variety. Available at: https://variety.com/2017/ biz/news/oprah-winfrey-leadership-academy-for-girls-10-year-anniversary-1202510605/.

Says, K. (2016). 8 young people who are changing the world. [online] More than Motivation: Study, Career and Life Inspiration. Available at: https://www.opencolleges.edu.au/blog/2016/04/26/lw-young-people-changing-the-world/.

Schild, D. and McDowell, E. (2020). 20 fashion trends from the 1990s that should make a comeback. [online] Insider. Available at: https://www.insider.com/best-90s-fashion-trends-2019-7.

Schnitzer, K. (2019). CEO Whitney Wolfe Herd is rethinking work-life balance at Bumble. [online] Ladders | Business News & Career Advice. Available at: https://www.theladders.com/career-advice/ceo-whitney-wolfe-herd-is-rethinking-work-life-balance-at-bumble.

Scholastic. (2018). Marley Dias Gets It Done. [online] Available at: https://kids.scholastic.com/kids/book/marley-dias-gets-it-done-by-marley-dias/.

Schooneveld, A. and Ogila, I. (2018). How 5 Teenagers Created a Revolutionary App to Fight FGM. [online] Compassion Australia. Available at: https://www.compassion.com.au/blog/how-5-teenagers-created-a-revolutionary-app-to-fight-fgm.

Schulman, M. (2015). Women in the 60's. [online] Historycentral. Available at: https://www.historycentral.com/sixty/Americans/WOMEN.html.

Schwanke, C. (2011). 1960s Hippie Fashion. [online] LoveToKnow. Available at: https://womens-fashion.lovetoknow.com/1960s_Hippie_Fashion.

Scobie, O. (2020). Duchess Kate Reveals the Survey Results That Will Shape Her Future Work. [online] Harper's BAZAAR. Available at: https://www.harpersbazaar.com/celebrity/latest/a34799293/kate-middleton-5-big-questions-survey-results/.

Scott, E. (2019). Transgender model Andreja Pejic in a Bonds lingerie campaign – is the revolution here? | Elfy Scott. [online] The Guardian. Available at: https://www.theguardian.com/global/commentisfree/2019/mar/07/transgender-model-andreja-pejic-in-a-bonds-lingerie-campaign-is-the-revolution-here.

Sessions, D. (2013). 1940s Fashion: What Did Women Wear in the 1940s? [online] Vintagedancer.com. Available at: https://vintagedancer.com/1940s/what-did-women-wear-in-the-1940s/.

Seth, A. (2013). Philanthropists of the Year: PRIYANKA CHOPRA. [online] HuffPost. Available at: https://www.huffpost.com/entry/philanthropists-of-the-ye_b_4347376.

Shafak, E. (2018). Elif Shafak on Ways of Knowing and the Women in Her Life. [online] Literary Hub. Available at: https://lithub.com/elif-shafak-on-ways-of-knowing-and-the-women-in-her-life/.

Shafak, E. (2019). What we want: to prioritise tackling inequality. [online] New Statesman. Available at: https://www.newstatesman.com/politics/2019/12/what-we-want-prioritise-tackling-inequality.

Shah, V. (2019). A Conversation with Elif Shafak. [online] Thought Economics. Available at: https://thoughteconomics.com/elif-shafak/.

Shenoy, S. (2018). Why Women Still Feel Valued by their Looks and How to Change That. [online] Available at: https://thriveglobal.com/stories/is-beauty-boss-why-women-still-feel-valued-by-their-looks-and-how-to-change-that/

Shepard, M. (2021). How Nobel Peace Prize nominee Ilwad Elman has left her mark on Somalia—and the world. [online] Macleans.ca. Available at: https://www.macleans.ca/news/world/how-nobel-peace-prize-nominee-ilwad-elman-has-left-her-mark-on-somalia-and-the-world/.

Shortyawards. (2019). Mari Copeny - The Shorty Awards. [online] Available at: https://shortyawards.com/11th/littlemissflint.

Skin deep and meaningful. (2021). Herald Sun, 25 Jul., p.4.

SLU.SE. (2020). "Insects are our future" | Medarbetarwebben. [online] Available at: https://internt.slu.se/en/news-originals/2020/2/insects-are-our-future/.

Smith, M. (2020). Sinéad Burke: "My goal was to change the entire fashion system." [online] The Guardian. Available at: https://www.theguardian.com/fashion/2020/nov/01/sinead-burke-my-goal-was-to-change-the-entire-fashion-system-#:~:text=%E2%80%9CI%20understood%20that%20one%20of.

SodexoSTOPHunger (2016). 2016 Sodexo Stop Hunger Foundation Growing Together Honoree, Katie Stagliano. [online] Youtube. Available at: https://www.youtube.com/watch?v=jfxQc0H707o.

Soley-Beltran, P. (2004). Modelling Femininity. European Journal of Women's Studies, 11(3), pp.319, 323.

Sorensen, B. (2020). Art and Mass Media: Barbara Kruger. [online] jmartmanagement. Available at: https://www.jmartmanagement.com/post/art-and-mass-media-barbara-kruger.

Specter, E. (2019). At 29, Ilwad Elman Is Helping to Rebuild Somalia. [online] Vogue. Available at: https://www.vogue.com/article/ilwad-elman-interview.

Stafford, Z. (2016). The Oprah Winfrey Show: "Hour-long life lessons" that changed TV forever. [online] the Guardian. Available at: https://www.theguardian.com/tv-and-radio/2016/sep/08/oprah-winfrey-show-30-year-anniversary-daytime-tv.

Standard Digital Videos (2020). "I-CUT App" University Students Launch App to aid fight against FGM in Kenya. Youtube. Available at: https://www.youtube.com/watch?v=RClGIlY5akk.

Steinbach, A. (1991). Wolf VS "Beauty Myth" Feminist sees conspiracy in stress on appearance. [online] Baltimore Sun. Available at: http://www.baltimoresun.com/news/bs-xpm-1991-06-23-1991174002.

Stella McCartney Cares. (n.d.). Pink. [online] Available at: https://web.archive.org/web/20211014222112/https://www.stellamccartneyfoundation.com/pink

Stellamccartney.com. (n.d.). About Stella McCartney | Stella McCartney US. [online] Available at: https://www.stellamccartney.com/us/en/stellas-world/about-stella-mccartney.html.

Stellamccartney.com. (n.d.). Measuring our Impact. [online] Available at: https://www.stellamccartney.com/gb/en/sustainability/measuring-our-impact.html#:~:text=To%20measure%20our%20environmental%20footprint.

Stellamccartney.com. (n.d.). Social Sustainability | Stella McCartney US. [online] Available at: https://www.stellamccartney.com/us/en/sustainability/social-sustainability.html.

Stern, C. (2021). Oprah details childhood abuse on Instagram and in new book. [online] Daily Mail Online. Available at: https://www.dailymail.co.uk/femail/article-9525681/Oprah-details-childhood-abuse-revealing-grandma-whupped-regularly.html.

Story TIme w/ Kayla (2021). The Girl Who Became the Change by Khloe Thompson | #ReadAloud. [online] Youtube. Available at: https://www.youtube.com/watch?v=mfFCTiF5eDU.

Sturges, F. (2020). Elif Shafak's How to Stay Sane in an Age of Division guides us through extraordinary times. [online] Inews.co.uk. Available at: https://inews.co.uk/culture/books/how-to-stay-sane-in-an-age-of-division-elif-shafak-review-emotions-642043.

Stutman, M. (2016). Khloe Kares - 9 Year Old Khloe Thompson "Kares" for the Homeless. [online] InspireMyKids. Available at: https://inspiremykids.com/khloe-kares-2/.

Stutman, M. (2019). Ruby Kate Chitsey - 11 Year Old Helps the Elderly One Wish at a Time! [online] InspireMyKids. Available at: https://inspiremykids.com/ruby-kate-chitsey-11-year-old-helps-the-elderly-one-wish-at-a-time/.

Suhrawardi, R. (2016). Diversity in Fashion: Are Millennials and Social Media the Answer To Changing Beauty Ideals? [online] Forbes. Available at: https://www.forbes.com/sites/rebeccasuhrawardi/2016/05/23/diversity-in-fashion-are-millennials-and-social-media-the-answer-to-changing-beauty-ideals/.

Suleman, A. (2018). How Fashion And Beauty Brands Embrace Diversity In Their Marketing. [online] ZD Blog. Available at: https://zilliondesigns.com/blog/fashion-beauty-brands-diversity-marketing-designs.

Sullivan, R. (2020). New Barbie dolls feature vitiligo and hairless models in bid to boost diversity. [online] CNN. Available at: https://edition.cnn.com/style/article/barbie-vitiligo-hairless-dolls-wellness-scli-intl/index.html#:~:text=New%20Barbie%20dolls%20feature%20vitiligo%20and%20hairless%20models%20in%20bid%20to%20boost%20diversity&text=The%20maker%20of%20Barbie%20dolls.

Sunrise (2021). *Huge increase in teen girls wanting cosmetic injectables.* [online] cs-cz.facebook.com. Available at: https://cs-cz.facebook.com/Sunrise/videos/huge-increase-in-teen-girls-wanting-cosmetic-injectables/2819959321590321/.

Sykes, P. (2020). how do we know we're doing it right? UK: Penguin Random House, pp.42, 47.

Tamaki, J. (2019). The Turkish Novelist Elif Shafak Wants You to Read More Women. The New York Times. [online] 26 Dec. Available at: https://www.nytimes.com/2019/12/26/books/review/elif-shafak-by-the-book-interview.html#:~:text=The%20Turkish%20Novelist%20Elif%20Shafak%20Wants%20You%20to%20Read%20More%20Women.

Tansley, P. (2020). Standards need to lift in cosmetic surgery. Herald Sun, 23 Dec., p.20.

Tay, A. (2020). Barbie introduced their 2020 Barbie Sports Toys Range. [online] 2CENTS. Available at: https://www.2cents.my/2020/03/26/barbie-introduced-their-2020-barbie-sports-toys-range/.

Taylor, E. (2018). How Kate Middleton's Idea May Have Just Changed Britain for the Better. [online] Vogue. Available at: https://www.vogue.com/article/how-kate-middleton-heads-together-idea-may-have-just-changed-britain-for-the-better.

TEDx Talks (2012). TEDxMogadishu - Ilwad Elman - In Memory of My Father, I Returned to Rebuild Somalia. [online] Youtube. Available at: https://www.youtube.com/watch?v=hBqdyn_V7VE.

The Fashion Folks. (2017). 21th Century Fashion History: 2000-2010 | The Fashion Folks. [online] Available at: https://www.thefashionfolks.com/blog/21th-century-fashion-history-2000-2010/.

The Guardian. (2016). Girl's drive to find 1,000 "black girl books" hits target with outpouring of donations. [online] Available at: https://www.theguardian.com/books/2016/feb/09/marley-dias-1000-black-girl-books-hits-target-with-outpouring-of-donations#:~:text=Children%20and%20teenagers-.

The Guardian. (2021). We all learned to love nature in lockdown. Now let's turn that into practical action | Bella Lack. [online] Available at: https://www.theguardian.com/commentisfree/2021/mar/30/nature-lockdown-government-environmental-crisis.

The Hero Effect. (2017). Katie Stagliano. [online] Available at: https://www.heroeffect.com/heroes/katie-stagliano/#:~:text=Katie%20Stagliano%2C%2018%2C%20is%20a.

The STEAM Connection. (2021). The STEAM Connection. [online] Available at: https://steamconnection.org/.

Thebookseller.com. (2020). Penguin Life scoops debut from teen environmentalist Bella Lack | The Bookseller. [online] Available at: https://www.thebookseller.com/news/penguin-life-scoops-debut-teen-envronmentalist-lack-1215030.

Thebroad.org. (2018). Untitled (Your body is a battleground) - Barbara Kruger | The Broad. [online] Available at: https://www.thebroad.org/art/barbara-kruger/untitled-your-body-battleground.

Thefamouspeople.com. (n.d.). Who is Stella McCartney? Everything You Need to Know. [online] Available at: https://www.thefamouspeople.com/profiles/stella-mccartney-5469.php.

Theresa, D. (2020). These sisters dream of a plastic-free world. [online] The New Indian Express. Available at: https://www.newindianexpress.com/cities/thiruvananthapuram/2020/jan/11/these-sisters-dream-of-a-plastic-free-world-2088086.html.

Times Of Israel (2016). Israeli women — and tech — connect African villages to water, electricity. [online] Timesofisrael.com. Available at: https://www.timesofisrael.com/israeli-women-and-tech-connect-african-villages-to-water-electricity/#:~:text=A%20charity%20led%20by%20Israeli.

Times, T.B. (1918). Women Dress: War Time Fashion. [online] Chronicling American Digital Newspapers. Available at: https://library.ccsu.edu/dighistFall16/exhibits/show/women-and-dress--women-s-contr/item/104.

Tonkin, C. (2020). The art of matching patients to clinical trials. [online] Information Age. Available at: https://ia.acs.org.au/article/2020/the-art-of-matching-patients-to-clinical-trials.html.

Topsfield, J. (2016). Bye Bye plastic bags: Sisters' remarkable fight to rid Bali of rubbish. [online] The Sydney Morning Herald. Available at: https://www.smh.com.au/world/bali-tourists-bagged-to-support-girls-monumental-plastic-rubbish-goal-20160311-gng8xs.html.

Tracey, E. (2013). Cerrie Burnell: Disability is not a negative label. BBC News. [online] 19 Nov. Available at: https://www.bbc.com/news/blogs-ouch-24988596#:~:text=Having%20a%20disability%20is%20not.

Trenoweth, S. (2021). Grace Tame's courageous journey has already achieved greater justice for survivors of child sexual abuse - now, she has a platform like no other. [online] Now To Love. Available at: https://www.nowtolove.com.au/celebrity/celeb-news/grace-tame-66974.

Tsoulis-Reay, A. (2018). What It's Like to Go Through Life As a Really Beautiful Woman. [online] The Cut. Available at: https://www.thecut.com/2018/04/what-its-like-to-be-a-really-beautiful-woman.html.

UKEssays (2018). Ideological Messages Behind Barbara Krugers Work Art Essay. [online] UKEssays.com. Available at: https://www.ukessays.com/essays/arts/ideological-messages-behind-barbara-krugers-work-art-essay.php.

UN Women (2021a). Yo soy Generacion Igualdad Julieta Amara Martinez. [online] UN Women | Americas and the Caribbean. Available at: https://lac.unwomen.org/en/noticias-y-eventos/articulos/2021/04/yo-soy-generacion-igualdad--julieta-amara-martinez.

UN Women. (2020). Girls to know: The next generation is already leading the way. [online] Available at: https://www.unwomen.org/en/news/stories/2020/10/compilation-girls-to-know.

UN Women. (2021b). Take five: "Girls' empowerment and inclusion in decision-making processes is a transformative force in achieving a sustainable and equal future." [online] Available at: https://www.unwomen.org/en/news/stories/2021/8/take-five-julieta-martinez.

UNICEF India (2014). UNICEF Deepshikha event with Priyanka Chopra. [online] Youtube.com. Available at: https://www.youtube.com/watch?v=u0jMQCXFNB8.

Unladylike. (2020). Episode 73 Transcript: How to Tilt the Lens with Sinead Burke. [online] Available at: https://www.unladylike.co/episodes/073/sinead-burke

Vanessa Van Edwards (2016). Beauty Standards: See How Body Types Change Through... [online] Science of People. Available at: https://www.scienceofpeople.com/beauty-standards/.

VELVET Magazine. (2018). Stella McCartney Cares Green: In support of a sustainable fashion industry. [online] Available at: https://velvet-mag.com/stella-mccartney-cares-green/#:~:text=Stella%20McCartney%20Cares%20Green%20aims.

Vidyasagar, A. (2019). For Disability Activists, 3 Weeks In Oregon Is A Game Changer. NPR. [online] 13 Aug. Available at: https://www.npr.org/sections/goatsandsoda/2019/08/13/749371398/for-disability-activists-3-weeks-in-oregon-is-a-game-changer#:~:text=Disability%20activists%20from%20around%20the%20world%20attended%20a%20seminar%20in%20Oregon..

Vincent, K. (2017). Manuri Gunawardena on Australian Leadership: "The most important qualities Australians seek from their leaders are courage and authenticity." [online] Australianleadership.blogspot. com. Available at: http://australianleadership.blogspot.com/2017/07/manuri-gunawardena-on-australian.html.

Vintage Dancer. (2017). 1960s Fashion: What Did Women Wear? [online] Vintagedancer. Available at: https://vintagedancer.com/1960s/1960s-fashion-womens/.

Vintage Dancer. (2019). Fashion in 1918 - Women and Men During WW1. [online] Available at: https://vintagedancer.com/1900s/1918-fashion/.

Vintagedancer. (n.d) 1990s Fashion | 90s Fashion Trends for Women. [online] Available at: https://vintagedancer.com/vintage/1990s-fashion-90s-fashion-trends-for-women/.

Vintagedancer.com. (2020). 80s Fashion— What Women Wore in the 1980s. [online] Available at: https://vintagedancer.com/1980s/80s-fashion-what-women-wore-in-the-1980s/.

Vintagehairstyling (2020). Red Lipstick and a Woman's Right to Vote. [online] Bobby Pin Blog / Vintage hair and makeup tips and tutorials. Available at: https://www.vintagehairstyling.com/bobbypinblog/2020/08/red-lipstick-and-a-womans-right-to-vote.html.

VOA. (2009). Oprah Uses Power of Media to Change Lives. [online] Available at: https://www.voanews.com/a/a-13-2007-01-26-voa42-66691912/558641.html.

Vogue Runway (2020). Today on Good Morning Vogue: Kerby Jean-Raymond on Why This is His Last Interview (For a While). [online] Facebook. Available at: https://www.facebook.com/VogueRunway/videos/today-on-good-morning-vogue-kerby-jean-raymond-on-why-this-is-his-last-interview/370427943976913/

W Magazine (2014). Log into Facebook. [online] Facebook. Available at: https://m.facebook.com/wmagazine/photos/pb.40621875003.-2207520000.1419131640./10154852383830004/?type=3&source=43.

Wallace, F. (2018). Kate Moss retracts her famous quote: "Nothing tastes as good as skinny feels." [online] Vogue Australia. Available at: https://www.vogue.com.au/fashion/news/kate-moss-retracts-her-famous-quote-nothing-tastes-as-good-as-skinny-feels/news-story/69 dbba57b1771fb6ad4534810ea9a2f5.

Wasley, K. (2021). Fashion Week Yet Again Showed Me The Lack Of Size Diversity In Australia & I'm Tired Of It. [online] Pedestrian TV. Available at: https://www.pedestrian.tv/news/fashion-week-no-size-diversity-australia/.

WBLS (2019). Game Changers: Marley Dias and the #1000BlackGirlBooks. [online] Youtube. Available at: https://www.youtube.com/watch?v=eV-tMaj1VXA.

Wells, G., Horwitz, J. and Seetharharaman, D., 2021. Bad Influence. The Australian, pp.p. 12-13.

Whatkatewore (2020). The Duchess Launches New Initiative Helping Babies & Young Children. [online] What Kate Wore. Available at: https://whatkatewore.com/2020/08/04/the-duchess-launches-new-initiative-helping-babies-young-children/.

White, C.C.R. (1997). AT TEA WITH: Alek Wek; When Fair of Face Looks African. The New York Times. [online] 16 Nov. Available at: https://www.nytimes.com/1997/11/16/style/at-tea-with-alek-wek-when-fair-of-face-looks-african.html.

Whitefield-Madrano, A. (2017). FACE VALUE : the hidden ways beauty shapes women's lives. Simon & Schuster, p.13.

Whyte, S., Brooks, R.C., Chan, H.F. and Torgler, B. (2021). Sex differences in sexual attraction for aesthetics, resources and personality across age. PLOS ONE, 16(5), p.e0250151.

Wightman-Stone, D. (2019). Stella McCartney launches #ThereSheGrows charity initiative. [online] FashionUnited. Available at: https://fashionunited.com/news/fashion/stella-mccartney-launches-thereshegrows-charity-initiative/2019030126468.

Wijsen, M. and I. (2016). Our campaign to ban plastic bags in Bali. [online] Ted. Available at: https://www.ted.com/talks/melati_and_isabel_wijsen_our_campaign_to_ban_plastic_bags_in_bali?language=en.

Winfrey, O. (n.d.). Oprah on the Most Valuable Gift a Loved One Can Offer. [online] Oprah.com. Available at: https://www.oprah.com/omagazine/what-oprah-knows-for-sure-about-adolescence.

WIRE, B., 2021. Chicago-Based Herrendorf Family Foundation Joins the Oprah Winfrey Charitable Foundation to Launch Scholarship Benefiting Chicago Youth. [online] Businesswire.com. Available at: https://www.businesswire.com/news/home/20210930005225/en/Chicago-Based-Herrendorf-Family-Foundation-Joins-the-Oprah-Winfrey-Charitable-Foundation-to-Launch-Scholarship-Benefiting-Chicago-Youth

Witcomb, G. (2019). Barbie at 60: instrument of female oppression or positive influence? [online] The Conversation. Available at: https://theconversation.com/barbie-at-60-instrument-of-female-oppression-or-positive-influence-113069.

Wolf, N. (1990). The Beauty Myth : How Images of Beauty are Used Against Women. London: Vintage Classic, pp.12, 73, 109, 127, 270.

Wolf, N. (2014). The Beauty Myth by Naomi Wolf, A Singapore Writers Festival 2014 Lecture. [online] Available at: https://www.youtube.com/watch?v=q3joFixoxhM

Wolfe Herd, W. (2020). Bumble - Bumble's founder and CEO Whitney Wolfe Herd talks building Bumble — and fighting for gender equality. [online] Bumble Buzz. Available at: https://bumble.com/en/the-buzz/a-letter-from-whitney-wolfe-herd-founder-and-ceo.

Women's Agenda (2019). The story of Ruth Handler: Creator of Barbie & co-founder of Mattel. [online] Women's Agenda. Available at: https://womensagenda.com.au/latest/the-story-of-ruth-handler-the-creator-of-barbie-co-founder-of-mattel/.

Wonder Crate. (2019). Kids Making a Difference: Khloe Thompson, Founder of Khloe Kares. [online] Available at: https://www. wondercratekids.com/2019/04/14/kids-making-a-difference-khloe-thompson-founder-of-khloe-kares/.

World Health Organization (2011). World Report on Disability. [online] www.who.int. Available at: https://www.who.int/teams/ noncommunicable-diseases/sensory-functions-disability-and-rehabilitation/world-report-on-disability.

Yarosh, D. (2019). Perception and Deception: Human Beauty and the Brain. Behavioral Sciences, 9(4), p.34.

YAYOMG! (2020). GIRLS WHO SHINE: Khloe Thompson, Founder of Khloe Kares. [online] Available at: https://www.yayomg.com/girls-who-shine-khloe-thompson/.

Young Women (2021). Revista_UNO35_ENG - COLLABORATION and VOICES from YOUNG WOMEN as a PATH TOWARD HOPE (51/60). [online] Uno35. Available at: https://uno35.uno-magazine. com/1261176/index-51.html.

Zargani, L. (2021). Prada Group Intensifies Commitment to Diversity, Equity and Inclusion. [online] WWD. Available at: https://wwd.com/ sustainability/social-impact/prada-group-intensifies-commitment-diversity-equity-inclusion-1234821972/.

Zuckerman, S. (2019). Full STEAM Ahead with Danielle Boyer: STEAM Connections. [online] SOLIDWORKS Education Blog. Available at: https://blogs.solidworks.com/teacher/2019/05/full-steam-ahead-with-danielle-boyer-steam-connections.html.

Shawline Publishing Group Pty Ltd
www.shawlinepublishing.com.au

SHAWLINE
PUBLISHING
GROUP

CPSIA information can be obtained
at www.ICGtesting.com
Printed in the USA
BVHW030931181122
652269BV00016B/421

9 781922 850546